E PLURIBUS OMAHA
Immigrants All

By Harry B. O...

in collaboration wit...
Donald H. Erickson

W.M.R.QUICK SC

Published by Lamplighter Press
HISTORICAL SOCIETY of DOUGLAS COUNTY
Omaha, Nebraska

Lamplighter Press
Historical Society of Douglas County
Historic Fort Omaha
5730 North Thirtieth Street, Building 11B
Omaha, NE 68111-1657

ISBN: 1-930644-04-3

Contents

PREFACE

This book is not a history of Omaha, merely a description of some of the people who have lived in it. There was no Omaha a century and a half ago. Now the city boasts of over four hundred thousand people. Who are they? Where on earth did they come from?

Available for our research were the archives of the city and its universities and especially those of the Historical Society of Douglas County, which enjoys the role of custodian of the **Omaha World-Herald**'s clipping files accumulated over the years. This was a special blessing for us.

Much of our work involved selecting appropriate individuals to personify each ethnic group and gathering the stories of such persons with tape recorder, pen and paper. Sometimes we were given printed family stories to digest.

We have been fortunate enough to find photographs, not only from the Historical Society of Douglas County, the **Omaha World-Herald**, the Nebraska State Historical Society and the Jewish Historical Society, but also from the Durham Western Heritage Museum which houses the priceless Bostwick-Frohardt photographic collection. Persons interviewed have provided others.

Two faithful employees of the Historical Society came to our aid when we needed them, Deirdre Routt and Bob Bailie. Deirdre put our computerized text into the proper form for printing. Bob magically transformed, through digitalization, the many old photos we handed him for insertion into the text and on the book's cover.

We are deeply grateful for the sincere interest in our project by our friend, Jim Clemon, who particularly approved and endorsed our selection of the book's title. We needed the spiritual boost of his advice and counsel and gratefully appreciated his patient editing of each chapter as it was written. Such commitment to the project was invaluable.

INTRODUCTION

Omaha is not merely a piece of real estate. It is a parcel of America where thousands of people have freely chosen to put down their roots and form a community. For a few hundred years it has been called home by people of many different cultures and ethnic groups.

This book attempts to weave some of the stories of Omaha's immigrants into a fabric that reveals the depth of character and color of its populace and its strength as a political and social unit. Reflecting a rich and continuing heritage springing from old immigrants, as well as new, these stories are proud bits of evidence that our democracy, only two hundred years old, is working well. Its fabric, although stretched from time to time, does not break.

Even before the Europeans came in 1854, the Otoe and Omaha Indians lived here for two hundred years and were visited from time to time, not altogether amicably, by the Sioux. All of these tribes had replaced other native Americans, the remnants of whose mound houses still can be found in the loess hills north of Florence, as well as up and down the Missouri River.

After 1854, each new arrival also has in some measure enriched society as a whole. The newcomer, usually with nothing other than his language, religion, physical brawn and a desire to be free, somehow adds a new tint to the social fabric—an indefinable hue that enhances, however slightly, the portrait of the city.

Many of the whites, who politically formed and thereafter ran Omaha in the 1850s and who owned all the real estate, were of British, German and Irish extraction, the Byron Reeds, the Augustus Kountzes and Ed Creightons. Arriving a few years later were other Irish, many of whom worked for the Union Pacific laying the rails that finally linked America's East and West coasts.

The railroads, in turn, fostered all sorts of industry, including the packinghouses where cattle and other livestock were killed in great numbers for Eastern markets. Once the news got out, the good pay of these slaughterhouses attracted hundreds of Europeans of every

Introduction

description, as well as African-Americans recently freed from Southern slavery.

Later on, folks from Latin America arrived at Omaha's door to replace the Europeans as railroad and packinghouse laborers. Even more recently, Asians from Vietnam, Thailand, Korea and elsewhere in the Far East have joined the Chinese and Japanese who for years have lived in Omaha.

With the exception of a few prominent glitches, during the past one hundred and fifty years all of these people have mingled amicably. While many have shared a common religion, usually Christianity, most have insisted in establishing a church of their own ethnicity, which they could huddle close to in their own neighborhoods.

One might wonder how such groups have fostered a tolerance for one another not found abroad. Although there is a constant interaction among them, they live in a placid setting not to be found were they similarly situated in Bosnia, North Ireland, Southern Lebanon or other trouble spots of the world where endless wars, riots and religious strife seem destined to ravage the peoples and the land. Why has Omaha, and the rest of America, escaped this turmoil?

One reason stands out bright and clear. America emerged from the womb washed in a tradition of Anglo-Saxon law that placed particular emphasis on personal liberty. Very quickly, the founding fathers made this tradition manifest in the Constitution of 1789 and the Bill of Rights, as contained in its amendments. As every citizen knows, the First Amendment to the Constitution makes it abundantly clear that government has no business interfering with free speech, free press and matters dealing with the free exercise of religion.

Although America is governed by the will of the majority, this will is reined in by these protective prohibitions, which for two hundred years have guaranteed these freedoms. Few seem to remember that for centuries in diverse realms throughout the world, and, indeed, in the American colonies themselves, such liberties were unheard of. This included the right to worship God however, whenever and wherever one pleased, or not to believe in or worship God at all.

Introduction

We contend that this separation of church and state is what has enabled every ethnic group in Omaha, however rambunctious, to rumble around and spout off without any real threat that a religious majority might some day pull a government gun and throw such nonbelievers in jail for failing to believe in its sacred dogma. Today it is hard for us to believe that in Puritan New England the Quaker could not establish his simple meeting house, and in Catholic Austria the Hapsburg emperor welcomed no Protestants.

A second reason for the existence of such tolerance may be found in the very number and diversity of such groups. There are some in Omaha who in Europe are traditional rivals: Croats and Serbs, Ulster County Irish and Southern Irish, for example. But there are a host of others: Poles, Lithuanians, Germans, Czechs, Greeks, Rumanians, Hungarians, Italians and more recently, Mexicans and many from the Near East and Asia. Yet, with little rancor, these people have shared together the problems of a new country and a new language, the struggle drawing them all the closer to one another.

Indeed, this relative harmony has promoted a general lack of fear of one group for another, and without the germinating soil of fear, hate is difficult to grow. Each passing year finds each group of people seeming more and more to enjoy and respect the distinct ethnic attributes of the others. From time to time they join in common folk festivals, participate in each other's dances and eat each other's food, apparently gaining strength from their very diversity.

As the generations go on, and English slowly replaces each of their native tongues, there has been a great deal of melting in the pot. More and more, the groups think of themselves not as Lithuanian-Americans, Mexican-Americans or Polish-Americans but simply as Americans who happen to live in Omaha.

While we have set down our stories of many ethnic groups, we regrettably have omitted others that are as important to the city as the ones we have written about. Although their numbers are relatively small, their presence also adds color to the cloth. They, too, make us richer by their presence.

Introduction

For example, although few Baltic peoples other than Lithuanian have come to Omaha (Finns and Estonians are scarce), the city has been a refuge for quite a few Latvians escaping from Russian domination. After World War II, John Ritums arrived from Latvia to establish a first-rate contracting business, as well as to serve on the city council.

Furthermore, although no large colony of Norwegians settled here, some prominent among them have made the city their home. Lloyd M. Peterson was one. Born in Hartington, Nebraska of ancestors who had immigrated to Nebraska from Norway during the 1860s, Lloyd, a poor dust bowl farmer, arrived in 1935 at age twenty-three ready to work long hours at forty cents an hour. Over the years he distinguished himself as the board chairman of many businesses and charitable institutions, among them the Omaha Real Estate Board, Omaha Building Owners and Managers, Morning Star Lutheran Church, Immanuel Hospital and Fremont Midland College. In 1964, the Norwegian crown named him vice counsel of Norway. Together with his brother Harold, he ended up owning the Barker Building.

Many other countries sent their citizens to Omaha in numbers too small to form readily identifiable colonies, yet their emigrants made a mark. One need not look too carefully to find in his neighborhood a person of Ukrainian, Hungarian or Bulgarian descent; a person from some Near East country, such as Iran or Syria; a new immigrant from Thailand or Korea; or a person from some Latin American country other than Mexico. All of a sudden one realizes that such a person has become a member of the Omaha City Council, or a prominent doctor, lawyer or restauranteur.

Today, many immigrants are political refugees. The lady in New York Harbor still opens her arms to them. Along with the rest of the country, Omaha is ready to receive them and help them make a home among us.

Our sincere hope is that this book will allow each Omahan to learn more about the fellow citizens who may reside outside his particular neighborhood—their ethnic backgrounds, their customs, their aspirations and their forms of religion—and thereby better appreciate what each of us gets to enjoy by living among such diversity. When he does, he may suddenly realize he has the whole world right here at home.

THE AMERICAN INDIANS: NATIVE AMERICANS

From their chiseled position in the pink marble above the south portal of Omaha's Joslyn Memorial Art Museum, these words sing out:

In the morning of time they came.
Their drums were beating. Their hearts were high.
The land summoned them and they loved it.

Long before the coming of the Spanish and French to mid-America, Native Americans roamed in the Omaha area. These early people appeared for a time and then vanished, leaving to the archeologists only traces of sunken mound houses and artifacts of stone and bone. They apparently occupied these houses in the loess bluffs only as long as timber and game gave them support, before moving up or down the Missouri River for better resources.

In historic times came the Omahas, whose name the city would adopt as its own. Some scholars say it means, "the people who move upstream" and describes a portion of the route the Omaha tribe took to get here from the East. As there are no written records, fixed dates are impossible, yet some two hundred years prior to 1854 the Omahas established villages on the west side of the river, some near the location of the present city.

Tradition has it that they were at one time part of a greater tribe consisting of Omahas, Poncas, Osages, Kansas and Quapaws. In the course of time and travel, while retaining a common language and cultural heritage, they broke away from one another due to accidents and quarrels.

Driven by wars from an earlier home in the Ohio River Valley, the mother tribe migrated west. Encountering the Mississippi River, part of it moved upstream, the *OO-Mah-Has*; part traveled downstream, the Quapaws. The upstream branch thence moved up the Des Moines River and its tributaries until it reached the Missouri River, which it crossed to claim that portion of eastern Nebraska bordering the

Native Americans

Missouri between the Niobrara River on the north, the Platte River on the south and a line some two hundred miles to the west.

In this region, when not on the hunt for buffalo, the Omahas lived in villages composed of domed dwellings made of sod and timber, each accommodating as many as four families. A circular opening in the center of the roof served as a chimney and gave light to the interior. Facing east, a six-to-ten-foot-long passageway provided an entrance. The skins or blankets hung at the outer and inner parts of this entrance afforded double protection against wind and cold.

Sod dwellings of the Omahas

Fires were kindled in a hollowed place in the center of the floor. Around the walls were arranged platforms made of reeds, on which robes were spread for use as seats by day and as beds by night.

Fifty to one hundred structures would be grouped together to form a village, always near both running water and convenient timber and usually near high hills from which lookouts could give notice of approaching enemies.

As agrarians, the Omahas raised large quantities of corn, beans, pumpkins and melons in sheltered valleys and bottom lands, using as hoes the shoulder blades of elks. The pumpkins they cut up in festoons to dry for winter use; the corn and beans, once dried, they stored in caches outside the lodges. The women did most of this agricultural work and called on the men only when help was needed.

Each family had its own garden, for as a tribe the Omahas raised nothing in common. Once a family chose a piece of ground for such use, its possession was respected by the others.

Providing meat and skins was another matter. Killing game was a tribal affair. Hunting was no pastime but an annual duty regulated by tribal ceremonies and led by men duly appointed and under serious obligations. The hunt occurred every summer, with most of the tribe moving out many miles with tents and tent poles pulled by ponies. Only the infirm and sick were left in the village under a special guard of warriors.

While engaged in this annual hunt, the tribe would camp by pitching their tepees in a large circle. In conformity with Indian custom, the Omahas were divided into subgroups or *gentes*, each *gens* having a distinct name, mythical origin and sacred symbols. The Omaha tribe had ten *gentes,* each of which had a fixed place in the tribal circle, whose opening was always to the east.

Part of an Omaha village, circa 1860

Native Americans

Inside the south side of the circle stood three sacred tents. The tent just south of the opening was dedicated to war ceremonies, the other two to the sustaining of life and to providing places for the safekeeping of the sacred pole and sacred white buffalo hide.

The men and older boys did the more dangerous work of finding, rounding up and killing the buffaloes. They also were in charge of skinning the hides and bringing them back to the encampment. There the women took on the arduous task of scraping and cleaning them, preparing them for final tanning once the tribe had returned to its village. The women also jerked the meat, cutting it into thin strips for drying in the wind and sun.

The Omahas did many things by fours. On their way home from the hunt, for example, while within a four-day march to their village, they would halt long enough for a four-day thanksgiving to celebrate their success. Only then would they scatter to their homes for yet another ceremony of thanksgiving, this time a private one.

The Omahas felt deeply the presence of *Waconda*, the Great Spirit or Great Life Force. Like all Native Americans, they were a spiritual people attuned to the forces of nature. And they looked upon nature subjectively. They considered all life as one and related and saw every living thing as part of themselves.

Eating the products of the earth and the flesh of animals was essential to their bodily vigor. Yet, since all things on earth and in the sky were permeated by the same life force that they were conscious of within themselves, their will, spirit and power to operate likewise were strengthened by the spirit and power of the bird, animal or plant they ingested.

A relatively peaceable tribe, the Omahas never warred with the white man, even as he disturbed their farms and their hunting as he moved west during the first half of the nineteenth century. Their only real enemies were the Sioux, whose occasional raids caused them much misery. They even got along with the warlike Pawnees whose lands lay more than two hundred miles to the west. Indeed, they often shared with this tribe the good buffalo hunting in central Nebraska, both north and south of the Platte River.

The Omahas were generous and hospitable. A tribute is owed to them for their treatment of the Latter-day Saints, the Mormons. In 1845 non-Mormon Americans (gentiles) had driven these people across Iowa from well-established homes on the banks of the Mississippi in Nauvoo, Illinois. Learning of the suffering endured by Brigham Young and his flock during this harsh winter trek across Iowa, in their compassion the tribe allowed these white men to reside for several years on the west side of the river, first at Bellevue and later at winter quarters in Florence and as far north as DeSoto.

At the same time, to the lasting credit of the Mormons themselves, despite the distinct likelihood of raids by the Sioux on their west bank communities, the Mormons honored a request of the United States to send a party of two hundred men to California to fight its war against Mexico.

The Omahas have had some excellent leaders. Notable among the early head tribal chiefs was Big Elk (*Ong-pa-tung-ga*), the third in a line of chiefs by that name. Many notables passing through his region admired him. Among those who commented on his natural abilities were explorer Major Long, artist George Catlin, pathfinder General Fremont, scout Kit Carson, Prince Maximilian, Karl Bodmer and Brigham Young. He also found warm friends in trading post owner Peter Sarpy and missionary priest Father DeSmet.

Big Elk foresaw the extinction of the buffalo herds as an eventual consequence of the white man's coming. Using his influence to prepare his people for survival, he pushed them into more extensive farming. As early as 1836, for example, when the Omahas joined with other tribes in ceding to the United States lands claimed by them east of the Missouri River, Big Elk used the money received from the United States to buy for his tribe both farm machinery and the services of a resident blacksmith.

Despite his efforts, the white settlers traveling west through Omaha's lands often imperiled Big Elk's tribe's entire supply of food by destroying their fields of beans and corn and mercilessly killing

Native Americans

off their game. At the same time, the new emphasis on farming over hunting made Big Elk's followers objects of distrust by those Indians, even within the tribe, determined to live in the old way.

And, to make matters worse, the Sioux became ever more hostile. An 1845 report to the Secretary of War from the Indian Commissioner read:

> *The Omahas are a peaceable people and have ever been the friends of the whites. From their exposed position of poverty, not being able to procure firearms, they are rapidly being reduced by the frequent attacks of war parties.*

Big Elk died in 1853 after a life of service to his tribe. But before his death, he visited Washington and took part in some of his tribe's treaties with the United States. Upon his return he addressed the Omahas as follows:

> *My chiefs, braves and young men, I have just returned from a visit to a far-off country toward the rising sun, and I have seen many strange things. I bring to you news which it saddens my heart to think of. There is a coming flood which will soon reach us, and I advise you to prepare for it. Soon the animals which* Waconda *has given us for sustenance will disappear beneath this flood to return no more, and it will be very hard for you.*

Big Elk wisely made provision for the reins of the head chief to be passed upon his death to an adopted son, a half-breed, Iron Eye (*Esta-Ma-Za*), known to the whites as Joseph La Flesche. This transfer of power was consented to by all Omaha chiefs as well as Washington authorities who sent Iron Eye papers bearing the great seal of the United States.

Although the new chief had no education and could neither read, write nor speak English, Indians and whites alike admired him as a

16

man of thought and good judgment, an unlearned, natural philosopher. Like Big Elk before him, he was determined that the tribe should be brought as soon as possible to abandon the Indian mode of life, go to farming and send its children to school. Half the tribe agreed with him; half disagreed, mainly in opposition to the education of the children.

Until 1854 the Omahas remained determined to abide in the land of their fathers, resisting all pressure and offers to go to Indian Territory (Oklahoma). Yet in that year they decided to sell their lands to the United States, reserving for themselves a portion on the Missouri River lying some eighty miles north of Bellevue.

The treaty containing the terms of the sale was duly executed with *X*'s by Iron Eye and six of his fellow chiefs, all in front of witnesses. It also was signed by George W. Manypenny, Indian commissioner and, ultimately, by President Franklin Pierce before being ratified by two-thirds of the Senate.

In return for an agreement by the United States to pay an aggregate of eight hundred and seventy thousand dollars over a period of years, other sums, large and small, and other promises made, the Omahas relinquished all their rights to their lands west of the Missouri River. They reserved for themselves only a small rectangle of land bordering the river in the northwest corner of the present state of Nebraska, about three hundred thousand acres. The tribe thus ceded to the United States about four million acres of land for less than twenty cents an acre.

During the early years under Iron Eye's leadership, tribal members cleared ground for tillage of corn in the new reservation and erected houses and schools. As good hunting first diminished and then ceased altogether, the proceeds from the sale of increased yields of corn to buyers in neighboring Sioux City allowed them to purchase meat products to take the place of the buffalo.

Among the chiefs who traveled to Washington to sign the treaty was White Horse (*Shongaska*), also known as Logan Fontenelle, the only one among them with any kind of formal education. His father,

Native Americans

Chief Logan Fontenelle

Lucien, a descendant of a distinguished French family, had picked the life of a trapper in the wilderness over a sophisticated existence in New Orleans or St. Louis. Appropriately, he had chosen for his mate Logan's mother, Bright Sun (*Meumbane*), one of Big Elk's daughters.

Born in 1825, Logan was reared in the two cultures, French and Indian. While Lucien was in Bellevue between trips to the Rockies to trade for furs, Logan and Bright Sun resided with him near Peter Sarpy's trading post in a more-than-fancy house Lucien had built and furnished in the white man's fashion. However, while Lucien was off on his long trips west, Bright Sun and Logan lived the life of the Indian with Bright Sun's own family in a nearby Omaha village.

Although Logan spent a few youthful years in St. Louis perfecting his French and learning English and the white man's manners, he grew to prefer the Indian life, especially the hunt. With stature slightly below the medium, he stood straight as an arrow. With prominent, dark, piercing eyes and long straight hair, he was deemed courteous and polished in white society. But among his mother's people he was a true Indian. His cousin tells us that although he was alert and generous to a fault to his friends, to his enemies (the Sioux) he was as relentless as he was unforgiving.

After the treaty party's return from Washington, the Omahas were ordered to remove to their new reservation. Fontenelle made a vigorous protest against it until the government should take steps to protect his tribe against raids by the Sioux, an obligation clearly stated in the treaty. By 1855 the Omahas' population had diminished to a little more than a thousand members, yet the Sioux at that time were roaming all over northern Nebraska.

When no protection appeared, Fontenelle spoke to his people

assembled in Bellevue. It was murder, he said, to place the unarmed and defenseless Omahas directly in the path of their hereditary enemies. Then, placing his hand on his revolver, he uttered these words: "This is good for six Sioux anyhow; we will go and meet our fate."

In meeting his own fate he delivered half his promise. A short time later, when the Omahas were on a hunt out of their new reservation, a party of Sioux overwhelmed them. *Shongaska* fell. His fellow tribesmen found his dead body surrounded by three of the enemy taken with his six-shooter.

His remains were returned to Bellevue for burial near his home in what is now Fontenelle Forest. Mourning Indians, many French traders and other whites from near and far honored him at a funeral presided over by a friend and neighbor, Stephen Decatur (only remotely related to the famous U.S. naval hero), who read the Episcopal burial service at his grave.

The transfer of title of Indian lands to the United States in 1853 now made possible the creation of Omaha City, as it was first called, directly across the river from what was then called Kanesville, now Council Bluffs, Iowa. The new city grew rapidly, especially after successfully competing with other new towns cropping up along the west bank of the Missouri River. Each wanted to be the eastern starting point of the railroad designed to connect the West and East coasts. Not only did Omaha win out in this regard, but for a while was the site of the capitol of the new Nebraska Territory.

Over the past one hundred and fifty years, many Native Americans have visited the city; some have come to stay. Arriving from every part of the country and from every tribe, they have helped staff Omaha industry. Many left their reservations during periods of war to take defense jobs in the city or to enlist in one of the armed forces. Today many are located, some permanently, some temporarily, in older areas near downtown Omaha and in South Omaha's older ethnic areas.

In the course of the years, Native Americans have so intermarried with persons other than their tribe, or even their race, that few

Native Americans

presently can claim to be of full blood, yet all remain proud of their Indian heritage. It has been estimated that as the century ends, Omaha can claim twenty-five hundred to four thousand persons of Indian blood. If one tries, he can discover them in almost every profession, business and trade, but he will be hard-pressed to find them as a group, since they live scattered throughout the city.

One Omaha collection point is the Ponca Health and Wellness Center at Twenty-sixth and J streets, a government-funded clinic offering free health care to all members of federally recognized Indian tribes. Tribal and clinic officials use traditional and modern methods to treat the Native Americans.

Reginald Buckman and the Ponca Health and Wellness Center sweat lodge

Along with the usual health care of scalpels, syringes and prescription drugs administered by Dr. Tawfig F. Ansari is the use of a genuine sweat lodge, a handmade pipe and herbal tea provided by Reginald Buckman who is of Sioux ancestry. Twelve of the clinic's seventeen employees are Indians who serve over eighteen hundred registered tribal members.

20

Native Americans

Some Native Americans have become prominent members of the community. One such is Charles Trimble, the thirteenth child of a Lakota Sioux mother and a white father. Born in the village of Wanglee, South Dakota, on the Pine Ridge Sioux Reservation, Trimble was schooled by Catholics in their Holy Rosary Mission, now Red Cloud Indian School, located on reservation land one hundred miles southeast of his birthplace.

Later he graduated from the University of South Dakota at Vermillion and served in the military before attending graduate school in journalism. Serving as editor of an Indian newspaper inspired Trimble to form the American Indian Press Association, joining Indian publications throughout the United States. Success with this led to national stature as a director of the National Congress of American Indians.

Having given of his time as a past president of the Nebraska State Historical Society and on the boards of a variety of non-profit organizations, Trimble currently focuses his attention on the John G. Neihardt Foundation. As a part of his work he is developing literary talent among Indian youth of high school level.

Very much a fan of Black Elk, a prominent Nebraska Sioux holy man, he believes that Neihardt's was the perfect pen to translate Black Elk's utterances and catch the spirit of his philosophy for the world.

No account touching on the relation of the Native American to the Omaha community would be complete without a reference to a dramatic event involving the Ponca tribe and one of its leaders, Standing Bear (*Mochunozhi*).

In 1868, the army established headquarters for the Army of the Platte at Fort Omaha (first named Sherman Barracks, then Omaha Barracks), five miles northwest of the new city. Named as the fort's commanding officer was Brigadier General George Crook, who became a participant in a trial that eventually brought a great victory for Native Americans.

During this era the United States was busy making treaties with many Indian tribes, among them the Poncas, whose rights were thus

Native Americans

reserved in 1858 to their old village sites north of the Niobrara River. Despite this solemn pact and with no knowledge or consent on their part, in 1868 some negligent U.S. agent drafted a treaty that granted the Sioux a large reservation of land erroneously including these ancestral Ponca lands. Yet no one informed the Poncas.

In 1877, issuing no warning and giving no reason, government officials told the Ponca chiefs that they must exchange their tribal lands for ones in Oklahoma and move to Indian Territory. Their loud protests did not prevent them from being escorted forthwith to Oklahoma to find a new reservation.

Nevertheless, instead of picking out new reservation lands, they picked up and went home. In the dead of winter and with only a few dollars and a blanket each, they walked five hundred miles back to their native lands on the Niobrara. The United States Indian agent was waiting for them. Summoning the military, this time he escorted the entire tribe, almost seven hundred persons, back to Indian Territory.

The change from a cool climate to a warm and humid one caused much suffering. Within one year a third of the tribe was dead, the remainder sick or disabled. Among the dead was the son of Chief Standing Bear.

Believing he could not bury his son away from his ancestors and even though it was January, the father took his son's bones and, gathering his immediate followers, left the "hot country" for the long trek back to the Omaha reservation where they hoped to find help. When they reached the reservation in May, penniless, near starvation and with bloodied feet, their Omaha relatives took them in and readily granted them loans of land and seed. They started to plant.

To no avail. Soldiers again appeared to arrest Standing Bear and his party and return them once more. While on their way back to Oklahoma, the prisoners camped at Fort Omaha, where General Crook saw them and heard their story.

Crook was revolted by his military orders to remove them. There is some evidence that he described the Indians' plight to Thomas Henry Tibbles, the assistant editor of the **Omaha Daily**

Herald. In any event, Tibbles learned somehow of the Poncas' misery and immediately sought the help of two prominent Omaha lawyers, John Webster and Andrew Jackson Poppleton.

The lawyers knew what to do. On behalf of Standing Bear and his party, they petitioned for writs of habeas corpus in the United States District Court and named Crook as defendant. The petition asserted that the Indians had broken no laws and were entitled to be released by the court.

General George Crook

The district attorney defended the actions principally on the ground that, whatever the circumstance, the Indians had no right to such remedy. The Constitution assures the right of habeas corpus only to "persons," the defendant argued, and an Indian was not a "person" within the meaning of the law.

The matter came before Judge Elmer S. Dundy. During the course of the hearing, the testimony of Standing Bear and members of his tribe revealed not only the unlawful transfer of Ponca lands to the Sioux, but the extent to which the Poncas, like the Omahas, had attempted by their farms, schools and churches on their reservation lands to adapt to the white man's culture, to give up their tribal structure and to be farmers, merely, each working his own tract of land.

During the two days of testimony by both Poncas and Omahas, Standing Bear, himself, wearing the full regalia of a tribal chief, uttered these words to the court:

> *My hand is not the same color as yours, but, if you pierce it, I shall feel the pain. The blood will be the same color. We are men, the same God made*

23

Native Americans

Chief Standing Bear

us . . . All I ask is what is mine—my land, my freedom, my dignity, as a man.

After eloquent legal arguments of counsel and after much research and deliberation, Judge Dundy decided that an Indian was, indeed, a "person" within the meaning of the law and that there was no authority under the laws of the United States to remove forcibly the prisoners to Indian Territory. In a landmark decision later upheld by the United States Supreme Court, he ordered their release.

After the trial, Standing Bear sought out Tibbles for a private conversation. With only an interpreter in attendance, he addressed him thus:

> *When I was brought here as a prisoner, my heart was broken. I was in despair. Then you came. From that time until now you have not ceased to work for me . . . I remember the dark day when you first came to speak to me. I know if it had not been for what you have done for me, I would be a prisoner in the Indian Territory, and many of these who are with me here would have been in their graves . . . I owe this all to you. I can never repay you for it.*

The following winter Standing Bear told his story to audiences in many Eastern cities. Publicity caused the United States Senate to order an investigation of the Ponca removal. Ultimately, those Poncas who chose to remain in Oklahoma were given good lands; Standing Bear and his followers recovered their old lands on the Niobrara and lost property was paid for.

In 1926, Congress finally passed a statute making all Native Americans citizens of the United States.

REFERENCES

BOOKS

Charvat, Charles. **Logan Fontenelle**. Omaha: The American Printing Company, 1961.

Fletcher, Alice C. **Omaha Tribe of Indians**. Washington, D.C.: Judd and Detweiler, 1885.

Fletcher, Alice C. and Francis La Flesche. **The Omaha Tribe.** 1911. Reprint. 2 vols. Lincoln: University of Nebraska Press, 1992.

Giffen, Fannie Reed. **Oo-Mah-Ha (Omaha City)**. 1908. Reprint. Omaha: River Junction Press, 1998.

Tibbles, Thomas Henry. **Standing Bear and the Ponca Chiefs**. 1880. Reprint. Lincoln: University of Nebraska Press, 1985.

INTERVIEWS

Trimble, Charles. Interviews by Harry B. Otis. October 24, 1997, and October 30, 1998.

MISCELLANEOUS

Ponca Health and Wellness Center. Pamphlet. Omaha.

United States of America and the Omaha Tribe of Indians. **Treaty**. Washington, D.C., 1853.

United States of America and the Ponca Tribe of Indians. **Treaty**. Washington, D.C., 1858.

NEWSPAPERS

Blackwood, Kendrick. Article describing Ponca Health and Wellness Center activities. **The Omaha World-Herald**.

THE COLONIAL DESCENDANTS

Colonial descendants are those whose ancestors emigrated to the thirteen original colonies before 1776 from some part of the British Isles: England, Scotland, Wales and North Ireland. They considered English their native tongue, and most were Protestants. In a word, they were WASPS, white Anglo-Saxon Protestants, a moniker hung on their progeny.

These descendants were born in the early part of the nineteenth century on the Eastern Seaboard in states created after the American Revolution. All had primary school training of some kind; many came to Omaha with college educations and some, having trained as doctors, lawyers, dentists and clergymen, had professional talents. Most arrived with some money in their pockets, ready to meet the challenge of building a new city.

Their ability to speak an American vernacular of English gave them an overwhelming advantage. Quite naturally, along with some Germans and Irish who also were first settlers, they were destined to be Omaha's early leaders.

Who were these young Americans, those whom Horace Greeley of the **New York Herald Tribune** admonished to go west and grow up with the country? Most of them, in their early twenties, came to Omaha from farms of every eastern state with an immense desire to get rich.

Although possessing definite advantages, they were just as much strangers to Omaha as those from foreign countries. Like the foreigners, they had to work their way up. Many succeeded, and some, like the early territorial governors, later would be honored by having Omaha streets named after them. Quite a few would grow wealthy enough to reside in huge, Victorian houses built in the various gold coast districts that developed from era to era.

Yet there were no guarantees. Like fellow immigrants from foreign lands, they faced the same muddy streets, inadequate housing and desolate landscape. More than one asked himself why, indeed, he

EDWARD CREIGHTON

EZRA MILLARD

SAMUEL MERCER

JOHN WEBSTER

JESSE LOWE

ANDREW POPPLETON

BYRON REED

BISHOP
ROBERT CLARKSON

Early pioneers of Omaha, inset: Byron Reed's Real Estate Office, circa 1860

had left his verdant eastern home to come to this land of sub-zero winters and oven-like summers where the mosquitos thrived, the saddles were hard, the beds narrow and the hot-water baths few. While dealing with raw whiskey, demanding Indians and rough characters, each had the opportunity to learn first-hand about bed-rock friendship, shaky government and swift justice.

Space permits us to list only a few of the more prominent among them.

Enos Lowe, an original pioneer of Omaha, was born in North Carolina in 1804, grew up in Indiana and received a medical degree in Cincinnati, Ohio. He was at Kanesville (now Council Bluffs) in 1853 when he and some friends, even before the territory was established, organized a ferry company and participated in laying out Omaha City. He later played a prominent role in securing the building of the Union Pacific Railway bridge at the Omaha site, a matter critical to the city's development.

Jesse Lowe, Enos's younger brother, is reputed to have given the city its name. He became its first mayor when it was chartered by the territorial legislature in 1857.

A. D. Jones, a colorful character, crossed the Missouri River to Indian Territory in 1853 with two friends in a leaky scow, surveyed a portion of the future city and staked out a claim to a part of it for himself. Following the transfer of lands to the United States in 1853 by the Omaha tribe and the passage of the Territorial Organic Act, Jones was hired to make a survey of the whole site—three hundred and twenty blocks. As the appointed postmaster in the new territory, he kept the mail in his hat.

Andrew Jackson Poppleton, a member of the Michigan bar, came to Omaha in 1854 at the age of twenty-four to set up a general practice in the brand new community. After serving in the first two sessions of the territorial legislature, he was elected mayor of the city and later appointed, along with J. Sterling Morton, to serve as United States senator. As his law career progressed, Poppleton's practice increasingly involved the affairs of the Union Pacific Railroad, yet

Colonial Descendants

he found time to help draft the revised statutes of Nebraska when it became a new state in 1867.

Another lawyer, James M. Woolworth, arrived in Omaha in 1856 at age twenty-seven to become Omaha's first city attorney, as well as the first chancellor of the new Episcopal diocese of Nebraska. His business ventures in livestock and banking made him a wealthy citizen.

Dr. Samuel D. Mercer, after serving as an army surgeon during the Civil War, came in 1866 to practice medicine in Omaha at the age of twenty-four. He organized the Nebraska State Medical Society and the Omaha Medical College. His successful practice led to the role of chief surgeon for the Union Pacific. He platted the Walnut Hill addition where his large brick residence at Fortieth and Cuming still stands. His descendants control a large part of the Old Market district of the city, a part of his real estate holdings.

Ezra Millard arrived in Omaha in 1856 at age twenty-two. Ten years later he organized the Omaha National Bank (now US Bank). He helped establish a cable railway company. In 1870 he was elected mayor of Omaha.

Two other Omahans arrived about a decade later than the earlier ones, but were no less celebrated, John Lee Webster and Robert Harper Clarkson.

Webster arrived at age nineteen in 1869 after service in the Civil War and postwar studies leading to admission to the bar. His was a distinguished legal career during the latter half of the century. His pro bono efforts on behalf of Standing Bear and his Ponca tribesmen, along with those of A. J. Poppleton, opened the gate to civil rights for Native Americans.

Clarkson, born in Gettysburg, Pennsylvania in 1826 and ordained as an Episcopal priest in 1851, came to Omaha at age forty in 1866 to serve as the missionary bishop of Nebraska and Dakota. He was a man greatly admired by all Omahans, as much for establishing hospitals and schools as for setting up churches in Nebraska and Dakota cities. Under his auspices, Omaha's Trinity Episcopal Cathedral, still standing, was completed in 1882 at Eighteenth and

Capitol. He and his wife are buried in its churchyard.

Byron Reed was only twenty-six when he reached Omaha in 1855 from service as a telegrapher in Cleveland, Ohio. He was born in Darien, New York, of Puritan ancestry. Before his trek to Omaha, he worked for a short while for the **New York Tribune,** reporting the events of the border ruffian war concerning slavery in bloody Kansas. He founded the Byron Reed Company in 1856 and achieved great success in real estate and international fame for coin collection.

These and many other early Americans were on hand to provide a welcome to all the citizens from other countries who have graced the city. Rough as the early years may have been, considering the establishment of clubs to enforce illegal real estate claims and physical brawls in the territorial legislature, these colonial descendants, especially the lawyers, started it out on the right foot by bringing to Omaha a knowledge of the nation's Anglo-Saxon system of laws necessary for the establishment of a sound society.

Cyrus Morton

Typical of these young men, but perhaps not so well known, is Cyrus Morton, of Scotch-Irish heritage, born in a log cabin in 1831 on a West Virginia farm. He headed west at age twenty-two to buy an Iowa farm, leaving home with enough money to pay the expenses of the trip, plus three hundred dollars in twenty-dollar gold pieces, the proceeds of a loan from his father, which his mother sewed into his belt.

Cyrus and a fellow traveler, John Marsh, rode the train to Rock Island, Illinois, crossed the Mississippi River by ferryboat and commenced a long walk across Iowa from government land office to land office looking for a good farm each could afford to buy. Their first stop was Iowa City. Finding the country all settled up and farms worth from ten to twenty-five dollars per acre, each placed a change of clothing in one of their two heavy satchels, and, leaving the balance of their effects in storage subject to their later order, resumed the walk to Fort Des Moines, the next office.

Disappointment again. Finding no suitable land out of Des Moines, off they walked west. Yet, even after having discovered affordable parcels in Cass County, Iowa, they reached the Council Bluffs land office to be confronted with a change of procedures requiring an expensive three-week wait for proposed purchases. Nothing to do but cross the river to find temporary work.

A sometimes muddy, sometimes dusty 1854 Omaha contained about a thousand people, many in tents and wagons, uncertain as to whether to stay or go on to California. Before finding work, Morton and his friend entertained themselves for a few hours viewing an inebriated early acquaintance, William P. Snowden, auction off an Indian pony, and watching Native American teenagers with bows and arrows shoot at coins lodged in split sticks whose ends were stuck in the ground. An Indian could claim any money he knocked out of the stick.

After a half-day's work in laying a floor in a cheap house for which each received one dollar, Morton and Marsh found two-week's work on a farm owned by Harrison Johnson, which lay between Twentieth and Twenty-seventh, Farnam and Leavenworth streets. Johnson and his wife became their fast friends. The two West Virginians intended to return home after buying the Iowa land they had chosen, but two weeks stretched to a whole summer when a temporary closure of the land office botched their ability to buy the farms they wanted.

It was at this point that Morton made a decision that tied him, however loosely, to Omaha. He paid one hundred dollars for a squatter's right to one hundred and sixty acres of land located three miles southwest of Omaha. He would own it to the end of his days.

But to live, he and Marsh had to work. Using three to four yoke of oxen provided by their employer, they broke the prairie soil of most of Johnson's tract. Morton drove the oxen, and Marsh handled the plow. Every night the grazing beasts would stray all over town; every morning the two would have to round them up before eight o'clock in order to resume the sod busting. This was not easy work.

One noon, when the men were eating their dinner, some Pawnee Indians stole a file, hammer and wrench left with their plow. Overtaking the thieves at a little creek where Leavenworth now crosses Twenty-fourth Street, they confronted them with sufficient sign language to make them understand they meant business, yet finally had to be content to recover only the stolen hammer from under one Indian's blanket.

Completing their sod breaking job, the two young adventurers decided to explore the Platte River valley. There, in the fall, they built the first cabin near the future site of Fremont on a land claim they had filed. Nevertheless, with winter coming on, they returned to Omaha to board with the Johnsons and assist with winter chores, including hog butchering.

It was well they had returned. While they were working, a winter storm blew in cold enough to freeze the pork they were piling in the back end of the kitchen. There it lay frozen all winter, to be chopped apart with an axe, a little at a time.

The winter proving exceptionally cold and snowy, Morton took time off to make a sled whose runners he cut from a forked elm tree. Its sale to the sheriff of Douglas County for sixteen dollars gave him more money than he had seen in a long time.

A major job was to cut and haul cordwood which Johnson sold for from seven to ten dollars per cord. Marsh cut; Morton hauled. When through with the day's haul, Morton daily would bring his boss back home from a session of the legislature of which he was a member. At that time the governing body met in the old Pioneer block between Eleventh and Twelfth on the north side of Farnam Street. Morton learned a considerable amount that winter listening to the arguments of members, "some of which were more forcible than elegant."

In the summer of 1857 the men helped Johnson make hay and in the fall harvest grain, before returning home to West Virginia for the winter. It was during this period that Morton preempted the quarter section of the squatter's claim he had purchased in June of 1856. To do so, the law required him to furnish his land with a house having a floor, door and window and to live in it for five days and nights. To bear witness for each other, a friend of his and he took turns living in each other's shanties for the required periods.

Upon his return to Omaha, Morton experienced a series of adventures. First, Johnson asked him to assist him in a two-week chase after a horse thief. Their horses carried them, without success, as far south as Leavenworth, Kansas. Next, gold fever struck both Morton and Marsh, causing them to buy oxen and milk cows for a proposed trip to the Pike's Peak goldfield strike. Before leaving, however, they changed their minds when they saw disappointed miners streaming back to Omaha.

This was just a start. In September 1860, in company with Johnson, they got up an outfit for hauling goods west. It took thirty-five days for three ox wagons with shelled corn to reach Denver. In 1861 they made two more trips with wagons now loaded with bacon, yet started the second trip too late in the fall to avoid snow and lots of problems. Back in Omaha and undiscouraged, they exchanged their cattle for mules and made five more trips in 1862.

Now Morton, at least, was ready for high adventure. During the summer of 1862, gold was discovered at Bannock in Beaverhead County, Montana Territory. The lure of gold and the fear of being drafted to fight a war against his fellow Virginians were sufficient incentives for him to head west. For the next five years, until he got off a boat that took him from Fort Benton to Omaha, he led the life

34

of a prospector.

For five years he walked more miles than most of his contemporaries traveled in a life time. Then, as now, Bannock, Montana, was a long way from Omaha, especially for one following plodding oxen. Furthermore, Morton had to acquire more new skills than most. One minute he was using his resources to salvage cooked bacon from a Denver warehouse, totally destroyed by fire, which had housed the provisions he had stored for his trip west. The sale of this bacon more than put him back on his feet. The next minute he was salvaging the iron tires of a government wagon which had been abandoned after a fire and discovered by him on his way to the goldfields. The sale of the scrap to a Bannock blacksmith netted nine dollars in gold dust, the first he had seen.

While he was actively mining the many different claims he purchased at Bannock and later at Last Chance Gulch near Helena, his ingenuity allowed him to recover gold where others failed. Furthermore, he always was on the alert to turn a dollar through the sale of scarce commodities, buying and selling flour and other provisions with the guile of a Turkish merchant.

By now he knew something about how to build cabins. Against a harsh Montana winter, he and others built a double log cabin with a stone fireplace, where, in beds three feet off the ground and covered with buffalo robes, they slept comfortably in forty-below weather.

Not that his life was a bed of roses. Sometimes there were Indians to contend with, some justifiably on the warpath. A diet of biscuits and bacon fat and the company of rough miners could become monotonous. But he had periods of respite in Salt Lake City where he could enjoy the fresh peaches provided by Mormon wives and hear Brigham Young preach a sermon or two in the new tabernacle.

In the fall of 1867, Morton and a friend, selling whatever interest they had in the mine they were then working, headed for a boat at Fort Benton, advertised to take them down the Missouri River to Omaha for one hundred dollars in greenbacks (fifty dollars in gold). The sixty-day trip from September to November involved many

View of Capitol Hill from downtown Omaha, circa 1865

incidents, including daily grounding on sandbars and a futile search for a prisoner who had escaped from the boat at Yankton. Nevertheless, Morton at last got home, glad to turn over his hoard of gold dust to Ezra Millard, pay four dollars a day for a room in the Cozzen's House, get a new suit of clothes and again see his old friends, the Johnsons.

Now it was time for a trip back to his West Virginia home to visit his parents once more. There Morton pleased his father by repaying with interest the early loans, both the one for three hundred dollars and a later loan that had allowed him to preempt the one hundred and sixty acres. Also, he was able to pay off John Marsh for his interest in the property.

He returned to Omaha in 1869 to start improvements. For this purpose he bought and broke four mules and two breaking plows, and got John Marsh to build him a house. That season he broke sixty virgin acres of sod; the next season he plowed the rest. In the meantime, his father died. Heeding his mother's request to return to live with her and his sister and manage their farm, he rented out his Omaha property in order to spend the next five years in West Virginia.

While home, he married Marsh's sister, and Marsh married his. Although the two couples planned to return to Omaha together when the time was right, to the bitter disappointment of everyone, family matters forced the Marshes to remain back East. While still farming his family's West Virginia farm, in 1874 Morton had acquired forty additional acres of land in Omaha adjoining his original quarter section. Twenty of these new acres bordered Center Street. He was anxious to return to his two-hundred-acre farm.

For a month after the couple moved to Omaha, they occupied but one room of the Marsh-built house that housed the tenant farmer. After Morton built another small house for the tenant, they occupied the whole of the older house, whose address became 4601 Center Street, and were able to move in all their furniture and other household effects brought from the East.

At last Morton could farm his own land with good Virginia corn seed. He planted twenty acres. Alas, on June 14, 1875, came grasshoppers in swarms great enough to obliterate the corn rows. The locusts, as they called them, liked the Virginia seed better than the local variety. That year he made only half a crop.

As the years went on, while Cyrus farmed, Mary bore two sons, Mark and George, the latter in 1877. As his health gradually failed, Cyrus more and more had to rely on these sons and others for the farm work. The boys had been prepared. Cyrus was a firm believer that growing boys should work hard. His favorite saying was, "A change in work is as good as a rest for a growing boy." Such "rests" involved raising poultry, tending vegetable gardens and herding cattle.

In the belief that occupancy of higher ground would help his health improve, he built for his family a new house at 4602 Center Street, directly to the north of where he lived. Mary occupied it until her death. It stands to this day.

Although Mark Morton, like his father, chose to go west and grow up as a rancher near Sterling, Colorado, his brother, George, remained

37

Colonial Descendants

in Omaha to become a dealer in real estate. Prominent in civic affairs, he was a driving force in the creation of the city's planning commission. A firm believer in public parks, against strong opposition he was instrumental in the passage of legislation requiring developers to dedicate portions of their platted properties for recreational use. In 1954 he donated to the city four acres of his own land for park and playground.

In 1923 and 1925 George Morton and others platted Morton Meadows from part of the two-hundred-acre farm he had inherited from his father. Standing at 4201 Poppleton, his was the first house built in the new addition.

As the twentieth century died away, Cyrus's grandson, Charles, a retired Omaha architect, still resided in the city, almost one hundred and fifty years from the time that his grandfather came looking for land. This stretch of time covers most of Omaha's history. Colonial descendants like the Mortons had an unusually strong influence on the city's growth. Three generations of Mortons personify the dedication and hard work this class of immigrant produced. In the fabric of the city, they and the others wove a strong and durable strand in the tapestry that is Omaha.

REFERENCES

BOOKS

Dustin, Dorothy Devereaux. **Omaha and Douglas County: A Panoramic History.** Oakland, CA: Windsor Publications, 1980.

Morton, Cyrus. **Autobiography of Cyrus Morton**. Omaha: Douglas Printing Company, 1895.

Sorenson, Alfred. **History of Omaha**. Omaha: Gibson-Miller-Richardson Printers, 1889.

INTERVIEWS

Morton, Charles. Taped interview by Harry B. Otis. February 13, 1999.

NEWSPAPERS

McMorris, Robert. *City Was Allowed to Grow with Adept Anticipation.* **The Omaha World-Herald**. October 24, 1970.

My First Job. **The Omaha World-Herald**. June 12, 1960.

Nielsen, Nathan. *1856 Omaha City of Transients*. **The Omaha World-Herald**. June 27, 1959.

THE IRISH

The Irish were among the first Omahans. Once congressional passage of the Kansas-Nebraska Act in 1854 permitted new settlements on the west bank of the Missouri River, Irish immigrants poured in to help build the new city.

Omaha's first contractor was James Ferry, an Irishman who constructed most of its early buildings, including the first territorial capitol. While Ferry was so occupied, his wife delivered a daughter, Margaret, Omaha's first white child.

Other Irishmen came close on Ferry's heels. Some were affluent; others poor. A few were Protestants; most were Catholics. Yet almost all were friends, united in an unending desire for an Ireland free of British domination.

Under Father John Cavanaugh, the Catholics built their first church in 1856. St. Mary was but a modest frame building topped by a wooden cross. Later came St. Philomena, a church that became a cathedral and later a cherished parish for Omaha's Italian population who renamed it St. Frances Cabrini.

Among the wealthier Irish coming to town in the early days were Edward Creighton and John, his brother, arriving from Ohio to supply miners with picks, shovels and other equipment for the Colorado gold rush of the late 1850s. Different opportunities soon came their way.

Edward Creighton no sooner started a lumber business than he abandoned it in favor of telegraphy. Having successfully strung telegraph lines in Eastern states, as well as from St. Louis to Omaha, he dreamed of a line coast to coast.

To make arrangements and show that the route was feasible, he rode a horse to Sacramento, California and back before starting to string wires between Omaha and Salt Lake City. At the same time, his partners brought the line from Sacramento to the Mormon capital. By October 28, 1862, the new service was in place.

This activity produced a coast-to-coast telegraph service for the nation and a pocket full of Western Union stock for Creighton. The telegraph not only put an end to the Pony Express but contributed directly to President Lincoln's decision to make Omaha the starting point for the Union Pacific Railroad.

Telegraph line construction

The fortune Creighton created allowed him to join the German, pioneer Kountze brothers in founding the First National Bank of Omaha, the First National Bank of Denver and another in Central City, Colorado. While other Creightons served these banks as managers, Edward entered the ranching business and also dealt in Omaha real estate. He became a wealthy man. Unfortunately he died early, in 1874 at the age of fifty-six.

His wife and brother carried out his dying request. Denied more than a fifth grade education, Creighton had dreamed of founding a place of higher learning for others. Four years after his death, the two used his money and their own to create Creighton College, which would become Creighton University. A few years later his estate funded Omaha Creighton Memorial-St. Joseph Hospital .

James E. Boyd arrived in America at age twenty-three from the Irish county, Tyrone, amd traveled by foot from the east coast in 1856 to find work in Omaha as a carpenter. A few years later saw him grow wealthy as a contractor, grading three hundred miles of track for the Union Pacific. Unlike the Creightons, he left no lasting monument such as a university or a hospital, yet during his day he was twice elected mayor of Omaha and once, in 1890, governor of Nebraska.

Meanwhile, he organized the Omaha Gas Works, the Omaha and Northwestern Railroad Company (building a road to Blair), helped create one bank and became president of another. Later he opened the state's second packinghouse. And in the course of his career, he built two opera houses in Omaha, one of which burned in 1893 and was rebuilt.

Less prominent early Irish sweated mile after mile with picks and shovels building the Union Pacific Railroad to Promontory Summit, Utah. After the railroad was completed, many returned to live in Omaha where the road had had its beginning. Here they found work in the U.P. shops or jobs in the slaughterhouses blossoming in South Omaha. Some opened saloons to assuage the thirst of these workers and serve the other immigrants swarming into the city.

While some Irish came directly from their land of origin, a majority, many second generation refugees of the 1840s potato famine, drifted into Omaha from the east coast of the United States. The Yankee population of New York City, Boston and Philadelphia had seldom extended them cordial receptions and often had frustrated their search for jobs. Too much religious and ethnic prejudice existed; too many eastern companies posted signs on their doors: "Irish need not apply."

Not so in Omaha. Here the city welcomed all newcomers. Here there was a fair chance for everyone. In the early days, the city's rapid growth meant plenty of work.

For a short time the Irish clustered in Sheeleytown, an area near the Sheeley Packing Company at Twenty-fourth and Bancroft. But after a few years they scattered throughout the city and into every social level, leaving the Sheeley district to Polish immigrants.

It was well they dispersed, for later in the century both they and other immigrants were not without their Omaha detractors. During

Irish

job scarcity, caused by the depression of the 1890s, a bigoted organization called The American Protective Organization cited them as targets in a failed effort to drive them out of town.

Piper Denny Moriarty from the Omaha Pipes and Drums with Dualta Dancers, Claire Haire, Amy Landholm and Patricia Palma

Yet the frontier was a great leveler. Omaha always has been essentially democratic. It readily accepted and assimilated the ebullient Irish who invariably infected fellow Omahans with their Celtic charm, winning them over as friends and neighbors. Their presence has played a major role in creating Omaha's lasting reputation as a place of friendly people with hometown virtues.

Of course it was an immense help to the early Irish that they all spoke English. The many stories they told of the old country—often related in an incomparable brogue over a glass of beer—was their method of endearing themselves to the natives and to the other immigrants, softening cultural differences.

One wag announced to his fellow Omahans: "In this country ivery man's just as good as ivery other man and, for that matter, just a little bit better!"

Whether it was the consequence of bitter memories of the potato famine or the result of other influences, most new Irish immigrants chose city life over farming. An Irish friend once told Omaha writer, Bob Reilly, that it was the land that had betrayed them. In any event, they tended to enter business and politics.

Thus Thomas J. O'Connor (no kin to his namesake who held the post a hundred years later) became register of deeds to head a long string of Irish taking government positions. And many besides Ed Creighton became bankers: John McCormack, Central National Bank; Frank Murphy, State Bank of Nebraska; John McShane, Union Stockyards Bank; H. F. Coad, Packers National Bank; and John Rush, Nebraska Savings and Exchange.

It is notable that the leading founders of the Union Stockyards Company in 1885 were all of Irish descent: John A. Creighton, John A. McShane, Frank Murphy and John H. Donnelly. South Omaha packinghouses were the creations of other native Irish. Sir Thomas Lipton, an Irishman born in Scotland, was an early Omaha meat packer. He later sold out to a Chicago company formed by Armour, later the Armour-Cudahy Company, and returned to tea peddling. Edward A. Cudahy, a young Irish immigrant, arrived in Omaha to run the new enterprise. Ultimately he bought Armour out. Many other Irish were engaged either as meat packers or ranchers.

Robert McMorris reports in the **Omaha World-Herald** on November 19, 1961, that one hundred years earlier Ben Gallagher had rolled into town with a lunch basket filled with sandwiches and a twenty-dollar gold piece sewed into the lining of his coat. He apparently ate the sandwiches before parlaying the twenty dollars into a fortune as the head of Paxton and Gallagher Company of Omaha, coffee roasters and leading wholesalers of groceries and hardware.

International fame came to other Irish-Omahans: Msgr. Edward Flanagan who founded Boys Town and W. H. Jeffers who, after working his way up from the bottom, became president of the Union Pacific. "The Irish built this railroad," he remarked, "it's time they

Irish

Father Flanagan

got to run it."

In more recent years President Harry Truman chose a man of Irish descent, eminent Omaha lawyer Francis P. Matthews, to serve the United States, first as Secretary of the Navy and second, in fulfillment of his lifelong ambition, as America's ambassador to Ireland. Matthews died in 1952 while on leave in the United States from his ambassadorial duties.

Following his death, his son, Frank Matthews, Jr., while in Dublin to help pack up his father's belongings, convinced yet another son of Ireland, John Mulhall, to come to Omaha. Mulhall proved to be one of the most delightfully effervescent Irishmen ever to grace the city. His friend, author Bob Reilly, calls John a version of the *sennachie*, the Irish storyteller who snuggled up against the turf fire in the old cottage days, preserving the history and the literature of the people.

John was born in 1922 in Tinahely, Wicklow County, when the new Republic of Ireland was scarcely a year old. His father, James, farmed about sixty acres of land and raised sheep and cattle; his mother, Bridget, reared three sons (John was the oldest) and four daughters, while tending to a garden and hordes of chickens. His brothers are still on the farm; his sisters long ago married and found homes in Dublin and London.

Situated immediately south of Dublin, Wicklow County is one of Ireland's fairest. Its beautiful wooded hills slope down to the Irish Sea, and the landscaped gardens at their feet provide a backdrop to seaside towns. Tinahely lies inland in the southwest part of the county at the foot of the Wicklow Hills.

John and his brothers were not without work to do, what with milking cows twice a day and tending the sheep, cattle and other livestock. The farm prospered while John was a young lad during the 1920s, yet its very success helped increase the problems of the new country. Other customers were hard to find for its agricultural products when England's new tariffs, reared against them following the political separation, barred their normal flow to that country. It took time to find alternative markets for Irish produce in America, France and elsewhere.

Yet there was time and money enough for John's education. After primary school in Tinahely, he graduated from a Catholic secondary school in Wexford, the county to the south.

Then fortune brought him a scholarship to Dublin University. Of course, it was for horticultural studies, as Ireland's economy, grounded in the export of foodstuffs, forced it to emphasize agricultural research above all other pursuits.

After qualifying for admission (one had to speak Gaelic to enter), John received an associate degree. However, he graduated during the worldwide depression of the 1940s that produced a glut of unsaleable foodstuffs in Ireland as well as everywhere else. For a time he had to find a living back on the farm.

> *I remember as a young man driving cattle all over the bloody countryside trying to sell them, John recounts. My dad said one day, "I think, John, that we'll have to get them shod"—as you would horses, because we were driving them so many places trying to sell them.*

Then, following a stint of work raising vegetables for a company started by an Irish agricultural minister, John took an exam for the position of head groundskeeper for the U.S. Embassy in Dublin, a place in the seventy-acre Phoenix Park previously owned by the British viceroy who ran the country before Ireland was freed.

Over approximately three hundred and fifty other applicants,

Irish

John won the competition. The embassy awarded him the prestigious job, provided him with living quarters and paid him a salary in U.S. dollars, a boon in those days. It provided a new experience and a decent living for him and his new wife, Maureen, from county Rosconmon.

Outside the ballroom of the fifty-room embassy building, where Winston Churchill once had resided, stood a three-story conservatory containing many and varied plantings, everything from palm trees and apple trees to roses and other flowers. With the help of fifteen laborers, John was in charge of maintaining this and the rest of the embassy grounds, twenty-five acres of greenhouses and a sophisticated garden enclosed by high walls. Believing that only a native Irishman had the sensitivity to handle the problems involved, the embassy wisely made John solely responsible for this horticulture.

Although his position inevitably put him in contact with all sorts of people: ambassadors from other countries, kings, queens, dukes, government officials, American congressmen and movie stars, none impressed him as much as Clare Hughes Matthews, the wife of the ambassador. She also had ancestral roots in the Emerald Isle. In his Irish brogue John speaks of her reverently:

> *[She] was one of the finest human beings that I ever encountered anywhere in the world—classy in every sense of the word. I didn't know Nebraska at all, but she tried to explain it to me, and so did her husband.*
>
> *She was an extraordinary person. This lovely lady by her husband's side would always have the right thing to say. The beauty, the proper beauty of language, and making the person with her—whether it was the highest dignitary in the world or the lowest person in it—make them feel comfortable and at home. She had that beautiful charm that is intellectual and very midwestern. She is one of the reasons I came to this country.*

Mrs. Matthews was still in Ireland when her husband died. President Truman not only sent a bomber from Greenland to bring her and her daughter, Marguerite, back to Washington, but also met the plane when it landed.

Since Mrs. Matthews already had sold Mulhall on Nebraska, Frank Jr. had little trouble convincing him to come to Omaha. John knew that the America he saw depicted in the movies was over-painted and inaccurate, yet he sensed that a real opportunity lay waiting for him.

With his wife's blessing, the two embarked on the journey that many others had taken before them, this time trading John's good-paying job and solid pension for the dream of a career in a new land.

They arrived in Omaha in 1953 with John having less in his pocket than the five hundred dollars Ireland permitted him to carry out of the country. After Matthews helped him find a three-hundred-dollar a month job with Omaha's park department, he and Maureen gently merged into postwar Omaha.

John had been with the city only a year and a half when he was hired away by Father Carl Reinert, president of Creighton University, who boosted his monthly pay to three hundred and fifty dollars. The two men fitted each other to a tee. In the course of time they became the best of friends. They both loved music as well as growing things and began to sing together, John driving Reinert crazy by hitting the top notes precisely on key.

Mulhall was determined to change the appearance of the campus. In a short time all sorts of things began to happen. Good things. First, Reinert and Mulhall, acting through the college board, got the city to vacate California Street. No more streetcars or buses rolling through the campus. Second, the magic doings of contractor Peter Kiewit and railroad president John Kenefick caused blacktop to be stripped from the vacated street and other areas so that John could plant things.

Now John was able to put down soil and flowers and lots of trees. Behold, a campus. He had helped to produce the nice walking area he wanted for the students. It was a large boost for Creighton and a great spiritual reward for him.

Irish

After a few years, John and Maureen were able to take the oath making them citizens of the United States.

In the late 1950s they lived in an apartment near Fiftieth and Underwood, expecting their second child and badly needing a house. Although John was doing some landscaping business on his own during his off-hours, the couple had little ready cash and even less credit.

To remedy the second problem, John borrowed one thousand dollars from the First National Bank and immediately repaid it with interest. Then he borrowed three thousand dollars. Having found a house for fourteen thousand and five hundred dollars at Fifty-first and Burt that fitted his needs and holding the three thousand dollars needed for the down payment, he now approached the mortgage loan section of the bank for a loan of the balance.

All was well until the mortgage agent learned that Mulhall's down payment for the house had come from the proceeds of another loan from the same bank. Appearing in the angry agent's office, John informed him that he had seven thousand dollars in a Dublin bank account which was blocked from removal by the Irish government (Matthews later got the money released for him). Upon hearing this news, the banker's ire abated.

John took the initiative, saying: "As crotchety as you may seem to me and as gullible as I may seem to you, we may yet become friends." At once the two men started to philosophize. Before long the agent announced: "Damn you, I am going to lend you the money!" And he did.

When John moved his family into the Burt Street house he suddenly had three jobs: the one at Creighton, a growing off-hours landscaping business and a remodeling effort. For three years he ripped out and replaced walls, painted, papered and otherwise restored a forty-year-old dwelling, performing tasks he had never before tackled.

His two eldest sons retain happy memories of their Burt Street lives: kindergarten days at Dundee School and early years at St. Margaret Mary Church School.

After a few more years, it was time to move again in order to find a nursery for John's growing business. He needed a place for his trucks. Profitably selling his Burt Street house, with the help of the Security National Bank he acquired a half-acre plot at Sixty-ninth and Blondo that boasted a building with a shop and office below and a dwelling place above. The business and the family moved in.

The demands of a growing nursery business were immense. Above all it needed space and lots of it. Over the ensuing years John bought and sold many parcels of real estate before finally rooting the business firmly at One hundred twentieth and Maple streets.

Today sons Sean and Dan Mulhall guide the business with the help of three hundred employees while their wives rear eight more Mulhalls, each family contributing four future gardeners. John's eldest son, Jim, practices medicine in Kansas City, Missouri, while his third son, Kevin, works as a CPA consultant. All four sons are graduates of Notre Dame.

No longer in active control of his business, John now has time for his church, St. Pius the Tenth at Sixty-ninth and Blondo, and Omaha betterment groups. His greatest concern is for Creighton University's trees and gardens, but he also

John Mulhall

Irish

loves to play golf and banter with his friends over a beer or two.

Above all things, he is a spiritual person. He daily rises early, drives to the little office he reserves in the nursery and takes long solitary walks. There is nobody around in the early morning—nobody on the street—eerie silence everywhere. He meditates and communes with God. His habit is then to return to his office and write something, often poetry.

Tranquil now the morning air,
The silence sweet and so serene.
Snow lies on the meadows where
the flowers of summer once have been ...

John has had a long-time love affair with Nebraska. Everything Clare Matthews told him about it has turned out to be true. He is taken by its simple, open radiance. He loves the clouds and the thunder rolling over the plains. "Everything about it is beautiful," he says, "especially out west in the Sandhills."

John's spirituality, humility and the irrepressible Irishness of his accent and demeanor have made him a worthy successor to all the Omahans of Irish descent who preceded him: Creightons, Boyds, Gallaghers, McShanes, Cudahys, Flanagans and those of lesser fame. It was inevitable that he would kindle friendships with hosts of Omahans of every stripe.

In 1997 he was named Businessman of the Year by the Rotary Club of Omaha. Receiving a standing ovation at a luncheon attended by most of his family, his parish priest, and two hundred Rotarians, he paraphrased a fellow countryman, William Butler Yeats: "Say not where my glory begins or ends. But say that my glory is that I'm amongst such friends."

REFERENCES

BOOKS

Day, Catharina. *Ireland*. In **Cadogan Guides: A Catalogue.** London: Globe Pequot Press, 1996.

Illustrated Guide to Ireland. London; New York: Reader's Digest, 1998.

Larsen, James H. and Cottrell, Barbara J. **The Gateway City: A History of Omaha**. Boulder, CO: Pruett Publishing, 1982.

INTERVIEWS

Mulhall, John. Taped interview by Harry B. Otis. January 10, 1997.

Mulhall, Sean. Taped interview by Harry B. Otis. May 20, 1997.

NEWSPAPER

McMorris, Robert. *Railroad Brought Wave of Irish*. **The Omaha World-Herald**. November 19, 1961.

PERIODICALS

Coad, Ralph G. *Irish Pioneers of Nebraska*. **Nebraska History Magazine**. Vol. 17, 1936, pp 171-7.

Reilly, Bob. *Mulhall the Storyteller*. **Creighton University Window**. Summer Issue, 1994.

Sorenson, Alfred. *Biographical Sketch of Edward Creighton*. **Nebraska History Magazine**. Vol.17, 1936, pp 163-9.

THE JEWS

About two thousand years ago, ancient Romans swept the Jews from their homeland in Jerusalem. Since then, the Jewish people have roamed the earth seeking a haven, or at least an accommodation, from the gentile world surrounding them. Seldom have they found either.

Despite brief periods of tolerance over the centuries, such as the edicts of Pope Gregory during the seventh century and of Charlemagne and his sons during the ninth, which temporarily freed Jews from economic and religious persecution, history reveals little gentile consideration for them. Especially after the eleventh century, few Jews escaped ill treatment from Christian neighbors. Crusaders on their way to the Holy Land ravaged them and stole their property. Local potentates in every European country barred them from crafts, agriculture and most forms of commerce. Then, between 1200 and 1600 A.D., the rulers of England, France, the German duchies, the Papal states, Naples, Venice, Spain and Portugal drove them from their borders.

They mainly fled to East Germany and to Central and East European countries, including Poland and Russia, where, although increasingly forced into ghettos, they found some measure of comfort.

Neither the Renaissance nor the Reformation, nor even the eighteenth century Enlightenment, brought much abatement to their suffering. The promises of relief made by religious leaders such as Martin Luther and by political reformers such as Napoleon were short-lived. And even in democratic England, no Jew, until 1858, could take an elected seat in Parliament.

The Jewish experience in America, especially after the American Revolution, proved to be different. Jews were among the first Europeans to arrive in the New World. Three Jews (albeit Catholic converts) were members of the crew of Columbus's first voyage in 1492. Jews driven out of Spain by Queen Isabella in the same year

Jews

and driven out of Brazil by the Portuguese later on, received a reception, however lukewarm, in New Amsterdam in 1684. In addition, England's Duke of York, taking over the colony from the Dutch a year later, was to permit religious worship "for any persons whatever," which was a big concession in those days.

With the passage and acceptance of the U.S. Constitution came additional relief. The new republic promised more than mere toleration, as expressed by George Washington in a letter to the Jews of Newport, Rhode Island:

> *All possess alike liberty of conscience and immunities of citizenship, and the Government of the United States which gives to bigotry no sanction, to persecution no assistance, requires only that they who live under its protection shall demean themselves as good citizens.*

Rose Blumkin's parents, the Goreliks

Those more recently finding a haven in America are Jewish survivors of the Holocaust. Numbered among them choosing Omaha in the late 1940s is Joseph Fishel, a survivor of Auschwitz and Dachau. Still other Omaha refugees from those and other Nazi death camps are Joseph Polonski, David Richman, Benjamin Josen, Roman Amster, Carl Rosenberg, Erwin Eisenberg, his wife Bella, her mother and others.

Julius Meyer, early Omaha resident and Indian interpreter

As these escapees related their horror stories to the citizens of their adopted city, Jews and gentiles alike rose to embrace them and help them to establish homes and businesses. They became cherished members of the community.

Jews have been Omahans since 1854. They helped found the city and cause it to grow and prosper. From Jonas L. Brandeis to Rose Gorelik Blumkin, most entered poor, and some became rich. Even though the Jewish community nurtured them, they excelled principally by their own ingenuity and sweat.

Often arriving unschooled and illiterate, they spent a century and a half seeing to it that their children had schools in which to learn and synagogues in which to worship. Loving their adopted city, they worked mightily to advance its interests. In doing so, they have contributed oceans of time and money to its arts and professions.

Jews of different origins came to Omaha. Some of the early ones were descendants of the Sephardic Jews whose ancestors had settled in colonial America. Most, however, were those who escaped

Jews

an anti-Semitic Germany after 1840 and a vicious, pogrom-ridden Russia after 1880.

At the time of the American Revolution, Jews in America numbered about three thousand, only one percent of the population. Mostly Sephardic Jews from Spain and Portugal, they actively fought for American independence. Several died for it.

German Jews, who markedly increased the population after 1840, soon sprinkled themselves throughout the United States. Thus some were present to help Omaha become a city. Originally young, unmarried men traveling the streets in the junk business with horse-drawn carts or on foot with peddler's packs, they soon established stores on the city's main thoroughfares selling hardware, clothing, jewelry, groceries and almost everything else.

Omahans became accustomed to seeing store fronts labeled J. L. Brandeis (originally the Boston Store), M. Hellman, Julius Meyer and so on. By 1870, on lower Farnam and Douglas streets, Jews owned and operated about half the Omaha clothing stores. Many of

Temple Israel, Twenty-third and Harney streets

the proprietors lived in rooms over their places of business or in apartments nearby.

An active religious life was out of the question for these early Jews. For the first fifteen years there was no rabbi in the community. Wives were imported through marriage brokers to be joined in matrimony by a visiting rabbi or by a judge and a knowledgeable member of the Jewish community.

Formal religious services came slowly. Rosh Hashanah services in 1867 were conducted in the home of a restaurant owner. The following year Omaha Jews formed the congregation of B'nai Israel, later becoming Temple Israel.

In 1884 Jews started a Sunday school and later erected Omaha's first synagogue at Twenty-third and Harney. Its members later, in 1908, would move their place of worship to a more substantial building of Byzantine architecture at Park Avenue and Jackson (later sold to the Greek Orthodox Church), and in 1953 to one at Sixty-ninth and Cass.

Young Jews also created local chapters of fraternal organizations, Kesher Shel Barzel and B'nai Brith, and a Young Men's Hebrew Association. They also joined Masonic lodges.

Jewish philanthropy started early. Prominent Jews organized in 1869 a Hebrew Benevolent Society. Among them were Edward Rosewater, a Bohemian, who founded the **Omaha Bee**, and J. L. Brandeis, a German, who started a department store that survived for the next hundred years.

Balls, fairs and a variety of events raised funds much needed by the Russian immigrants who began to descend on Omaha. Coming after 1880 in vast numbers, these poor, uneducated and unskilled refugees put an immense burden on the Omaha Jewish community charged with finding them housing and work. Nevertheless, with the help of Jewish agencies in New York and other port cities, Omahans settled many hundreds of Jewish immigrants, both in Omaha and in other Nebraska communities, adopting a one-on-one program of sponsorship and settlement.

Jews

Their form of religious worship and the extent of adherence to traditional Jewish customs separated these newer Jewish immigrants from the old. Because they were Orthodox Jews, the religious activities of these Eastern European immigrants differed markedly from earlier Jews who had adopted the customs of the nineteenth century Reform movement.

The newcomers yearned for their own synagogues. Through the turn of the century they established them, principally in the area lying just north of downtown Omaha where the new Jewish population was beginning to concentrate.

Many of the newcomers found a friend in Rabbi Henry Grodzinsky, "a bearded patriarch with a most musical voice," who was greatly loved and respected by all Omahans. He arrived in 1891 and became a force in the Orthodox community, keeping it in balance by settling many disputes among its people who had originated in many different Eastern European countries.

Rabbi Henry Grodzinsky

Our Story, published by the Omaha Section of the National Council Of Jewish Women in 1981, describes the Omaha Jewish community between 1885 and 1925. Photographs and the vignettes of sons and daughters of immigrants graphically reveal the impact of Omaha on their daily lives. For most, Europe became only a bitter memory.

Graduating from public schools, Jewish offspring became doctors, lawyers, journalists, engineers, rabbis, businessmen, scientists and scholars. At least one, Lawrence Klein, received a Nobel Prize in economics.

As time passed, a Jewish Community Center arose for the use

of all Omahans. The brick building housing it at Twentieth and Dodge, built in 1922, was replaced by an even larger one on One hundred thirty-second south of Dodge in 1975. Widely used as a meeting place for persons in all walks of life, it houses Jewish memorabilia of every kind and provides a place for many activities, lectures, sports, theater and the like.

Such was the Omaha that Holocaust survivors found following World War II.

The stark horror of the Holocaust was such that it seems impossible that even one person could survive it, let alone immigrate to Omaha to establish a successful business. Joseph Fishel was such a person.

He appeared in Omaha in 1947 against stark odds. Barely twenty-seven years old, he had borne the Nazi brutality of Dachau and Auschwitz death camps and had miraculously escaped the fate of six million other European Jews. Upon his death in 1994, he was a successful Omaha businessman, survived by three exceptional children, Norman, Renee and Eadie.

Born in Bendzin, Poland, for ten happy years Joseph lived a middle class existence in a small, nearly half-Jewish village. His relatives lived nearby in a close loving relationship; he could meet any of them he wanted by merely walking out in the street. His Polish gentile neighbors treated him in a mixed fashion, sometimes tolerating him and sometimes, in the case of teenagers, chasing him and beating him up for being a Jew.

During the week Bendit, his father, ran a shirt factory, delivering shirts to the Polish equivalent of a Woolworth store. As a master shirt cutter, his better-than-average income allowed the family to live and eat well and to enjoy some luxuries.

On Saturday, following services of *Shabbat*, Bendit often would take his children to soccer matches, warning them not to tell their more religious mother, Rifka, of such sacrilege. When the weather was right, he and the children would walk to a nearby lake for a swim.

Jews

In 1931, after a week of suffering from a gall bladder attack, Bendit died, and a series of trials for the Fishel family began. Unable to run the shirt factory on their own, they sold its machinery piece by piece until there was nothing left.

Joseph and his brothers and sisters had to quit school. Each got a job and contributed to the family larder as they could, yet there were days when they had to go to work without food. Fortunately, Joseph's school allowed him to complete his education tuition-free, and for two years the family's landlord delayed collecting rent payments.

By 1936 they had enough to pay the landlord and satisfy their other creditors, for by then Rifka had opened a little restaurant and had begun feeding Jewish soldiers in the Polish army. Profits from this and the children's odd jobs made their life comfortable again.

Joseph was a handsome youngster of medium height and slender build. His deep brown eyes and black hair set him apart from the other young people of the village. His body was agile, his mind

Baruch, David and Joseph Fishel in front of their home in Bendzin, Poland

quick. He could best the others in sports and outwit any bothering bully. How could he have known that these qualities would save him in the years ahead?

To survive stints at Auschwitz, Dachau and other horror camps took not only luck, but physical stamina and mental ingenuity. Despite more than four years of confinement, near starvation, beatings, deprivation of sleep, exposure to the elements and mental distress, he never openly expressed any resentment towards his oppressors or a desire for revenge. His wife Helen would go into a justifiable rage whenever, in later times, she spoke of the treatment. Yet even in Joseph's taped recital of his life under the Nazis, he reports, but never whines.

From September 1939 when the SS came to his village, filling his synagogue with Jews and burning them all to extinction, to the last days of the war when an American patrol found him sitting under a tree near Stuttgart, his shoes too tattered and his body too weak to permit him to continue the death march his jailers had ordered, Joseph overcame every brutal thing the Nazis dreamed up.

Soon after the German invasion of Poland on September 1, 1939, like all his fellow Jews, he was forced to wear the yellow Star of David fixed to a white band around his arm, marking him as one to be chased and beaten when the police wanted someone to clean the police station nearby.

Joseph's ingenuity revealed itself early on. His voluntary offer to clean the station daily and to polish the Nazis' shoes relieved him from further harassment. It also produced some extra bread for his hungry family.

As time passed, conditions worsened. Jews formed breadlines daily for the few loaves that kept them from starvation. The Nazis would shoot every fifth Jew for any unruliness in line.

Yet it was the behavior of many of his Polish gentile neighbors that distressed Joseph the most. He could never understand why these people suddenly would turn on him and his fellow Jews.

Jews

Even before the Nazis had imposed the armband requirement, they could readily learn who in the village was Jewish by merely asking a gentile. Seeking to curry favor, some Poles would go out of their way to point out Jews. Worse yet, one of his close friends before the invasion now turned his back on him and refused even to speak to him.

A year went by. Came October 5, 1940, and a knock on the door. The Germans wanted one hundred and fifty Jewish laborers for an ammunition factory in a distant town and a like number for the construction of barracks in another. Joseph's luck held. He was sent to a camp named Bautrup-Saybusch to build barracks in neighboring villages. His ten-year-old brother was not so lucky. His lot was the ammunition factory. Within a few months he died in the dangerous business of producing bullets for the Germans.

For two-and-a-half years, between October 1940 and April 1943, Joseph and three or four other friends of the same age built barracks for the German army. Under light guard, they were fed adequately and even allowed visits home. These three-day trips, in the company of their guard, allowed them to help keep their families alive, as the pilfered bread and salami they carried would last them three or four months.

This quiet period ended. Passover in April 1943 was the last time Joseph was to see his mother. By July of that year every Jew in his village had been taken to Auschwitz.

As for Joseph, in April he and his friends were returned to Saybusch to face a vastly different life which now became one of beatings and misery. Several inmates died when a sadistic SS guard substituted their bodies for the horses used to pull the construction materials the barracks required. Their friendly guard had been arrested and sent to Auschwitz.

Yet, within four or five weeks, Joseph's cunning overcame the new guard. By bribing him with bread, butter and eggs obtained from contacts he had established with Polish merchants, Joseph convinced him that his best interests lay in letting up on the prisoners.

64

The harsh treatment stopped. By June the guard even allowed them to play soccer with a team from another camp.

This endurable interlude ended in July when storm troopers came to whisk the inmates to various concentration camps. Joseph ended up in Gradditz in a six-floor brewery filled with three-tiered wooden bunks. With no hay to lie on, he was forced to sleep on the bare boards of one of these, covered only by a thin blanket. The brewery provided the housing for slave labor that was employed in a factory many miles distant. The guards enforced discipline by banging inmates on the head with shovels.

Gradditz was Hell. Up at four A.M. for the daily head count, to stand outside until five A.M. regardless of the temperature; one-hour walk to the train depot; forty-five-minute train ride to the camp; forty-five-minute walk to the big factory; eight hours work; little food. Then the long trek back to the brewery.

Returning one night, the miserable group discovered the bodies of three of their comrades hanging from a tree outside their barracks. The men had been caught and shot by the SS for trying to escape. Later, when the guards suspected an escape effort by Joseph himself, they delivered a hundred lashes to his bare back. He nearly died; for two weeks he couldn't walk. Only the succor of fellow inmates and a friendly doctor saved him.

December 1943 brought a typhus epidemic. Every day inmates died. Survivors stacked their bodies like cord wood against the brewery wall. Very few in the camp of twenty thousand lived, but Joseph, though he prayed for death, was one of them.

His good fortune was to run into an acquaintance from his village, a big cook in the camp named Meyer, who offered him security. Meyer kept his word. One day Joseph appealed for protection against the blows of a *sheba*, a Jewish bully foreman charged by the SS with the duty of harassing the other inmates. After beating up the *sheba*, Meyer announced that if ever again he hit anyone from Bendzin, he would kill him. No more blows for Joseph.

April 1944 brought another move, a sinister one. Along with

other inmates, Joseph was ordered to strip and don some rags the SS provided. To the men this meant Auschwitz and death. Unbelievably, as part of a maintenance crew they were shipped to Annaborg, a gathering area for concentration camps. The guard was lax. For a few months Joseph was free to barter and trade his few remaining possessions with other inmates and even with gentiles, Polish and foreigners.

Prayer was part of his life. Aware of the September date of Yom Kippur, on that day he carefully refrained from eating his only food, the miserable quarter loaf of bread allotted to him. This fast brought him spiritual relief. Later, he and a few others discovered a room where they could lock the door and find comfort in a few minutes of prayer together. "We knew we were Jews, " he said.

September came and another traumatic move. The Nazis loaded the entire camp into boxcars and sent them, this time, to Auschwitz. Upon their arrival, the inmates' first sickening sight were carloads of dead bodies awaiting cremation. Dog-leading SS guards, shouting, "*Schnell! Schnell!*" immediately ran them into camp for haircuts, shaves, tattoos (identification numbers) and prison garb.

Surrounded by fellow inmates with similar striped prison clothing, Joseph spent the next four or five weeks in a bare, wooden, three-tiered bunk, smelling the sickening odor of the crematorium and awaiting his fate. He was fully aware of the alternatives. Would he be sent to Dachau where he heard the Germans needed workers? Would he be selected by the evil Dr. Mengele for use as a medical guinea pig? Would he be consigned to the gas chamber?

Joseph speaks in his taped interview:

> *And we had selections every day. There was an SS man by the name of Mengele, Dr. Mengele, and he was a son-of-a-gun. He was the one that made the selections. If he didn't like the way you looked, he told you to go to the left. So he picked every third or fourth or fifth guy he didn't like. He told them to*

go to the left, and they went to the gas chambers, yet we didn't know where they were going.

They wanted carpenters for Dachau. Although Joseph knew nothing of the trade, if they wanted carpenters, he was a carpenter. Any place would be better than Auschwitz.

He was wrong. Dachau proved to be far worse, but not at first. Dachau was divided into little camps called *lagas*. Joseph's bunch of inmates, twenty-six in all, were ordered to do all the dirty work of the camps, a task, however, that permitted them access to the common kitchen where they could steal enough food to meet their needs during the winter days ahead.

This duty ended in November 1944 when they were confined in *Laga* Number One, the most miserable camp of all. There they found no bunks, tiered or otherwise. Sixteen men slept on the dirt floor of a little room, each with one blanket and a piece of wood for a pillow. Their only heat was a small coal stove.

Their job now involved the construction of concrete bunkers. Each night from eleven P.M. on, after walking forty-five minutes to the work site, Joseph and his comrades unloaded sacks of cement in the below-zero winter weather. Every night, walking to and from work, men died. The inmates had to carry the bodies back to the barracks.

In his tape, Joseph speaks as follows:

> *We used to go home in the evening, or in the morning whenever we came home walking, we were all wet and sweaty, and full of mud, so that by the time we came home we had to clean the mud off our shoes so we could get up in the morning and go to work. Sleep, we didn't get too much, we must have gotten about four or five hours every night. And on Sunday they used to make us clean the barracks, and everything was cleaned, spotless clean. Every time they had something else. We couldn't rest, there was*

Jews

no way we could sit down and relax and stay in the barracks.

Spring of 1945 came. The increased Allied bombing raids so frightened the German construction workers that many didn't show up. Relaxed vigilance by the SS guards gave Joseph the chance to sneak away to a concrete bunker and sleep until it was time to return to his miserable lodgings.

At the very end, on the night before April 26, 1945, the SS marched the whole barracks to the main Dachau camp. They were to be executed in a gas chamber, they were told. Instead, they were crammed into a small room where there was no space to sit or lie down. "People were dying just like herrings, standing up."

The next day started a death march. Day and night the SS trekked the Jews through Germany. The guards said that they were on their way to Switzerland. Every day men died.

Joseph survived, partly due to a soup made of bread that he and a few friends were able to steal from an SS bread truck whose sleeping driver the men had overcome during a rest break. By May 2, he was sitting under the tree where the American patrol found him.

From this point on, only good things happened to him: he met Jewish doctors, Jewish chaplains and even Jewish friends from Poland; he went to a synagogue in Stuttgart where he met his future wife, Helen, and he even found his brother, David, and his cousin, Sima, both now free.

Before long he and Helen were married. The two then lived in Germany for more than two years before discovering that Joseph's long lost uncle Hermann and his aunt resided permanently in Omaha. They would sponsor his wife and him should they want to come to America!

After having lost her first baby, Helen was now pregnant with her second. Yet to America they came. After spending some days in New York City to marvel at the sights, they made the long trip to

Omaha. Uncle Hermann met them at Union Station to take them to his home at Thirty-first and Decatur for a party with all his friends. Quite a commotion, but they loved every minute. Almost everyone at the party spoke Yiddish. They felt at home.

For a while Joseph worked for Uncle Hermann, who was a wholesaler of things in general, including nuts. A fellow employee was Hermann's son-in-law, Rudy Fox, who became Joseph's fast friend. After a year the new immigrant found a better paying job with the Hinky Dinky Company at two dollars and fifty cents an hour.

Joseph Fishel

By this time the couple lived in an apartment, scarce in those days, above a store on Sixteenth Street opposite the post office. Shouldering bananas all day was tough work for Joseph, and the apartment, shared with cockroaches, was less than ideal for Helen, but the two loved their new city.

Many Omahans went out of their way to help them. Art, a one-armed black coworker, became Joseph's ideal. Despite his handicap, Art could carry produce better than anyone else and was a living model for the newcomer.

Joseph's biggest barrier was learning English. Some people, such as a postal worker, would humiliate him for his inability to use the English word for something, like stamps. But most people were helpful. Bus drivers, for example, would readily drop him off at an address that someone had written for him on a piece of paper.

Nevertheless, the inability to communicate depressed him. In order to learn how to speak, he and Helen sat glued to the radio every night. At least she soon learned so much of the language that in a few months she could cover for the two of them in most situations. Echoing the words of hundreds of immigrants, in his taped statement Joseph exlaims: "Believe you me it was very, very miserable. If I would have had a ticket, money to go back to Germany, I would have. But thank God, I didn't."

They didn't have much money. It was hard to shell out cash for a crib when Norman was born in October. Yet they were able to save regularly, buying postal savings bonds with forty-five of their sixty-dollar weekly income. They found a house for sale for one thousand dollars. With seven hundred dollars of their savings and three hundred loaned to them by Uncle Hermann, they bought the house. They fixed it up, and rented part of it to another uncle and aunt who had come from Poland. Two years after arriving in America, Joseph was a landlord! No more cockroaches.

Joseph's new house was located on Nineteenth Street north of Decatur in a predominantly Jewish neighborhood sprinkled with Italians, Irish and blacks. He was happy that on the same street a house had been converted to an Orthodox synagogue. In another nearby house resided a *shokat*, an Orthodox Jewish butcher, and next door to him, a Jewish grocer. These businesses purveyed kosher food to customers who spoke nothing but Yiddish. This eased Joseph's pain in his slow search for English. Yet maybe it slowed the search.

In the mid-1950s, Hermann moved out to a new home in the Country Club addition near the new Beth Israel Synagogue on Fifty-second Street. Almost ready to retire to Florida, he sold Joseph not only his business but his house at Thirty-first and Decatur as well.

Now Joseph and Helen were even closer to a community that was almost entirely Jewish Orthodox. They lived near North Twenty-fourth Street. Everywhere were Jewish stores: bakeries, grocery stores, butcher shops, tailors, hardware merchants plus lots of Yiddish. Even the American Jews could speak some of it.

In 1960 another move, this time to Seventy-fourth and Page, a few blocks north of the Crossroads Shopping Center. By now Joseph had confined his prospering business to the wholesale distribution of nuts. He called it Herman Nut and Supply Company and caused a picture of his father, Bendit, to be placed on every metal nut container.

The social life of Joseph and his wife revolved around the synagogue, bowling and games of all kinds. With their friends they sometimes played poker three times a week, everyone screaming at one another in Yiddish and possibly losing one dollar and twenty-five cents in the process. As a seasonal business, the nut factory was shut down during the summer, which allowed frequent visits to race tracks: Ak-Sar-Ben for horses, North Sioux City for dogs. Occasionally they made it to Las Vegas.

Finally, the Fishels were able to send all three children to college: Norman went to the University of Iowa and Renee to Ohio State. Eadie attended the University of Wisconsin before residing nine years in Israel where she met her husband, Eitan Tsabari. Today Eitan teaches at the University of Nebraska at Omaha, while, until recently, Eadie and brother Norman ran the nut company.

Bonded by fire, the Omaha survivors of the Holocaust have met frequently over the years. Grateful for Omaha's warm reception, they have repaid her by their industry. Omahans are proud of these immigrants who chose their city as a refuge.

Omaha would be a poor place, indeed, without the all the Jews, of every kind and from every country, who have come for one hundred and fifty years to make a mark on our city.

Jews

REFERENCES

BOOKS

Larsen, James H. and Barbara J. Cottrell. **The Gate City: A History of Omaha**. Boulder, CO: Pruett Publishing, 1982.

Rosenbaum, Jonathan, ed. **Our Story: Recollections of Omaha's Early Jewish Community, 1885 to 1935**. Omaha: Omaha Chapter of the National Council of Jewish Women, 1981.

INTERVIEWS

Fishel, Joseph. Transcript of interview. January 10, 1989.

Fishel, Norman and Eadie F. Tsabari. Taped interview by Harry B. Otis. January 25, 1996.

MISCELLANEOUS

Rosenblum, Dottie, the Nebraska Jewish Historical Society. Conversation with Donald H. Erickson and Harry B. Otis. 1995.

Eisenberg, Bella. Conversation with Harry B. Otis. 1997.

THE GERMANS

Augustus Kountze

Long before the Revolutionary War, Germans settled in the American colonies, particularly in Pennsylvania, where they received a Quaker welcome. All became good citizens. Many fought and died for American independence. There even was a time when German language vied with English for acceptance as the national tongue.

During the second half of the nineteenth century, German immigrants entered the United States in a flood. They came from every part of Germany, and some from Russia, to seek land of their own, avoid the rigors of military conscription and escape religious intolerance.

Diverse forces attracted Germans to early Omaha, not the least of which was the publicity given the area by Prince Maximilian of Wied and his artist companion, Karl Bodmer, who visited the site in 1833 and returned to tell fellow Germans by words and paintings of its natural delights.

From Augustus Kountze, who came before Omaha was incorporated, to the German immigrants of recent years, the river city has always welcomed such newcomers.

The earliest immigrants, mainly from the north of Germany, Schleswig-Holstein, Saxony, Hanover and Prussia, were predominantly Protestants, usually Lutherans. Later arrivals often

73

Germans

were from the South, the Rhineland or Bavaria, or from Austria. For the most part, they were Roman Catholics.

German Protestants founded the Evangelical Lutheran Church of Omaha in 1858, which later became the Kountze Memorial Lutheran Church. German Catholics built St. Mary Magdalene's Church in 1868. Until World War I, sermons in many churches of both denominations were delivered in German.

In 1900, there were two hundred and two thousand German-Americans living in Nebraska, mainly in the larger communities of Omaha, Lincoln, Grand Island and Hastings. The 1980 census reveals that seven hundred and twenty-four thousand Nebraskans claimed German heritage, many having arrived during the post-World War II period.

There always have been more Omahans of German extraction than of any other ethnic group. Germans never established, as did the Italians, definite colonies or places of their own. They more readily assimilated with the general population, finding homes throughout the city.

Since basic English words are of Saxon origin, English may have come more easily to them than to other immigrants. Even though they taught their children German at home and in church schools, at least before World War I, they increasingly spoke English in their daily activities.

The efforts of Edward Rosewater, a Jewish immigrant from Bohemia, intensified Omaha's promotion when copies of his German language newspaper, ***Beobachter am Missouri***, found its way back to Germany. Later, Valentine J. Peter published the **Omaha Daily Tribune** and other newspapers in German which, widely circulated here and abroad, were beacons of light for Omaha.

Germans arrived with various talents, from banking to brewing. Far from illiterate, many had rich cultural backgrounds. Some were skilled craftsmen, artisans, tradesmen, musicians and artists. As early as 1857, the early arrivals even produced a play, Schiller's **Robbers**.

One early resident, Augustus Kountze, came in 1854 as the

Float in the German Day Parade, October 2, 1913

vanguard of four brothers who, one way or another, pioneered Omaha banking. After forming banks of their own, they joined forces with Edward Creighton to establish the First National Bank of Omaha.

Music was always a part of the life of the German settler, particularly the Southern German. In an era of the brass Um-pah-pah band, there was no lack of entertainment for the sippers of beer at the gardens established by Krug, Storz and the others. Social clubs, such as Omaha *Musik Verein*, German-American Club and Turner Hall, cropped up to provide places for homesick newcomers to talk, sing and drink beer together.

The beer was provided by some early German brewers. Fred Krug, immigrating to the United States in 1833 at the age of nineteen, came to Omaha in 1855 to build the city's first brewery. He operated it out of a twenty-two-by-forty-foot house he built with his own hands at Tenth and Farnam, delivering the beer to his customers by wheelbarrow. In later years the well-patronized beer garden he established in Benson became an amusement park and, still later, a city park named after Rachel Gallagher.

Taking over from Joseph Baumann, in 1876 another early brewer, Gottlieb Storz, built his own brewery, one that that lasted well into

75

Germans

the twentieth century. Gottlieb's progeny became local civic leaders and nationally recognized supporters of the American Air Force.

Two early Omaha immigrants from Northern Germany were Henry Eicke and Hans Glissmann. Eicke came in 1865 to help build the railroad; Glissmann arrived a few years later from Nordorf, Germany to deal in cattle and to marry Eicke's daughter. One day the Nordorf town square would sport a fountain emblazoned with Glissmann's name. In the meanwhile, he and fellow German immigrants, Grabows, Eickes, Armbrusts, Bocks, Dolls and Roots, would acquire farms west of Seventy-second and south of Pacific that would eventually turn into housing additions, golf courses, shopping centers and even cemeteries.

For the most part, these Northern Germans worshiped in Missouri Synod Lutheran churches. Living in an area not yet a part of Omaha, they often directed their interests away from the city. For example, they sought entertainment in their own *Deutsches Verein* in Bennington, Nebraska, rather than in the one on South Thirteenth, and established churches and schools in their own outlying neighborhoods. They helped make their community as renowned for dairy products as for beef cattle. One Glissmann is credited with introducing Holstein dairy cows to the area.

Over the years these farming families, intermarrying with one another and with the Anglo-Saxon population, disappeared as Germans and became German-Americans. Becoming citizens, they fought America's wars and embraced its customs. Yet they never forgot their own, remaining proud of the centuries of art, literature and music which Germany has given the world.

A person who identified perfectly with this German culture was Valentine Joseph Peter, a Bavarian.

His was quite a family. For over sixty years Valentine (Val) Peter made Omaha his home and the seat of publication of the **Omaha Tribune** and other German language newspapers from Baltimore to San Francisco.

At the same time, he and his wife reared a family of twelve

Val Peter Family, 1927

children, a baker's dozen, if we include their granddaughter, Valerie, who came to live with them when her own mother died prematurely. Their offspring, who became respected homemakers, priests, lawyers and businessmen, would one day carve their own firm niches in the community.

In May of 1889, the steamship *Damphfer Hermann* brought Val, his parents and two sisters to Baltimore, Maryland. They had immigrated from Steinbach bei Lohr/Main, Bavaria with few assets. Val's father at once moved his family to Rock Island, Illinois, to scrape out a meager existence before dying three years later of a heart condition. At age seventeen, Val became the sole support of his mother and sisters. To augment the Peters' dwindling savings, he found farm work at six dollars per month, followed by lumber mill labor with Weyerhauser at three dollars a week. Somehow the family survived.

As the breadwinner there was no day time for high school for Val, but in night school he learned English, mathematics and history. Then, finding a job as a printer's devil with Rock Island's semi-weekly

Germans

German newspaper, *Volkszeitung*, over the next five years he mastered not only the linotype, but every aspect of the printing business. His career was launched.

When in 1897 the Peoria *Taegliche Sonne* hired him at age twenty-two as city editor at seventeen dollars per week, he was the youngest editor of any Illinois paper. In the same year, he proudly took the oath to support and defend his adopted country and became a naturalized citizen of the United States.

He was also a frugal citizen. During the next five years, while still supporting his family, he saved a precious eight hundred dollars. He used this money in the foreclosure purchase of the now failing Rock Island *Volkszeitung*. With seven hundred dollars borrowed from the paper's owner he was able to make up the one thousand and five hundred dollars purchase price. At age twenty-seven he now was the youngest publisher in Illinois.

The turn of the century was a time of marvelous new machines, not only the linotype invented by Val's fellow German, Merganthaler, but popular things like telephones, sewing machines, typewriters and talking machines. The depression of the 1890s was over, yet things were cheap. Eggs were twelve cents a dozen and steak fourteen cents a pound.

German immigrant families, including the Peters, were cohesive and made their own entertainment. It was mostly music. Later Val Peter would have two pianos in his home. Singing societies were large, and their concerts well attended by Germans from miles around.

Across the Mississippi River from Rock Island lies Davenport, Iowa. There Theodore Reese and his family had immigrated in 1890 from Magdeburg, Germany, about eighty miles west of Berlin. Reese had studied music in conservatories at Cologne, Hamburg and Berlin. An accomplished composer and conductor, he became acquainted with all the music greats of nineteenth century Germany and was a protege of Hans Von Bulow, the first husband of Cosima Wagner, the daughter of Franz Liszt and later the wife of Richard Wagner. Papa Reese loved Wagner's operas.

Traveling groups brought German operas, operettas and plays to Davenport, a mecca for singing societies. Reese was in the thick of it all. Orchestras and vocal choruses answered to his baton; operas, grand and light, blossomed under his direction. His friend, Victor Herbert, once recommended him for the post of conductor of the Chicago Symphony. He refused the offer. His English was too poor, he said.

Theodore Reese

At one of the singing fests, Val met Reese's second child, Margareta (Greta). Despite Val's mother's disapproval, in 1906 Greta became his wife. Greta had sung in one or more of her father's operettas and thus had to be of "low moral character." And it didn't help matters that Papa Reese was considered a "free thinker" and a sometimes Lutheran.

Val just ignored his mother's objections. Following their Niagara Falls honeymoon, he moved his new wife into a tiny apartment above the print shop where at the end of the year she bore his first child, Carl, for *Grossmutter* Peter to fuss over.

During the winter of 1906, while on a business trip to San Francisco, Val discovered Omaha. News of the Bay City's earthquake had stopped him in Omaha. Impressed by its large German population, strong Catholic element and good schools, especially Creighton University, he decided to stay.

Soon he met the Festner family, owners of a weekly German newspaper, the **Nebraska Tribune**. In a few months he had bought the paper to join the ranks of earlier Omaha German language publishers: Edward Rosewater of ***Beobachter am Missouri***, a weekly that survived for eight years, and Charles Banckes of the **Omaha Post**, a daily that became a semi-weekly.

Germans

Val soon turned Festner's **Tribune** at 1307 Howard into a daily, re-naming it the **Omaha Daily Tribune**. Over the next half century, with the help of loyal employees such as Otto Kinder, the **Tribune**'s editor who would remain with him for many years, Val became one of the nation's leading German newspaper publishers.

In 1908 he moved his family to Omaha. While still in Davenport, Greta bore a second son, Theodore. Over the next nine years she would have a baby every two years, each one bringing *Grossmutter* Peter to Omaha to show Greta how to rear it.

These children were pre-World War I babies, some of whom were old enough to feel the weight of public persecution of German-Americans when the United States entered the war in 1917. As the publisher of a string of German newspapers, Val particularly felt the sting of the pervasive anti-German sentiment. Egged on by super-patriotic firebrands, the public was encouraged to see a traitor in every German and subversion in everything printed in the German language.

Omaha Daily Tribune Office and employees, 1307 Howard Street

Even though he was a naturalized citizen, and his wife and each of their children a citizen by birth, and despite the fact that every editorial written in every newspaper Val owned was pro-American and anti-German, bigots sent him hate mail. They threw red paint on his house. They accosted his newsboys and pelted his sons Carl, age eleven, and Ted, eight, with rocks, trying to knock them off their bicycles.

The Peters were not alone in this abuse. All traces of German became taboo. The German language no longer was taught in the schools; to speak German on the telephone was considered disloyal; symphonies refused to play music by German composers (even Mozart); sauerkraut was renamed liberty cabbage; ministers and priests who preached in German were challenged in their pulpits; even daschund dogs in the streets were attacked. An angry Omaha mob attempted to lynch a German immigrant; an Illinois mob succeeded.

In the midst of all of this, Val Peter went right on publishing the **Omaha Daily Tribune** and his other periodicals. Each night at home, with his foot-long shears, he would cut appropriate articles from American papers to be translated the following morning into German for inclusion in the **Tribune** and other works.

In a competition with other foreign language newspapers, he submitted editorials in support of the Liberty Loan. His was the first accepted by the Treasury Department. During World War II, four of Val's sons and four of his sons-in-law served their country in the military.

Carrying news from the old country, Val's papers helped new German immigrants overcome their feelings of isolation and homesickness in the strange new land, especially during World War I. It gave them a jump start in becoming what they all wanted to be—good Americans. Val never missed a publication date.

Two years after the Peter family moved to Omaha, father-in-law Reese brought his own wife and children to the city, moving them to Twenty-fifth and Dodge across from what was then Father Flanagan's

Germans

Val Peter Family, when Val Peter received an LL.D. from
Creighton University, June 11, 1953

Boys Home. Reese became the director of the Omaha *Musik Verein*, where he was especially active before World War I, a time of so many German songfests, throwing himself into his conducting like Arthur Fiedler, with his hair tossing. Music director, as well, for St. Mary Magdalene Church under Father Sinne, he wrote many musical Masses for its choir.

Val always admired and respected his father-in-law. They were good friends. In later years he even found Reese a room in his own crowded house at 809 Pine. From this abode, after a breakfast that he insisted on making himself, thus depriving the women of their kitchen, the retired musician would emerge every noon to join companions at the *Deutsches Haus* on South Thirteenth for the remainder of the day. Upon his death, Reese's family honored his written request to be buried from the *Musik Verein* with no religious ceremony. He was interred in St. Mary Magdalene cemetery in a lot Fr. Sinne provided for him.

During the years following World War I, while Greta bore six more children, the last, Eugene Walter, in 1924, Val not only acquired other German language newspapers throughout the United States, but also established two other businesses, a printing company, Interstate Printing, with his brother-in law, Ernie Reese, and a travel agency, the Peter Travel Bureau.

A growing family demanded larger quarters. At 809 Pine, Val found a house that proved to be incredibly expandable. Upstairs it boasted four bedrooms, a large bathroom and an unheated sleeping porch. Downstairs was a large living room, dining room, a huge breakfast room-kitchen and a sunporch.

Winter and summer the Peter boys, and sometimes their Reese boy cousins and assorted friends, slept in the sleeping porch in a series of beds on a first come, first served basis. The rest of the family and their German immigrant maids occupied the bedrooms. Until later years, there was only one bathroom.

The growing family required discipline. Everyone had chores. Everyone did his or her school homework between dinner and eight-thirty P.M., when it was lights out. In spite of occasional gripes, there was a strong feeling of unity and togetherness in the house. Fights were short-lived and no grudges remained.

The logistics of feeding the brood were challenging. Val made periodic visits to the packinghouses for meat, open-air markets for fruit and vegetables and grocery stores for periodic bargains on cases of canned goods. The milkmen of three dairies furnished milk.

809 Pine Street residence

Although Greta often had German girls to help her, she was the one

Germans

responsible for the good German cooking that poured from the kitchen. For many years the big meal of meat, potatoes and vegetables was eaten at noon. The adults and the older children sat in the dining room, the younger children in the breakfast room. Val often invited to these dinners his friends, priests and businessmen.

Every month Val would bring home from the Woodmen of the World Building a barber named Schrupp, who claimed to have cut the hair of Kaiser Wilhelm. One by one, every Peter child would sit in a high chair on the porch to be tonsured by this celebrity.

The Reese heritage assured that music was everywhere. It was in the family's blood and genes. At one time, no less than four of Papa Reese's progeny together played various instruments in the Omaha Symphony. Not only had a former owner of the Pine Street house left a Victrola and lots of German records, but Aunt Evelyn Reese appeared periodically to teach the violin to anyone talented. In addition, an Englishman, Mr. Duffield, taught piano to the Peter children, talented and untalented alike. After a few years, one of the two pianos was always in use.

Saengger-Halle, Seventeenth and Capitol, circa 1875

Val encouraged a couple of the boys to learn the clarinet and the cornet well enough to entertain on the street corners of little Nebraska towns, such as West Point. There he and his sons would travel to pitch German Day, always held in Omaha three days before Labor Day.

The boys also participated in the newspaper business, first as carriers, and later as part of the business itself. They worked early. Up at four A.M., they delivered their papers. Then, only after Mass at St. Joseph Catholic Church, did they return home for breakfast.

Because the travel agency required personal guidance of tourists on trips to Germany, Val, with Greta, was able to visit his relatives there and make other side trips. On one such trip he delivered the flag of his Omaha Rotary Club to the club in Zurich, Switzerland, whose members beamed at being addressed by an American in fluent German.

Education was important to Val. Remarkably, at a time when higher education for women was not stressed, all twelve children, girls as well as boys, graduated from Creighton University. And Greta saw to it that the children attended Mass regularly, wherever they might find themselves. It became part of their lives. One son, Paul, became a priest, as did a grandson, later.

Val was generous of his time and treasure. Like millions of other Americans, he felt the Depression and witnessed much suffering. There were always men coming to the door asking to do any kind of work for food. He would assign them some simple chore around the house, pay them a little something and have Greta give them something to eat. His son, Arno, said of him: "Father was always concerned about the needy, and whenever he could possibly help them, he would, if only with a free meal. My father never seemed concerned about money. He had faith, I guess."

His work in the community was likewise generous. Especially during the Depression, he was active in the direct relief provided to needy persons by St. Vincent de Paul Society, and for many years he was president of the German Relief Society.

Germans

Accolades and honors come to him as steadily as Greta bore him children. In 1922 he was appointed Nebraska representative for the German Consulate and the Austrian counsel-general. In 1950, with another Omahan, Burt Murphy, he was named by Pope Pius XII a Knight of St. Gregory. In 1951 his hometown of Steinbach, Germany named a street after him. And in 1953 Creighton University awarded him an LL.D., an honorary doctoral degree of law and letters.

He hated Hitler. Before World War II he successfully fended off Nazi attempts to control or acquire his German publications. At the same time he successfully assisted Germans to escape their Nazi-ridden country. For these efforts, Theodore Heuss, president of the Federal Republic of Germany, awarded him in 1975 the Officer's Cross of the Order of Merit.

He didn't live to see it, but would have endorsed enthusiastically the construction in 1967 of a new German-American Club Building on One hundred twentieth Street south of Center, where all of Omaha's German societies successfully created a common home. It was built with the personal toil and sweat of society members who decorated the central hall with the coats of arms of the various German provinces. Upon hearing the old songs sung in the new hall, Val and Papa Reese would have lifted steins of beer in its praise.

Yet their greatest pride would have been in learning that their progeny, Valentine Peter, would one day be the president of Omaha-treasured Boys Town. The appointment was a sure tribute to two families whose lives, like those of many other German immigrants before and since, materially shaped the city.

REFERENCES

BOOKS

Duffy, Valerie Peter. **"Memories" of : The Life and Times of Valentine Joseph Peter and Family**. 1987.

Larsen, James H. and Barbara J. Cottrell. **The Gate City: A History of Omaha**. Boulder, CO: Pruett Publishing, 1982.

Souvenir Book: 105th Anniversary of the German-American Society. January 14, 1989.

Souvenir Book: 110th Anniversary of the German-American Society. January 15, 1994.

INTERVIEWS

Crotty, Beverly. Taped interview by Harry B. Otis. September 15, 1997.

Grabow, Curt. Interview by Donald H. Erickson and Harry B. Otis. July 28, 1995.

Olk, Heintz A. Interview by Harry B. Otis. October 1997.

NEWSPAPERS

McMorris, Robert. *Germans Brought Taste for Music, Wines and Beer Gardens*. **The Omaha World-Herald**. November 5, 1961.

THE CHINESE

For more than one hundred years, Cantonese colors and written characters have brightened the walls of a few Omaha restaurants. From time to time, Chinese residents have given the city a further exotic tang by decorating their plain brick habitations with red and gold and placing out front wooden signs with finely carved Chinese characters trimmed in gold leaf.

With the passage of more liberal immigration laws, Omaha's Chinese now hail not only from Canton but from many of China's provinces. Today, one can find Chinese red and gold and beautiful bronze reliefs adorning a host of non-Cantonese Chinese restaurants whose owners speak Mandarin, now the official language of China.

In the early days, from all of China it was only the Cantonese who brought Omaha their language, their customs and, especially, their peculiar American-inspired cuisine of chop suey, chow mein, egg *foo-jong* and egg rolls. Along with these dishes, they brought their shy, restrained friendliness, intelligence and a diligent work ethic.

Many of these early people carried the name Chin. At one time Omaha had a Chin association made up of all Chinese who had Chin in their names, which was practically everybody. Whether or not you were directly related, you were treated as one of the family. A similar Omaha family were the Hueys.

The **Omaha World-Herald** articles of Robert McMorris and Edward Morrow report that Omaha in 1900, like many cities of its size, boasted a Chinatown. It was not like the ones of San Francisco and New York City, but consisted of a group of two hundred to three hundred Chinese who lived, together with other immigrants, in a four-block area around Twelfth and Douglas streets. Most of these Chinese worked in a half dozen restaurants and laundries. Some kept small shops which specialized in exotic foods and Cantonese art objects.

The first Cantonese drifted into Omaha shortly after the completion of the transcontinental railroad in 1869. Principally they had labored for the Central Pacific to build the line from Sacramento,

Chinese

California, to where it joined the Union Pacific at Promontory Summit, Utah. The Central Pacific hired them when no other group of workers was willing to bear the immense hardships and dangers involved in laying rail through the mountains. Finally, laid off from railroad duties, they sought work in Eastern cities, including Omaha.

Unlike most Europeans, these immigrants had not come to the United States with any intention of a permanent stay. Many of them had wives and children in China whom they intended to return to after accumulating a fortune in America. By Chinese standards, back home they could live a life of ease.

Wishing their children to be reared as Chinese, it fitted their plan to leave their families in China while they worked here, at least until such time as their offspring had thoroughly absorbed Chinese language and customs. They never intended to assimilate with the Americans whose culture was so different.

Joe Wah Lee, August 1900

For most, the fortune they dreamed of never appeared. There was no return to China for them; they continued to live where they had found work, remaining aloof from the Caucasians and close to one another in tight communities.

In California, if not in Omaha, their cultural differences and their willingness to work for wages lower than that acceptable to the average American caused friction. Perhaps a Chinese reluctance to mingle with Americans, immigrant or not, arose out of their treatment by the white man. Although the California gold strike and the construction of the transcontinental railroad made work

90

opportunities plentiful for them during the 1850s and 1860s, as time went on they competed more and more with Caucasian labor. Their intrusion was resented.

Labor unrest, coupled with a wide cultural and racial divide, made it easy for white politicians to accede to a public demand that the Chinese, even though they were competent and hardworking, be denied a part of the new American society.

California newspapers added fuel to the fire, calling Chinese "deceitful, vicious, criminal, cowardly and inferior from a mental and moral viewpoint." Before a congressional committee one witness even opined that the Chinese were "inferior to any race God ever made."

It didn't take long for California and the federal government to beat on them with restrictive legislation. In 1853, California taxed all Chinese four dollars per month for the privilege of mining. If they didn't mine, they paid a four dollar "Chinese Police Tax." No Chinese person was permitted to testify in court against a white man. Every Chinese male prisoner (the jails were full) had to suffer his queue being cut off (a gross indignity). An 1879 statute prohibited employment of Chinese by any California public office, corporation, attorney or contractor.

As for the United States, in 1882 Congress enacted the National Exclusion Act that prohibited further Chinese immigration and denied all persons of Chinese descent the right of citizenship. Not until 1943 was this act repealed.

For many years, Gin Ah Chin was the Chinese patriarch of Omaha. (In China, where according to custom the family name is placed first, he called himself Chin Ah Gin.) In 1840, with Gin and the rest of his family, his father had immigrated from Canton to Stockton, California to scrape a living growing potatoes. For a time he was successful, but when the rains failed to fall and the crop suffered, he urged his son to travel east.

Moving to Duluth, Minnesota, Gin started a restaurant; when Duluth proved too cold and snowy, he moved south to Omaha to start

Chinese

another. It was 1890. By then Omaha had a growing Chinese community.

An August 1900 edition of the **Illustrated Bee** reported a recognized leader of the Omaha colony to be Joe Wah Lee, the richest Chinese in Omaha and one thoroughly versed in English. He operated a restaurant on "East Douglas Street." Another prominent Chinese was Hong Sling. Having grown up in the service of the Union Pacific, Sling had been elevated to the position of passenger agent for that railroad as well as two others, the Chicago North Western and the Southern Pacific.

In these very early days, however, most Omaha Chinese supported themselves through the laundry business. By 1890, there were twenty such laundries. Then, in a few more years, a popular taste for Cantonese food spurred the creation of restaurants. By 1906 there were six, including the one run by Gin Ah Chin.

In 1912 Gin opened another, the Mandarin Café, which proved to be the most popular yet. To help run it, he employed not only family members, but other Chinese needing jobs. Finally, in 1921, Gin Ah Chin created a triumph of a restaurant, King Fong. It still reigns, ornamented in luxurious fashion on the second floor of 315 South Sixteenth Street.

Mandarin Café, 1409 Douglas Street

Those who have never visited King Fong have a treat in store. To climb up the steep, worn marble staircase, clutching a highly-polished brass handrail, is a small price to pay for what you get to experience. On your right, as you ascend, are glass-enclosed, museum-quality silk embroideries which, at the restaurant level, continue

Interior, King Fong Restaurant, 315 South Sixteenth Street

around the perimeter of a large dining room. Time has not diminished the beauty of these fabrics that were imported by Chin from Hong Kong in 1919 along with the rest of the room's fixtures.

And what fixtures they are.

With the help of a few wall lamps, the dining room is lighted by four overwhelming, hand-painted enamel chandeliers. The figurines on each fixture tell the story of a different Chinese opera, yet are so intricate that you wouldn't realize their purpose unless you climbed a ladder to observe closely the dragons and miniature play sets that make them up and see the texts in Oriental characters that tell the stories. You will wonder at their art, awed by the number of hours the artist must have taken to create them.

Next to meet the eye are more than twenty marble-topped, teakwood dining tables inlaid with chips of mother-of-pearl, still impressive despite missing a number of chips in each, the result of

Chinese

eighty years of souvenir-hunting by customers. A glance toward the rear of the room reveals various booths, the angles of which are adorned with golden camphor wood carvings of birds and fish extending from ceiling to floor. These have flown and swum for delighted customers for eight decades, yet still seem fresh and new.

Practically the same now as it was in 1921, this is no franchised restaurant. A mild, musty odor of rice, steamed vegetables and cooked shrimp pervades it. Whether one is a tea drinker or not, you are enticed to drink small cups of tea with your dinner or "iced cold beer."

It was over twenty years ago that Doug Smith in the **Omaha Spectrum** wrote:

> *King Fong's is a relic from a time and culture the franchiser wouldn't understand . . . in addition to its excellent food, [it] gives us a chance to let our imaginations run—to pretend we're bit players in an old Humphrey Bogart or Charley Chan film. And a chance to wonder at man, the marvelous maker of things.*

Although Gin Ah Chin continued to operate the café, he gradually sold part ownership rights to others, including members of the Huey family. His sons and daughters sought other careers. His youngest son, Carl, for example, was a graduate chemical engineer who ran the Omaha Treatment Plant for most of his life. Carl's wife, Jeanette, also of Cantonese descent, taught in the Omaha public schools for many years.

Eventually Gin turned over operation of King Fong to Sen Huey who, with his own family, managed it in the same fashion. In time, members of the Huey family became the café's cooks, waiters and other personnel. When Sen Huey retired in 1981, his daughter, Nancy, became manager, assisted by her mother, Yo, her brother and sister, and her aunts, Yo's sisters. They successfully operate it today, dishing out great quantities of rice and unlimited pots of tea to be poured into the tiny handleless cups.

Jeanette and Carl Chin

In addition to laundries and restaurants, the early Chinese community even had a tong, *On Leong Tong*, a sort of protective business association and fraternal society. Fortunately there was only one such tong. Things were quieter that way. Larger cities, where two or more tongs existed, sometimes saw tong wars and death.

For many years *On Leong Tong* found quarters in a narrow, three-story red brick building at 111 North Twelfth Street. Here its members could engage in diverse activities: meet for prayer and meditation in a shrine room containing a squat Buddha; "shoot the hip," i.e., lie on their hips in bunks while inhaling opium (freely obtainable in those days); or play a centuries-old Chinese game, *mah jongg*, or other games of chance.

One of the games was a complicated Chinese form of bingo which advertised possible winnings of five to ten thousand dollars. Records indicate that only one man ever claimed more than the minimum. When tong officials, deeming him a phony, rejected his ten thousand dollar claim, he complained to police. The ensuing raid led to jail for

Chinese

many Chinese.

The building, gaily decorated in traditional red and gold, also was used in the celebrations of the Chinese New Year. Robert McMorris reports as follows:

> *Long strings of firecrackers would stretch from the top of the On Leong Tong house to the sidewalk. When lit, the firecrackers would explode one after another in a manner guaranteed to frighten away all evil spirits for miles around. For added insurance against bad luck the Chinese colony staged lion dances and dragon dances.*

Since the tong building previously had been owned and used by Anna Wilson (Omaha's philanthropic madam whose Prospect Hill grave is mysteriously adorned each Memorial Day with roses), these firecrackers also must have scared away any would-be customers who somehow had failed to learn of the building's new use as tong headquarters.

The dragon costume used in the dances came from China and was irreplaceable. Its owner, a San Francisco Chinese-American group, shipped it annually to Omaha for a proper ushering in of the New Year. Apparently, the dragon finally died.

On special occasions, such as the Chinese New Year, the Chinese liked to gather at their tong for banquets. The principal fare consisted of vegetables most often provided by Sam Joe, an *On Leong* spokesman and another patriarch. Sam Joe, who raised Chinese style beans, lettuce, parsley, turnips, cauliflower and cabbage on a truck farm near Council Bluffs, shipped his products all over the Midwest. He was a close friend of Florian Newbranch, a longtime **Omaha World-Herald** reporter who often was his guest at tong affairs.

Another frequent guest was Edward Morrow, who in a 1978 **Omaha World-Herald** article described his experiences. The dinners were on the second floor of the tong building, the guests sitting at long tables. The banquets usually started at noon and lasted until five o'clock, "or as long as one could stand them."

> *The food was all right, though many dishes were mysteries to me. It was served in small portions in many courses. Usually, between courses, we had tea, a glass of rice wine or soup. It seemed to fortify one to try the next course.*
>
> *At the end of the room was a Chinese orchestra of about five pieces. It is hard to understand how agonizing this "music" is to Western ears. The musicians always played fortissimo. The music seemed to consist of squeaks or squeals on wind or stringed instruments, with drum beating a steady beat, (maybe today's rock fans, who like deafening noise and relentless beat, would enjoy it).*

Although the Depression wiped out most Chinese restaurants except King Fong, eventually a few other Cantonese restaurants appeared. One of them, Chu's Chop Suey and Steak House, was started in 1964 in the vicinity of its present location, 6455 Center Street, by Chu Huey and his wife Sun.

Chu's father, Chiang Hoy Huey, immigrated in 1909 to San Francisco to work in a laundry. In 1913 he returned to Canton long enough to marry before coming back to Omaha in 1915 as an active restauranteur. Like many of his kind, he left his wife in China, periodically returning to increase the size of his family.

Thus, Chu was born in Canton in 1934 but did not appear in Omaha until 1951 to live with his father. Perhaps he would not have come, even at that time, had the Communists not taken over the government of China. Upon his father's advice, in 1949 the whole Huey family had moved to a safe haven in Hong Kong where Chu applied for an immigration visa.

Chu arrived with no knowledge of English. For a year he worked at his father's Edward Café on Sixteenth Street while attending eighth grade, where he studied hard to learn the new language. Later, at

Technical High School, he was able to get a good grasp of it.

Then in 1952 his cousin, Sen Huey, gave him a job at King Fong where he worked until 1955, when he was drafted into the American army which sent him to Korea as a cook. During the two-year Korean service, while visiting his mother and the rest of his family in Hong Kong, he met his wife, Sun, whom he married in 1958. Upon his discharge from the army, the two returned to Omaha to start both a family and a restaurant. Both have flourished.

When Chu came to Omaha in 1951, he experienced little public prejudice. What little he did find took the form of once being denied free access to rental property. His father and he were forced to remain in their small, downtown, rented room after a prospective landlord, noticing their race, told them to leave at once a larger apartment they were attempting to lease. "People see us and don't understand about us," his father told him.

Regardless of this glitch, Omaha has fully accepted Chu and Sun, and, indeed, all persons of Asian descent, whose adjustment to Omaha has not been markedly different from the experience of other immigrant groups. And native-born Omahans of Chinese descent, who naturally speak English with little or no accent, have always been popular, especially with their contemporaries. Even Chinese immigrants who recently have arrived generally receive a warm embrace by the general public and apparently sense no discrimination.

During the past thirty years the number of Omaha residents who claim Chinese ancestry has increased from a few hundred to a thousand. In addition to swelling the student population of Omaha's colleges and universities and joining the ranks of many businesses and professions, these newcomers have created more than forty new Chinese restaurants in the greater Omaha area. Almost all specialize in the Mandarin (Northern Chinese) cuisine, and somewhat grudgingly include Cantonese fare as well.

Typical among these newer residents are Joseph Kuo and his wife, Alice, who arrived in 1978 to establish, over time, a string of eating places called The Great Wall. Having previously established restaurants in Chicago, he sought a new opportunity in Omaha where no Mandarin cafés had as yet appeared.

During his first two months in the city, though he desperately needed employees for his new enterprise, Joe failed to meet up with any Chinese who spoke Mandarin. Finally, a Korean grocery store owner informed him of a New Year celebration being planned by Chinese friends. It turned out to be a bonanza.

Fifty or sixty Chinese showed up. Many were older than Kuo; some were young students. All were from mainland China via Taiwan or Hong Kong. Like him, many of the older men were university graduates and had jobs at Omaha firms such as OPPD, InterNorth and Mutual of Omaha. Some were doctors doing research with the University of Nebraska Medical Center or Creighton University. From among the students Joe was able to recruit part-time help for his first Great Wall Restaurant.

But the New Year meeting produced much more than new friendships and some student employees. A church was born—a Christian church, The Chinese Christian Fellowship. It started with a Bible study group meeting at the home of one his new Chinese friends and ended with a church building of the group's own at Eighty-third and Blondo.

Over the years the fellowship slowly progressed from somebody's home, to Joe's first Great Wall Restaurant, to the basement of the First Presbyterian Church at Thirty-fifth and Farnam, to a small chapel in the First Christian Church at Sixty-sixth and Dodge and finally to its Blondo Street home. On an average Sunday, one hundred and fifty people form the congregation, mostly Chinese-Americans but two or three Caucasians as well. Services are conducted in Mandarin and repeated in English.

These new Chinese friends share Joe Kuo's goals. Most of them came from Taiwan to study here, get a job and in time obtain permanent residence status, a green card. They looked for the three Ps: Ph. D., property and permanent residence status. Joe had come in 1970 to study at Fort Hayes, Kansas, and had there earned a master's degree

Chinese

in mathematics.

America's recognition of Red China during the 1970s gave an impetus to Chinese immigration. With permanent residence, in five years these immigrants could become naturalized citizens and eligible to bring in their parents, siblings and children. After coming for studies in 1970, Joe returned to Taiwan in 1972 to marry Alice. During the following two years he taught math in a Taiwanese college before returning to the United States to study for a Ph.D. degree. But on his return to the United States, it was too late for any such studies. He had to support his growing family. Thus the restaurant business.

In 1973, while the two were still in Taiwan, Alice delivered their first daughter, Ingrid. Two more daughters, Ellen and Esther, later were born in the United States. In time the two older girls have graduated from Cornell University and Wellesley College. The youngest attends Brownell-Talbot school in Omaha.

Joe and Alice Kuo are proud to have been naturalized and, with their daughters, to be Americans. Joe calls America a super heaven.

When they appeared in Omaha in 1978, there were only three Chinese restaurants, all of which were Cantonese. Joe's was the first restaurant to offer Mandarin food, the spicier fare of Northern China. In the next twenty years, his one Great Wall would blossom into twelve restaurants, managed by relatives and friends. As his business grows, the managers operate the restaurants as interested parties.

With each passing year, Omaha welcomes new Chinese to the community. Some of them are young students here only temporarily to study at UNO or Creighton; some are older scholars here to do research work at the medical centers; some are businessmen here to start new enterprises; and some are here to join their relatives, Chinese-Americans already established in the city.

Just as their predecessors have enriched Omaha to its great benefit, all of these immigrants currently blend their own cultural values into the city's fabric.

REFERENCES

INTERVIEWS

Chin, Jeanette. Interview by Donald H. Erickson and Harry B. Otis. January 1998.

Huey, Chu. Taped interview by Harry B. Otis and Donald H. Erickson. June 10, 1998.

Huey, Nancy. Interview by Harry B. Otis. June 5, 1998.

Kuo, Joseph. Interview by Harry B. Otis. July 27, 1998.

NEWSPAPERS

McMorris, Robert. *Gay Dragons Once Danced in a Thriving Chinatown*. **The Omaha World-Herald**. December 6, 1961.

Morrow, Edward. *Omaha's Orientals*. **The Omaha World-Herald**. March 5, 1978.

Omaha Chinese Hold Feast Honoring 4—638th New Year. **The Omaha World-Herald**. January 28, 1941.

Smith, Doug. *King Fong—A Storehouse of Eastern Art*. **The Omaha Spectrum.** 1976.

Tong Building Will Tumble Down. **The Omaha World-Herald**. December 30, 1962.

THE LITHUANIANS

If any priest has ever deserved the title, pastor, it was Father Juozas Jusevicius. He immigrated from Lithuania to Chicago with his family at the age of nine. That city's Lithuanian community reared, educated and ordained him before he headed west to Omaha in 1932 to nurture the parish of St. Anthony of Padua. For almost thirty years he shepherded his Omaha flock of Lithuanian-Americans with a selfless diligence.

Father Juozas Jusevicius

When he arrived in the middle of the Depression, fewer than forty families supported the Thirty-second and S Street church whose debt was thirty thousand dollars and whose sanctuary was in dreadful need of repair. When he died of a heart attack in 1959, over six hundred parishioners supported the church, most of them refugee Lithuanians whom the Russians had driven from their homeland. In the meantime, Father Juozas and his parishioners had erased the early debt, faced the sanctuary with brick and built an enlarged church school.

In 1901, earlier Lithuanian immigrants founded the Society of St. Anthony of Padua, whose members had finally convinced a skeptical Bishop Richard Scannell to permit them a church of their own. He had questioned whether there were enough of them to support

Lithuanians

a Lithuanian-speaking parish. A written petition with many signatures (some of non-Lithuanians) indicated there were, and the church was organized.

In spite of their resolve "to praise God and confess in their native tongue," they had a tough time finding and retaining Lithuanian-speaking priests. Nevertheless, between 1900 and the end of World War I, under many such priests the church population bloomed to over two hundred communicants before the decline that followed the liberation of Lithuania from Russia under the Versailles Treaty.

Then, in 1932, Fr. Jusevicius appeared: a short, stout man with a full face, quiet brown eyes and the mien of a kindly monk. More frugal than the most frugal Lithuanian, he refused a salary, preferring to use whatever funds came his way to reduce the church debt or to fund the funeral expense of some impoverished Lithuanian family.

He didn't care whether his suit was always rumpled or that his socks sometimes had holes in them, so long as he could buy confirmation clothes for Lithuanian children whose parents were suffering from a prolonged stockyards strike or if he could take these children on a picnic or to camp.

Deeply concerned about the 1941 Russian invasion of his native land, which he saw recur in 1944, Fr. Juozas prepared to help his countrymen who were holed up in German refugee camps at the war's end. He awaited only the passage of an American law that would permit him to sponsor them. When the law was finally enacted and Archbishop Gerald T. Bergan asked him how many refugees he could accommodate, he was able to reply: "As many as you can send us." Refugees, who began arriving in Omaha in 1949, found him ready, with the help of his parishioners, to find them shelter and work.

Typical of these refugees was the family of Pranas Totilas.

In 1906, when Pranas was born, the Russian heel of the Czar bore down on his beloved Lithuania. In 1977, when Pranas died, it was the Soviet heel of Stalin and his successors. Only the oppressor had changed. In railroad boxcars, with doors nailed shut, these tyrants had shipped hundreds of thousands of Lithuanians to Siberian oblivion.

104

Fortune favored Pranas; he was not one of them. In 1944 he escaped from his homeland. Along with hundreds of other Lithuanians he eventually came to Omaha to live in peace for the rest of his life, only to die too soon to see his country finally break free.

For twenty-two precious years following World War I, Pranas and his wife Emilija breathed the air of Lithuanian freedom. The 1918 Versailles Treaty had broken the Russian yoke, liberating Lithuania and her sisters to the north, Latvia and Estonia. Until the Soviet invasion of 1940, these tiny Baltic states prospered and flowered.

On February 16, 1918, the newly formed Council of Lithuania accepted and publicly acclaimed Lithuanian independence. Despite Russian carping, from that time to the present day the United States has recognized its sovereignty and received its ministers.

In celebration, American Lithuanians in 1921 presented the country with a "Bell of Freedom," which her leaders immediately hung in the tower of the War Museum of the city of Kaunas. It rang every evening as a reminder of the words carved on its side: *Toll forever for the children of Lithuania. He who does not defend his freedom is not worthy of it.*

During these happy years, after graduating from eight years of high school in Jurbarkas, Pranas helped his father on the farm near his home before enrolling in the Lithuanian Military Academy. Upon graduation from the military academy, he accepted a commission in the Lithuanian Army, rose to the rank of captain and qualified for major just before the Russian occupation of 1940.

Emilija, his wife to be, trained as a nurse in Kaunas and worked in a hospital. In 1931, the two were married in Ukmerge where they continued to live and where, in 1934, Emilija bore a son, Algimantas (Al), and in 1937 a daughter, Jina.

Lithuanian independence did not come without terrible struggle. From the time Pope Innocent IV crowned Mindaugas the first Christian king in 1253, the tiny country has fought off Vikings and Germanic knights in the southwest, Poles on the south and Russians on the east. Even so, for a time during the fourteenth and fifteenth centuries

Lithuanians

it was one of the most powerful nations in Europe, territorially stretching from the Baltic nearly to the Black Sea.

Traveling monks early on brought Lithuanians both Roman Catholicism and the Latin alphabet. These they have held close to their hearts, never succumbing to attempts by czars and others to wrest them away.

A little over twenty-five thousand square miles in area, Lithuania is larger than Denmark, Holland, Switzerland or Belgium. Although it shares the same latitude as Southern Alaska, the Baltic Sea makes its climate milder, more like that of northern Wisconsin and Michigan.

It is an agricultural land of hay fields and beautiful birch forests; its capital, Vilnius, is one of the oldest cultural centers in Europe. At the invitation of the Lithuanians, Jesuits founded its university in 1579 and brought it Western European cultural trends and customs long before Peter the Great got into the act on behalf of Russia.

A typical Lithuanian is tall, attractive, blue-eyed, blonde and fiercely independent. Under nineteenth century Russian domination, Lithuanians staged many uprisings. After one such rebellion in 1863, the czar closed all parishes and schools, forbade the use of the Lithuanian alphabet and confiscated prayer books from the faithful. Books in Lithuanian were printed in East Prussia and smuggled in. During this period, many of the persecuted migrated to the United States, some to Omaha.

Following independence in 1918, Lithuania's economy prospered. The owners of its privately owned one-hundred-and-twenty-acre farms effectively used every bit of productive land for the best breeds of cattle and the highest quality seeds. The Lithuanians offered the world a renowned cheese, *Tilsiter.*

Then came World War II. In 1940, a deceitful deal with Hitler allowed Russia to move into Lithuania, unchecked. Commencing June 14, 1941, Soviet henchmen began arresting thousands of influential people, the intelligentsia who might try to frustrate the Soviet domination. They rounded up military officers, police officers, teachers, priests and other intellectuals for trips to Siberia for liquidation. In addition, they confiscated and burned Lithuania's paper currency and stole much of its gold reserve.

To escape a Lithuanian army officer's probable fate, Pranas quietly moved his family north to Emilija's hometown, Mazeikiai, close to the Latvian border. There her brother, Stasys Virkutis, found work for Pranas on the family farm and for Emilija in a hospital.

Yet they were not safe. During this period of Russian occupation, Pranas spent much of his time during the day hiding in the woods with other Lithuanian army officers, helping on the farm only at night. He was a *bourgeois* and fair game for deportation. The threat was real. Years later, Al Totilas relates the following:

> *One day a Jewish acquaintance from the village came to our farm with a list of families ordered to be rounded up by the Communists. They had ordered her to list all of the names of those in the neighborhood she knew, she said, and she was warning the Virkutis and Totilas families to be*

Totilas family portrait

prepared. Being our friend, she had put our names at the bottom of the list. This action may have saved us, for unlike the persons who rolled past their farm in trucks, screaming and crying for rescue on their way to the railroad yard, Russian agents never arrived at our door.

Shortly thereafter, Germany declared war on Russia. The advancing German army moved into Lithuania, pushing the Russians out.

For a while the German presence afforded some "relief." However, because Lithuania refused to fight against the Allies, Germany refused to recognize her as a nation, but was so occupied with the war that it let her people pretty much alone. Unless, of course, they were Jews. As elsewhere in Europe, they systematically liquidated these innocent citizens.

Al recalls one dismal incident:

During the German occupation my grandmother and I would sometimes bring food to the farm workers near the river Venta. One day we heard a barrage of shots from a nearby woods. Grandmother at once threw herself and me, her seven-year-old grandson, into a ditch where, crossing herself, she started to pray. "The Germans are shooting the Jews," she moaned. Finally the firing stopped.

The following day my mother, father and I went to the field where we found the bodies of the slain lightly covered with dirt. Among these shallow graves, as if substituting for urns of funeral flowers, we saw hair, combs and other personal items littering the entire area. I will never forget this.

The relief the German occupation afforded was short-lived. In 1944 the Russians came again, chased the Germans west, reoccupied the country and renewed their policy of persecution and annihilation. They now took over private farms for collectivism.

Learning he was on a Russian black list, Pranas decided it was time to leave his homeland. But how to leave? Having made great inroads against the Germans, Russian tanks now blocked any escape directly southwest into Germany.

Emilija's brother Stasys came to the rescue, offering a horse and wagon to carry the family and its possessions north to the Latvian port of Liepaja. The trip would be a short one. Pranas could ride a bicycle a quarter of a mile ahead of the rig to warn of danger.

The trip went well until one early morning. Awakening in a wooded area, the family heard the sound of a speeding German reconnaissance car. A quick hitch of horse to wagon allowed them to move out of the woods, only to discover the presence of Russian tanks. These caused the car to zoom back to the German lines with Pranas following, happy at not being fired upon.

Turning the rig up a hill, he found yet another peril at the top, a German 88-mm gun aimed straight at him. The gun crew's warning motions were unnecessary. The whipped horse ran as fast as she could. The family's luck held. Neither side fired. The German gun held the Russian tanks at bay and allowed the wagon to escape.

Before long other Soviet tanks started shelling their road. In the hopes of saving their only means of transportation, Pranas deposited his family in the shelter of a deep ditch and took off with the scared horse and bouncing wagon for a nearby spot on the other side of a hill.

As if on cue, on the left side of the highway being shelled, a German armored train suddenly appeared and fired upon the approaching tanks, causing them to retreat. During the quiet period that ensued, an anxious Pranas and a weary horse rejoined Emilija and her children in their temporary haven.

Eventually they reached the port of Liepaja, where they hoped to board one of the German ships waiting to carry German wounded and refugees to Danzig. Soon they were securely among the soldiers and

Lithuanians

hordes of Lithuanian and Latvian refugees who filled the vessels forming the convoy.

As they moved west along the Baltic coast, ship after sunken ship showed what air attack might do to their own ship, but a persistent fog saved them, shielding them from the enemy aircraft that constantly soared overhead throughout their voyage. Oblivious to danger and with the unconcern of youth, Al and Jina kept a constant watch on a German U-boat zigzagging ahead of them, now submerging, now surfacing, to their great delight.

The convoy reached Danzig without incident. Experienced railroad workers were in short supply in Germany where the Allies were destroying both rails and rolling stock faster than they could be repaired and rebuilt. The Germans needed Pranas's services.

From Danzig they were only too glad to take the family to Stargard, a rail center ten miles south. There Pranas worked until the Russian army came through on its march west; then it was off to Berlin in another escape.

Only the German need for railroad workers saved them. When the Russians came, many refugees were left to the invader's mercies while the Totilas family was moved south as part of the war effort. To avoid inviting air attack, the engineer stopped the train by day and pulled it by night. Arriving to find Berlin in shambles, the train continued to Ingolstadt, a rail center on the Danube river about sixty miles north of Munich where Pranas would work until nearly the end of the war.

Constantly bombed—British by night, Americans by day— Ingolstadt was where Pranas decided that escape from this incessant terror was worth the danger of being shot for escaping from the barbed-wire-enclosed compound. Since there were no guards, departure wasn't difficult. Nobody challenged the four as they walked to the railroad depot, boarded a small passenger train and traveled to Eggweil, a small village forty miles to the west where they found peace at last in a *gasthaus* owned by a farmer who offered Pranas work. Al recounts: "The first night we couldn't sleep—it was too quiet. Day and night we were used to going to an Ingolstadt air raid shelter. In Eggweil the only sound we heard was that of Allied aircraft flying over to bomb the city we had fled."

So they lived to the end of the war. Soon Jeeps and armored vehicles arrived carrying non-threatening Americans who chewed gum and held their weapons downwards as a sign of complete indifference to any danger. Al and Jina were amazed. American soldiers billeted in the ground floor of the *gasthaus* became the Totilas children's good friends and provided them with gum and candy.

When the war ended, Pranas had no thought of returning to his Soviet-dominated fatherland. He moved his family back to Ingolstadt, to a large German army barracks housing displaced Lithuanians, which was located in the fortress surrounding the older part of the city. There, with many other families, the Totilas family spent four years as refugees displaced by the war.

Despite Pranas's forced unemployment, the family bore up well in the Ingolstadt camp. Emilija's job as a part-time nurse provided a small amount of spending money; the Red Cross and other relief organizations gave them food, clothing and information concerning emigration possibilities; Pranas's weekly trips to the farm of his Eggweil *gasthaus* friend brought them fresh produce which could be exchanged for CARE-donated cigarettes.

The children's education was not seriously interrupted during this period. Soon after their arrival, Al enrolled in the first grade of an eight-grade high school, or *gymnasium*, organized by camp personnel. In addition, he learned to play the violin from a refugee friend, J. Remys. For her part, Jina studied ballet after school with a Ukrainian, a former ballerina from Kiev who had fled Russia.

In the displaced persons camp, everyone's sights were set on America. Around 1949 a family could immigrate there if it could find an American sponsor to assure that it would not become a public charge. Pranas's brother John and sister Rosalia, earlier escapees to Waterbury, Connecticut, came to the rescue.

Proposing to be their sponsor, John found work for them on a

Lithuanians

Connecticut tobacco farm. The Totilas family was soon on a ship headed for America.

After a few weeks on the tobacco farm, a letter from Pranas Odinas, a former Ingolstadt camp friend, summoned them to Omaha. Why not enjoy the higher wages of meat packing jobs? All the big packers were there, he told them, Cudahy, Swift and Armour.

Although it meant leaving a large established group of Lithuanian friends in Waterbury, the Totilas would move out West. The knowledge that many fellow displaced countrymen had preceded them calmed their fears of life in an unknown town with a strange Indian name.

The fall of 1949 found them in Omaha, practically penniless. But no matter. They had Lithuanian friends, a Lithuanian church with a warm and loving pastor and Lithuanian-provided temporary lodging in one room of a five-room house at Thirty-third and U streets. They shared this dwelling, owned by Pranas Odinas, for a few weeks with a half dozen other families.

Then they moved to a one-room loft over Draper's Garage at Thirty-third and Q where they lived for the following four years. A reward for the cramped living quarters were the jobs both Pranas and Emilija found at the Armour Packing Company. Each began earning one dollar an hour, Pranas cleaning machinery and Emilija cutting bacon.

Freedom was worth every bit of the hard work. Indeed, it allowed them almost at once, with their bare hands, to construct their own home. With money painfully saved from their Armour wages, they acquired a lot at 3413 W Street. Then with the help of a Lithuanian friend and a few electrical and plumber benefactors, over the next four years they slowly erected a house. It was pay as you go, no mortgage loan or other debt ever involved.

A night job enabled Pranas to work on the house during daylight hours, and each day after his classes at South High School, Al was free to lend a hand. It was a glorious day when, in 1953, they moved into the home in which they lived to the end of their days. Here the two parents reared their children free from the terrors of tyranny.

112

Lithuanians

The Omaha that the Totilas family found in 1949 was the residence of about two hundred Lithuanians from previous periods of immigration. After 1949, Fr. Jusevicius and his allies replaced this gradually diminishing group with a growing number of postwar immigrants.

It is small wonder that these refugees remember Fr. Juozas with affection. He sponsored them, fed them from his scanty resources and housed them in the basement of his church when he couldn't find other temporary shelter for them.

Typical among them was Romanas Drukteinis who, with his wife Joana and his daughters Virginia and Ima, had himself barely escaped the 1944 reinvasion of the Russians. Fr. Juozas sponsored him, found

Lithuanian dancers, left to right: Audrius Reskevicius, Roman Siciunas, Rimas Reskevicius, Judy Praitis and Irene Cernius

Lithuanians

him a job at Swift Packing Company and gave his family temporary shelter in the church basement before promoting more permanent living quarters in the home of a somewhat crabby Lithuanian woman parishioner of an earlier vintage. The Drukteinis family loved this selfless priest who would do anything to help them.

Between 1949 and 1950, six hundred and fifty-five Lithuanians arrived in Omaha. Like that of the Totilas and Drukteinis families, they all have stories of hard work, struggle and sacrifice during the early years in Omaha. Comfortable in their homeland, all came with little money and in their flight were forced to leave behind all but their most personal possessions. Even worse, most couldn't speak English, which was a huge emotional and practical barrier.

A most moving story is that of Julius Rukas, a Lithuanian Freedom Fighter. The war separated him from his family for sixteen years. Sweeping through his town, Ramygala, the Russians had captured his pregnant wife, Katryna, and his two-and-a-half-year-old son, Vidmantas. At the same moment, Julius had been herded west by the retreating Germans to work in Germany. Learning that someone had seen Julius in a nearby forest, the Communists jailed Katryna and beat her for days in order to force her to reveal his whereabouts. Their efforts were in vain, so they finally released her.

After a few months Katryna delivered a daughter, Laisvute. She struggled for the next twelve years to sustain herself and her two children, not knowing whether her husband was alive or dead. Only after Stalin's death did she receive news of him and learn that in 1950 he had emigrated to the United States, to Omaha.

Finally, following American intercession, the Russians allowed her to rejoin her husband. At Thanksgiving time in 1960, Julius and many fellow Lithuanians greeted Katryna and the two children at Eppley Airfield where, through tears of joy, he saw his sixteen-year-old daughter for the first time.

Sad to relate, what happened to waves of earlier Irish and Italian arrivals and to other newcomers also happened to the Lithuanians arriving in the early 1950s. Not every Omahan welcomed them and

114

was friendly. Many were bigoted. Some fellow workers mindlessly accused them of getting unfair income tax breaks just because they were new arrivals; others scornfully called them "Goddam DPs."

Even some earlier Lithuanians were cool to them. Perhaps less well educated than the newcomers, these older immigrants may have felt intimidated by the professional people who suddenly appeared among them, those who couldn't practice their professions here and thus entered the market for common labor jobs. Army officer Pranas Totilas and many others were perhaps seen as a threat to the old-timers.

Time diminished these resentments as these Lithuanian immigrants of the late 1940s melded with the community, yet to this day "DP" remains for them a term of derision, and memories of the taunt linger on.

How did these displaced Lithuanians cope? What tools did these families have?

First, they had the Lithuanian community itself, a group proud of its heritage and determined to maintain family values, centuries old. The love of these people for the United States, where most became citizens, neither softened their affection for their native land nor dimmed their desire to one day see it free.

A Lithuanian Refugee Community formed in 1946 was reorganized into the Lithuanian World Community in 1949 to preserve Lithuania's nationality, language, culture, religion and customs and to strive for her independence. In 1992, her stubborn insistence on severing ties with Russia played a huge part in the miraculous disintegration of the Soviet Union, an event cheered with joy in Omaha.

Second, they had their church. No one should underestimate its role in the lives of these people. Even before Fr. Jusevicius, St. Anthony Church had long been the hub around which the community turned. Nearly all incoming Lithuanians settled within its parish limits, and even though some moved to other parts of the city, they often returned, and still return, to attend church services within its walls.

Lithuanians

The newcomers were no exception.

Today St. Anthony is the only ethnic Catholic church in Omaha whose pastors, whenever possible, still say Mass only in the native tongue. St. Anthony continues this regardless of the difficulty of finding and holding Lithuanian-speaking priests. An excellent choir (now under the leadership of Al Totilas) sings Lithuanian hymns and helps to assure well-attended services.

Pranas, the extrovert, soon after his arrival made friends with all Omaha Lithuanians, as well as with many "American" coworkers at Armour's. He was not only an ardent church member but also belonged to diverse Lithuanian organizations. With some difficulty he learned English, but whether in English or Lithuanian, he reveled in discussing politics, particularly world politics, with his friends.

He constantly reminisced with fellow immigrants, recalling the underground activities in which they participated during the Russian and German occupations, the pilfering of war material from passing freight trains, the bombings and the pace of their lives in Germany during and after the war.

He was also an artist. He dabbled in all forms of graphic art: painting, drawing and sculpting. His developed skill enabled him to teach art at Al's school in the Ingolstadt camp and later to convey this discipline to his children, especially Jina.

Pranas was an excellent finish carpenter. In addition to his own house, Al and he personally would build three others during his lifetime. He loved Omaha. Like others who came from Lithuania, he enriched it.

Pranas was most proud of his role as first president of the Lithuanian veterans society, *LKVS Ramove*. Created in 1954 as a chapter of a national group earlier formed in Chicago, *Ramove* is made up of former Lithuanian army veterans whose goals are to restore independence to Lithuania (now achieved) and to assist former Lithuanian freedom fighters.

Civic minded, in 1955 the group gave hearty support to Omaha's centennial celebration. One member served on the anniversary

Lithuanian float at Omaha Centennial Celebrations, 1955

committee; others sponsored folk dances and similar activities. But the most fun came on July 17, 1955 when *Ramove* members picketed Soviet Foreign Minister Andre Gromyko at the Union Station. Everyone cheered when member Anatas Dubauskas gave a stirring speech, in Russian, denouncing the visitor. The event made the national press, and, to the delight of all, a photograph of the pickets appeared in **Newsweek** magazine.

Emilija's strong will and perseverance kept the family going during all of their troubles. Her calm demeanor had a stabilizing influence on them in times of crisis. Her training as a nurse assured Pranas and the children of proper diet and health measures even when food was scarce and unpalatable and medicine in short supply.

Before glaucoma blinded her, she was an avid reader of **Draugas**, the Lithuanian newspaper. Although she missed her homeland, she lived to see it free, yet she was too old and too weak to revisit it in its freedom.

The Totilas children had few problems integrating. Jina's early experience with the ballet in Germany stood her in good stead when it came time to participate in Lithuanian dance groups with Virginia Drukteinis and others. Her father's love of art affected her own career, for she became proficient enough to teach the subject at Boys Town. She eventually married a Lithuanian, became Jina Leskys, and now resides in Los Angeles where she continues her career in the fine arts.

Al met and married in Omaha his Lithuanian wife, Dana Arnauskas. Dana's recent death left him with their daughter, Silva, and two sons, Liudas and Jonas, who now have their own Omaha homes and families. He lives alone in a house improved by his own hand to double its original size. Retirement permits many camping and fishing trips with his progeny.

Al's love of music caused him to continue his violin studies in Omaha. His skill with the instrument improved to the point of his performing a recital at the Josyln Art Museum. His desire to play in the high school band caused him to take up the study of the French horn at South High. He considered a career in music but chose one in languages, adding Spanish acquired at Omaha University to his proficient Lithuanian and English.

Only recently retired from teaching Spanish at Burke High, Al continues as a devoted director of the St. Anthony choir. Every Sunday finds him there with his singers to support the Mass. Following Lithuania's independence in 1994, Al took part of his choir to the Lithuanian Song Festival in his native land. While there, he was able to visit his uncle, Stasys Virkutis, who had helped his family escape in 1944.

It was well Al went when he did, for Uncle Stasys died the next year. After the family's departure, the Communists had arrested Stasys and buried him in a Russian prison for seven years, releasing and sending him home only after someone finally determined he was only a simple farmer and no *bourgeois*.

In all this Stasys kept a sense of humor. Upon reuniting with his nephew, the first question he put to him was: "What happened to that mare I loaned your father for your escape?"

REFERENCES

BOOKS
Larsen, James H. and Barbara J. Cottrell. **The Gate City: A History of Omaha**. Boulder, CO: Pruett Publishing, 1982.
Sulkis, Benediktas C. **We Lithuanians**. Omaha: Taylor Publishing, 1984.

INTERVIEWS
Drukteinis, Johanna. Taped interview by Harry B. Otis. May 23, 1995.
Totilas, Al. Taped interview by Harry B. Otis. April 24, 1995.

THE AFRICAN-AMERICANS

Bearing Anglo-Saxon names, they came to Omaha with the earliest settlers. Some descended from those who had lived in America long before the Revolution, people who thoroughly had adopted American mores and customs, worshiped in mainstream American churches and celebrated every American holiday. Some of their ancestors had fought for America in each of her wars.

There were no language hurdles for these newcomers to Omaha. English was their only tongue. Unlike immigrants from foreign lands, they found no barriers to their advancement in a new growing community, save two: their skin was black, or a shade of brown, and

The Jerry Shores Family, early Nebraska homesteaders

their ancestors had been slaves. These facts alone stopped most of them, or at least slowed them down.

Even a lack of education was not a bottleneck for those coming from the Northern states. Many of them could read and write. Many of their brothers from the South, on the other hand, were illiterate. In the slave states to teach an African-American to read and write was a criminal offense.

Regardless of the sacrifice of a half million American lives in the Civil War, regardless of Lincoln's Emancipation Proclamation and regardless of Constitutional amendments freeing and enfranchising African-Americans, most Southern whites and many Northern ones have been slow to alter age-old attitudes toward them. Only grudgingly have African-Americans been accepted as social

121

African-Americans

equals, irrespective of their intellectual and cultural achievements.

Notwithstanding the differences between early white Omahans and the rainbow of ethnic groups that came from abroad after 1854, noting especially the gigantic language differences, most newcomers could ultimately cross the tracks and live on an equal footing with native-born white Americans. There was no such possibility for the dark-skinned, however. Until recent decades, human prejudice has effectively prevented assimilation into white society. Many states prohibited black-white intermarriage by law; all states blocked it by social taboo.

The most menial jobs have been the lot of the African-American, who otherwise has been hard put to build a business of his own. Often he has been unable to get bank loans at competitive rates, if at all, or goods for resale at competitive prices. Unlike immigrant Swedes, Jews, Germans or Irish, who often could get at least financial help from their own kind, ordinarily the African-Americans were unable to borrow much from their fellows. They were too poor.

So it was in Omaha. So it was elsewhere in the United States, North as well as South. And so it was where William Lawrence (W.L.) Myers was born in 1883 in a New London tar paper shack in the former slave state of Missouri. New London was merely an unincorporated scattering of shanties lying close to both Mark Twain's Hannibal and the plantation whose owner, less than twenty years before W.L.'s birth, claimed African-Americans as his property.

Not that the early realization of his status bothered W.L. much. How could a lad feel the weight of white man's prejudice while happily exploring what Twain called a "boy's paradise?" His terrain of deep woods, interspersed by prairies, limestone quarries and small rivers, was the same one known and loved by the storyteller.

Between episodes of school attendance, home chores and errand-running for the owner of the nearby Marvel plantation, W.L. was free to spend his daylight hours wandering the countryside.

With snares and slingshot he learned to take wild game. Among the deep woods of oaks and hickories, he found wild fruit, strawberries and bluefox grapes, and discovered the ripe cucumber taste of pawpaws and the bittersweet flavor of little purple blushed persimmons. Often he angled the Salt River for catfish, sunfish and perch, and when he occasionally could catch a wagon ride to the Mississippi River five miles to the east, he would fish for bullheads and swim in the quiet backwaters.

It was during these countryside jaunts that W.L. began shaping his future. His journeys often led to isolated places where dead birds and animals lay on the ground, cold, alone and unloved. Something called him to be their benefactor. Something moved him to mourn these dead creatures and to bury them. He felt good saying a few words over their graves.

What better path to a mortician's career.

W.L.'s skin color was very light. His ancestors were blacks, Indians and whites. His mother's mother had been a white girl, disowned by her parents for mating out of her race. In the boy's simple home, his own mother furnished the little he had in the way of food and clothing.

Under the strict rules of the simple school W.L. attended, he learned piety, good manners, reading, recitation, numbers and spelling. His schoolmaster may have given him a whipping from time to time, but this was a punishment common in all nineteenth century schools, regardless of the race of the scholar.

Adolescence brought W.L. closer to his chosen vocation. As time went on, new techniques in the art of embalming caused such schools to open in a few of the states. But where could a poor black youngster find the means to enter such halls of learning? He was determined to beat the odds. First he would have to earn the money, but somehow he would go to embalming school.

He began by burying Indians for the state of Oklahoma, a job few wanted. Later he found better paying, but backbreaking labor, in a coal mine in Buxton, Iowa. Between times he did odd jobs and saved his money. Finally, his hard work permitted entry to the Worsham School of Embalming in St. Louis where, before his money ran out, he completed several courses.

More education required more money. He found a job in a Minneapolis foundation and garment factory. For once his light-colored skin allowed him to fill a position ordinarily offered only to whites. His employer apparently believed him to be white. He worked there for eight years.

By 1908, diligence led to promotion. He was made a foreman. Early that same year he met and married his wife, Eunice (Essie). A few months later the couple learned that a baby was on the way. Things were happening.

Alas, nuptial bliss meant economic sorrow. Since W.L. had married a woman with a darker skin color, it suddenly dawned on management that he was indeed an African-American. They fired him for this reason alone, separating him from work for which he was fully qualified and had honestly earned.

With W.L. unemployed, the birth of the couple's first child, Florence, was both a joy and a burden. They found life further complicated when Essie again became pregnant that year.

W.L. and Essie Myers

Still dedicated to becoming a mortician, W.L. felt that it was now or never to complete his education. Having saved some money, he enrolled in the Barnes School of Anatomy in Chicago while Essie moved in with grandparents in Fulton, Kentucky, to deliver their second child, Hazel. The year 1910 saw the new baby born in the same year W.L. received a degree in embalming. Now their fortunes would surely rise.

A Muskogee, Oklahoma funeral director, having no license to embalm, needed W.L.'s help. By this time, with licenses from Oklahoma, Missouri and Arkansas, he fitted right in. He moved his family to Muskogee.

For the next eight years, not only did W.L. sign the director's papers as his embalmer, but also taught him the embalmer's art. Yet, in 1918 he received another blow. After having obtained his own license to embalm, the director fired him. Just as W.L. was recovering from a bout of typhoid fever, he had to start anew.

Licensed to practice in Missouri, W.L. returned to Hannibal to open a funeral home of his own. During this period Essie delivered a son, Bob. With a wife and three children to support, and recurrent health problems, life was tough.

To make matters worse, his doctor advised him to move north for his health. On his way to Minneapolis in an old touring car, filled with a wife, three children and all their possessions, he stopped over in Omaha to visit acquaintances. It was a lucky move. For sale by an estate were the ragged remains of a funeral parlor at 2528 Lake with a dwelling house next door.

The Myers had little money, but the seller agreed to accept payment for the property out of earnings from a new mortuary that W.L. would set up with the help of his Omaha friends. Best yet, his family would have living quarters until they got on their feet.

The W.L. Myers Western Funeral Home was born. W.L. had finally found a place to sink his permanent roots. Now he could further his education. A tireless reader, in order to increase his general knowledge and to learn all he could about running a business, he bought books and took correspondence school courses. These studies paid off. His business soon prospered.

African-Americans had come to Omaha as early as the late 1850s, part of the migration of freed slaves that left the South to find new lives, in Northern cities as workers and on the Western frontier as cowboys and homesteaders. Until the 1880s they came only in small numbers, many of them serving on railroad construction crews. Then, during an ensuing ten years of prosperity, the number of black citizens in Omaha increased to about four thousand, only to diminish during the economic slump of the 1890s.

During the latter half of the century, many prominent leaders appeared. For example, Dr. Matthew O. Ricketts, born in Kentucky of slave parents, moved to Omaha in 1890, graduated with honors from Omaha Medical College and practiced medicine in Omaha until 1903. Thereafter, he began two terms of service in the Nebraska Legislature, a role enabling him to open up positions for blacks in city, county and state government.

An occupational census of 1900 reflects an Omaha labor force of about two thousand African-Americans. Except for meat packing jobs, they were mostly in domestic and personal service. Some held jobs as porters and helpers on the railroads; a few had cherished jobs with the U.S. postal service and a scattering were professionals: doctors, lawyers, clergymen and musicians.

Apartheid was the norm. Even fire stations were segregated. Yet, in 1903, a time when blacks often were excluded from public service jobs, Emory R. Smith proudly became one of Omaha's first black policemen.

The year 1910 found several physicians practicing in Omaha: J.F. Hutten, M.O. Ricketts and August Edwards, all of whom had offices in downtown business blocks. Other downtown professionals were W.W. Peebles, a dentist and attorneys H.J. Pinkett, Silas Robbins and F.L. Smith. A funeral parlor, run by G. Wade Obee, was located at 1002 North Sixteenth Street.

Many other African-American businesses were located downtown, and many of their owners lived, as was the universal custom, next to or above their stores. It was not until the 1910s that such firms and their proprietors found new locations north of Cuming and as far north as Lake, between Twenty-fourth and Thirtieth streets. Black families followed.

Thus by 1921, when the Myers family came, most of the African-American population was located in what was, and is, known as the Near North Side. During the next forty years social pressure would cause this area to become a ghetto, and there, other than in a few blocks near the South Omaha stockyards, most of the city's blacks would reside. Although they might perform work in other parts of the city, it was in the ghetto that society, if not the law, required them to dwell, shop, worship, dance, attend movies and otherwise conduct their lives.

Yet it was not social pressure alone that walled them in. Until 1948, when the U.S. Supreme Court ruled them illegal, covenants restricting ownership of real estate to Caucasians, duly recorded in the Office of the Douglas County Register of Deeds, affected the titles of many Omaha properties, especially those abutting the ghetto. Violation of such covenants could produce judicially-imposed restraining orders.

Curiously, more whites than blacks worked and lived in this ghetto. At the time Myers bought his funeral home, numerous businesses, interspersed with family homes, lined the streets radiating four blocks from Twenty-fourth and Lake. Immigrants occupied most of them: Germans, Italians, Irish, Swedes, Poles, together with Orthodox Jews from European countries, especially Russia. Blacks owned or occupied only a relative few.

The speech on the street was polyglot, with Yiddish as the prevailing language. It was New York City's Lower East Side right here in Omaha. Every imaginable goods and services were for sale, and everyone did business with everyone else. This was good for the new mortician.

The Myers boys were among the very few black children attending Lake School during the twenties. They happily learned and played with Jews, Irish and Italians, unconscious of any differences. The boys felt no prejudice, at least until such time as Bob, proudly wearing his new white safety patrol belt for the first time, was jostled and laughed at by some older white schoolmates who asked: "Are you a nigger?"

Later the puzzled brothers would ponder why, although they could freely accept snacks at the home of an Italian buddy with whom they hiked and played, his parents had warned him never to accept food from the Myers family.

William Lawrence Myers was a handsome man, gracious and soft-spoken. A good conversationalist, he was well received by his black and white neighbors. Although it was not easy starting a new business in a new city, especially competing against a half dozen other black funeral parlors, by eating sparsely and otherwise scrimping, the family made out during those first trying years.

This situation soon changed. Since few blacks possessed Myers's education and experience, most competitors disappeared. A good many were mere fronts for white morticians seeking a share of black funerals. The community was quick to find them out and funnel its business to W.L.

By 1928, Myers Funeral Home had outgrown the Lake Street premises. W.L. relocated it to a new building at 2416 North Twenty-second Street. Then, in 1936, he doubled its size. Later on, Bob and Ken bought the lots north of the building for its better access to Lake Street.

From the earliest days, diverse spiritual forces sustained the Myers. Churches, as well as social and political clubs, became very important. W.L. joined the Mt. Moriah Baptist Church located at Twenty-fourth and Ohio, and later, after relocating his business, transferred his allegiance to St. John African Methodist Episcopal Church, next door. His youngest son, Ken, born in Omaha in 1923, went with him.

Founded in 1865, St. John AME, the earliest black church in Omaha, had served its parishioners at Eighteenth and Webster until the 1920s. Its congregation then commenced construction of its present building, a Frank Lloyd Wright-inspired edifice at Twenty-second and Willis streets.

St. John AME Church, Twenty-second and Willis streets

W.L. loved to sing in St John's choir. In fact, he enjoyed singing so much he regularly volunteered his voice to other choirs in the community, thus becoming very well known and loved.

Essie and son Bob, for their part, joined Zion Baptist at Twenty-third and Grant, an early Omaha congregation. To this day, in keeping with family tradition, Bob sings in the Zion choir as well as in the choir of Pilgrim Baptist, his wife's family church.

As it did for so many of their neighbors, the Myers' various churches provided a refuge for them, a constant source of solace. There the African-Americans could divulge grievances to their pastors, soothe feelings hurt by society's barbs, and share with fellow members their hopes for the future.

Along with the church were fraternal and other organizations. W.L., a member of the Elks Lodge, was also a Blue Lodge Mason who in

129

time attained the thirty-second degree of the Scottish Rite. Bob, also a Mason, was elevated to the thirty-third degree in 1977.

W.L.'s favorite social club was the Jolly Twenty. It convened monthly at the members' homes for games, discussion of social and civic issues and scrumptious meals. With their wives and children, its members met annually at a Bennington, Nebraska farm for huge, mouth-watering picnics.

On a more serious level, W.L. was a member of both the National Association for the Advancement of Colored People (NAACP) and the Urban League, each devoted to the interests of the black man. Like many fellow African-Americans, he faithfully served these organizations for years, demonstrating to his sons the vital role they played in the slow struggle for social and economic justice.

In 1955, death came to both the elder Myers. In 1950, they had passed the reins of the funeral home to heirs fully qualified to run it. Today Ken's son, Lawrence, operates the oldest black business in Nebraska.

The fifty years following W.L.'s death witnessed profound changes in the African-American community. Locally and throughout the United States, verbal and physical expressions of black frustration, some quiet and some militant, led to court decisions and legislative acts of dramatic scope.

The non-violent resistance preached by Martin Luther King and others found realization in lunch counter sit-ins, public transportation boycotts and marches. In time, the resistance became more militant. During the 1960s, Omaha and other cities experienced periods of violence, destructive of life and property. In the Near North Side, some white businesses, and some black ones as well, were looted and burned.

Whatever force caused it to be enacted, a federal civil rights law under the Johnson administration represented a significant step forward. Following its passage, an African-American could live anywhere he wanted, seek any job he desired, and not be denied the right to vote or hold office, at least according to the statute's wording.

And in the 1970s, by mandating busing, the federal courts implemented a U.S. Supreme Court order desegregating the public schools.

In all this change, the activities of Omaha African-American leaders were significant. A notable early champion was Whitney Young, director of Omaha's Urban League in the early 1950s, who later became famous as executive director of the National Urban League.

Omaha Urban League meeting, circa 1930

Later, Omaha civil rights activists were Charles Washington and Lawrence W.M. McVoy. The latter was president of Omaha's chapter of the NAACP during the 1950s. A more recent leader, Ernest Chambers, chosen by his people session after session to represent them in the Nebraska Unicameral, often has raised his voice in behalf of the black community, sometimes stridently and controversially, yet often effectively.

Elizabeth Pittman, a lady whose fellow students at Creighton

African-Americans

University once elected beauty queen, elevated her race in the public's eye. Together with her father, she practiced law with distinction for years before becoming the first African-American to be appointed to the bench. There she served the community as a first-rate county judge.

Another early supporter of African-American causes was Mildred Brown. After an apprenticeship period with C.C. Galloway, a businessman and fighter for civil right who owned and published the **Omaha Guide**, she started up a paper of her own in 1938. The **Omaha Star**, a weekly still being published, has served through the years as a voice of the black community.

Sports, also, have made a difference. African-American athletics has been an effective weapon against intolerance. Many first-rate athletes grew up in Omaha during this era, among them: Robert Boozer in basketball, Robert Gibson in baseball, Gale Sayers in football and Petey Allen, who won a place in the Softball Hall of Fame. Everybody loves a successful sports person. The respect all Omahans developed for these leaders had its own effect in softening latent racial prejudices.

The Myers family played its part in this slow implementation of civil rights. Especially Bob Myers. After Lake Elementary and Technical High School, he attended and received diplomas from Howard University and San Francisco College of Mortuary Science before returning to be a part of his father's business during the 1940s. His brother Ken followed a similar path, attending Howard University and St. Louis College of Mortuary Science.

Over the following forty years Bob plunged deeply into civic and civil rights matters. In addition to becoming a life member of the NAACP and serving as treasurer of the Urban League, he was active in the more militant 4CL movement of the 1960s.

While a member of Mayor Sorensen's Biracial Committee and his Human Relations Board, he somehow found time to be on the boards of both the Near North Side and Metropolitan Branch of the YMCA and a director of the National Council of Christians and Jews.

Arguably his most important service was on the Omaha Board of Education, between 1964 and 1969. Bob was the first African-American member. First appointed to fill an unexpired term, he was elected to a four-year term of his own in a city-wide vote. Once accepted, he tactfully demonstrated to the other board members the unfairness of their teacher-hiring policies. This was not easy; he plowed new ground but made some progress.

Some board members suggested that he sought reform too fast; most fellow blacks complained that he moved too slowly. Significantly, it was during his term of office that the board hired black school teachers for the first time ever. Furthermore, they scattered these teachers throughout the school district.

Enough to goad him to action was the way his own wife had been treated. Reared in Omaha, Bertha became an accomplished musician, playing both piano and organ. In 1951 she earned a bachelor of music degree from Northwestern University and thereafter taught music in the Detroit public schools for eight years.

Moving back to Omaha, she sought a job in the public schools, only to find that her teaching abilities and experience didn't count. The superintendent of schools refused to hire her as a music teacher, even as a substitute, except in all-black schools. Even when she later was allowed to teach full time at Howard Kennedy School, board policy precluded any advancement. Discouraged, she decided to obtain a masters degree in guidance and counseling and ultimately became the first African-American counselor at Central High School.

All of W.L.'s and Essie's children and nearly every one of their grandchildren and great grandchildren have earned college degrees at various universities, including Howard University in Washington, D.C. Bob's daughters have degrees in teaching and music; his grandchildren in criminal justice. One of Ken's daughters, Sibyl Myers, is a feature writer for the **Omaha World-Herald**. Another, Valarie Wilson, is co-owner and operator of a St. Louis advertising and marketing firm, one of the fastest-growing privately-held companies in the United States.

African-Americans

Although many African-American citizens still reside in the Near North Side, many now have homes in all parts of Omaha. Not only does the law require that they be free to buy or build wherever they desire, but many see a continual softening in the social prejudice that previously has inhibited them from doing so, even when they could afford it.

Robert and Bertha Myers, 1965

Yet even before the enactment of civil rights laws and other betterments, some of these citizens showed the ability to help themselves. Bob Myers took such personal action, breaking through the ghetto wall by guile.

In the late 1950s, with the help of a white banker, he financed the construction of a home for Bertha and himself at Fifty-first and Curtis, outside the invisible ghetto wall. Although the couple minutely planned the house, it was actually built and decorated by a white contractor on a lot whose title stood in the contractor's name under a silent trust.

This was a perfectly legal transaction, yet Bob and Bertha didn't dare show their faces to inspect the work, even at night, until the house was ready for occupancy. Only then did they move in.

A few days later Bob heard shots in the area. Were they warnings of neighborhood friction? Bob installed flood lights, controlled by a remote switch, on all corners of his house, placed a shotgun in a corner of his attached garage, put a loaded .38 handgun on his living room coffee table, and ordered a hired security guard to advise the world that any challenge to his possession would result in a free funeral for the invader, "with all the trimmings."

Silence reigned.

REFERENCES

BOOKS

Larsen, James H. and Barbara J. Cottrell. **The Gate City: A History of Omaha**. Boulder, CO: Pruett Publishing Company, 1986.

Shukert, Martin. **Patterns on the Landscape: Heritage Conservation in North Omaha**. Omaha: Omaha Planning Commission,1984.

INTERVIEWS

Myers, Robert. Interview by Donald H. Ericksen and Harry B. Otis. January 4, 1995.

Myers, Robert and Kenneth Myers. Interview by Donald H. Ericksen and Harry B. Otis. January 24, 1996.

Myers, Robert L. Interview by Dr. Dennis Mihelich. March 21, 1979.

MISCELLANEOUS

Evans, James C., of the Office of the Assistant Secretary of Defense. Letter to James Stewart Office of the Chaplain of the Archdiocesan Council of Catholic Action of Omaha. Notification of Defense Department Order barring discrimination in housing. March 8, 1963.

Myers, Robert L., Jizba, Jaro, et al. Correspondence. Concerning Myers property at 5120 Curtis, Omaha, Nebraska. February 16, 1965 to

African-Americans

November 15, 1966.

Myers, Robert L. Letter to Attorney General Robert Kennedy. Complaint about Offutt Air Force Base housing discrimination. January 25, 1963.

NEWSPAPERS

Group Told; Be Positive on Busing. **The Omaha World-Herald**. August 27, 1976.

Myers Honored for Distinguished Service. **Omaha Star.** November 18, 1966.

Reynolds, Cynthia Furlong. *Firm Didn't Grow; It Mushroomed*. **The Omaha World-Herald**. August 6, 1990.

Taylor, John. *Magazine Aims at Healthy Life*. **The Omaha World-Herald**. June 24, 1992.

United Voice on Racial Problems. **Omaha Star**. August 1, 1963.

Williams, Paul. *Why Bob and Bertha Myers Decided to Fight*. **South Omaha Sun**. March 11, 1965.

THE RUMANIANS

They hailed from Rumania, the land of gypsies, the wandering folk of middle Europe. Much like gypsies, from the minute they left for America, Alex Morar and Traian Posa were on the move.

Alexander Morar, called Alex, entered the United States in 1914 at age sixteen. For two years he lived from job to job. On his way out west, he arrived in Omaha out of money. A fondness for the city's fostering Rumanian community made him stay. All he wanted was to get rich enough to live a good life back home. He got rich enough, but by then he had lost a desire to live in his homeland.

Traian Posa, at age thirteen, left Rumania in 1906, earlier than Alex, yet permanently settled in Omaha much later. Until the early 1920s, he drifted in and out of the city and suffered more than his share of hard knocks. But by 1922 he was married, had an acceptable hold on the English language and could navigate on his own.

Rumania is shaped like a fat potato, surrounded by Bulgaria, Yugoslavia, Hungary, Ukraine, Moldova and the Black Sea. It is only four hundred and sixty miles long and two hundred and ninety-five miles wide, yet has a diverse geography and ecology. Both Alex's Rumanian birthplace, now called Dobrovita, and Traian's birthplace, Sebecu de Jos, are located in the center of the country on a very hilly plateau of wide valleys and extensive arable slopes. The Transylvanian Alps enclose them on the south; the Carpathian Mountains, on the north and east.

Much like Omaha, the area suffers warm summers and cold winters. With an average of twenty inches of rainfall, the plateau's fertile soil makes it highly suited for growing wheat and other grains. Fruit trees thrive, and the region's grapes produce some of the best wine in Eastern Europe.

Although Alex and Traian remained unacquainted, each loved Rumania and brought something of it to his adopted city.

On the day he waited for the train at Dobrovita, then called Comuna Tintir, Alex carelessly dropped his suitcase, dumping his lunch and

Rumanians

all his clothes on the station platform. For his mother this was an omen that he would never return. And he never did, at least in her lifetime.

For his first two years in America, he bounced from city to city practicing the trades of tailoring and barbering, from Ellis Island westward, finally landing in Omaha. He really intended to live in the "Wild West," somewhere in Wyoming or Montana, but the Omaha Rumanian colony quenched his thirst. Besides, he had, as yet, no hold on the English language. His new Rumanian friends found him a rooming house and a job at the Armour Packing Company. Even better, they helped him to learn English.

Mary and Alex Morar

Before long he had saved enough to open a tailor shop between Twenty-fourth and Twenty-fifth and Q streets, learn a little bit of English, and have his picture taken. Another immigrant, Mary Covrig, from Tirgumures, Rumania, was on her way to St. Agnes Lutheran Grade School when she spotted his picture in Japanese photographer Ishii's shop window. Could this be the handsome tailor she saw daily sitting in his Q Street shop working on suits? Would he be her future husband? He would.

The two met at a dance in the Rumanian Hall, fell in love, and were married in St. John Greek Orthodox Church at Sixteenth and Martha. When their first child was born in 1918, they named her Mary and gave her credit for ending World War I. Her brother Alex was not born until 1929.

The Morars were good Orthodox Christians. Soon after their marriage they joined St. Cross Rumanian Orthodox Church at Thirty-second and R. Although they sent their daughter Mary to a Lutheran day school, which many Rumanian children attended, when it came time for her confirmation, her father insisted that the St. Cross priest perform the rite. She was a Rumanian. Nothing but an Orthodox confirmation for her, he said.

Together with an active colony of over one hundred families, the Morars supported their Rumanian Orthodox parish all their days, Alex often serving as a church officer.

Priests and congregation at St. Cross Rumanian Orthodox Church

St. Cross retained its ethnic character until the end of World War II. During this period, most Omaha Rumanians inhabited an area between Q and P and Thirty-third and Thirty-sixth streets. Only after the war did they move slowly to other parts of the city and to other churches.

Over the years, Rumanian Orthodox priests, Fathers Cohan and Bideaux, took care of their flock's many spiritual needs and preached them many sermons, half in Rumanian and half in English. Only in later years did the church, still Orthodox, adopt English as the sole language for its services and change its name to St. Gabriel.

Rumanians

Fr. Bideaux had a voice one could hear two blocks away. Fr. Cohan would almost put himself and his congregation to sleep, yet he could express himself when he wanted to. One Sunday Mary Morar and other little children sat in the church balcony, laughing and making noise. Stopping his droning in midstream, Cohan screamed at them in his best Rumanian: "You young jackasses, shut up!"

The Morars always lived close to St. Cross, first at 3707 S Street, and later at 3716 U. Although they drew comfort from their own people, they yearned to become full-fledged Americans. Soon after their wedding, they attended night classes in English at Tech High School. The new language was tough to learn, but the hard discipline made them even more determined. In their home they decided to speak nothing but the language of their new land. Naturalization followed. In the early 1920s, on a proud day, a federal judge swore them in as citizens.

Alex lost no time establishing businesses in his new environment. Tailoring and barbering provided funds for a good start. Soon he was operating a pool hall on Q Street. By the late 1930s, he owned a nightclub on the highway to Offutt Air Force Base, the Black Cat. He later acquired the Golden Spike Bar at Twenty-sixth and N and the Rainbow Bar at Twenty-fifth and N, both victims of condemnation when Interstate Highway 80 and its access routes came through.

Like nearly all immigrants of their time, Alex and Mary prized thrift. Soon after their marriage, Mary found a job as a meat processor with Armour Packing and worked there for twenty years. Her frugality provided funds for the higher education of both children and grandchildren.

The Rumanian community of Alex and Mary's day loved to dance in the Rumanian Hall located near the church. Polkas, waltzes and *schottisches*, the folk music of the dancers' native land, relieved a lingering nostalgia. Alex himself played the horn, and Mary's uncle, the clarinet. Annual participation in Omaha's multiethnic gatherings let them show how proud they were to be of Rumanian descent.

Mary's cooking was part of this heritage. Her grandchildren loved her and called her MaMa Tina. She in turn indulged them with products of Rumanian recipes she carried in her head: cookies, cakes and good Rumanian rye bread.

Alex (TaTa Tina), likewise spoiled his grandchildren, giving them pop and potato chips when they stopped at one of his bars. Sometimes he would drop everything to take them to an ice cream stand or a movie.

Neither Alex nor Mary ever regretted their American destiny. They found many reasons to be grateful. During the 1960s they returned for a month-long visit with one of Alex's brothers. Although Rumania was under communist domination, this poor soul had refused to embrace the Communist party and was maltreated accordingly. The government had confiscated half his possessions and left him with only the worst part of the family farm.

Alex still held title to some land and a grocery store his parents had left him, but now, being a foreign national, he couldn't keep them. As he departed his native land for good, he gladly ceded to his brother whatever interest he owned.

Mary, the daughter of Alex and Mary, married Michael Covalciuc, of Rumanian descent. They had four daughters and a son. One of the four daughters, Margaret Munnally, having earned her Ph.D., served as senior vice president and dean of the College of St. Mary in Omaha. Their son, Michael, graduating from medical school, is now affiliated with the Mayo Clinic in Rochester, Minnesota. Another daughter, Mary Ann, and her husband, Ron Patton, own and operate Patton Equipment Company in Omaha.

Alex and Mary Morar, though recently deceased, are remembered by their fellow Omahans as energetic, intelligent, determined people who bettered both themselves and Omaha. They came to their adopted city poor and with no knowledge of the language, yet managed to prosper sufficiently to leave behind a legacy of brilliantly educated American citizens.

****

Rumanians

Traian Posa

Born on November 2, 1894, Traian Posa was only thirteen when his father, Josif, brought him to America on the steamship *Koln*. He left behind brothers, a sister and a teary-eyed mother, Anna. He missed them even before the train left the station of his little village. Yet his homesickness during the trip to Breman, his first train ride, was nothing compared to his seasickness during the subsequent fourteen days to the United States. A bad start.

Traian tried to tell himself that he was only following the trail of an older brother, Josif, whom their father had brought to the New World two years earlier. But that didn't help. When his father had returned to Rumania he had left his brother alone in Baltimore to shift for himself. Would they find Josif? Would his father abandon his other son to strangers speaking a language he couldn't understand? He was miserable.

In Baltimore they found brother Josif alive, well and working for a shoemaker. The three set forth for Indianapolis for the first of Traian's many adventures. There his uncle Stephan, an earlier immigrant, found them a few months' work in a canning factory. They were laid off when the season ended.

Hearing news of jobs in Omaha, father Josif and his two sons hopped a westbound cattle car for the good wages of the city's meat packers. The Swift plant provided work for all but Traian. He was too young. He had to work in a Rumanian grocery store.

During a very cold depression winter that saw thousands of unemployed in soup lines at the packinghouses, Traian delivered groceries and baby-sat the grocer's young daughter. While others suffered, he was able to earn seven dollars per month in wages plus his room and board. Even better, he lodged with a Rumanian-speaking family.

The following year, a Nebraska literacy law required all children under sixteen years of age to attend school. Herman Smith, a Harrison County, Iowa, farmer needed a boy to help on his farm and promised to see Traian educated. Traian lived here during the summer and winter of 1908, attending school in the town of Logan and doing farm chores.

While he was so occupied, his restless father returned to Rumania without him, and his brother moved to St. Joseph, Missouri to open a shoe repair shop of his own. It was a wretched time for Traian. At age fourteen, he was deep in the heart of America without any family members and very homesick. To make matters worse, his limited and broken English made learning very hard. Herman's two brothers didn't help. These fellow farm workers never ceased picking on him, teasing him and calling him an illiterate "foreigner." In January 1909 he fled back to Omaha, to the sympathy of the Rumanian grocer.

Fortunately, his friend found him new work with a farmer, John Ruff of Nehawka, Nebraska. During the next five years he really progressed, happily working on the Ruff farm during the summer and attending school in Nehawka during the winter.

With no Rumanians in the vicinity to talk to, it was sink or swim. His English and his fortunes improved. Because of his youth, he even learned to speak the new language with a barely noticeable accent. Even better, by the age of twenty he had earned enough money to afford a motorcycle, an Indian. John Ruff became his lifelong ally. Over the years Traian would visit the Ruff family many times.

In 1914, Traian reunited with his parents in Omaha. Returning to America for a third time, his father had now brought along his mother, Anna. So, for the first time in seven years, Traian could embrace his mother.

The three found jobs with Swift and lived together for a year before a layoff caused further moves. Traian temporarily returned to the Ruff home in Nehawka while Josif, always mobile, traveled with Anna to North Platte where he had found a job with the Union Pacific

Rumanians

Railroad.

Times were hard. Anna helped heat their modest quarters by gleaning coal spilled from rail cars onto the tracks outside of town. Life became more bearable when Traian joined them for a U.P. job as a machinist apprentice.

In 1916, with Swift again seeking workers, the ever-restless Josif returned his family to Omaha. The following year Josif, Jr. joined them temporarily, soon to leave for Australia and never to be heard from again.

In 1919, all three Posas decided to return to their native land. Josif was still dissatisfied with his lot; Anna couldn't adjust to America; Traian didn't want, just yet, to lose his parents. Anna missed her other children but wouldn't bring them here. Somehow the Posas failed to relieve their longing for the Old World by identifying with the Omaha Rumanian community which the Morars found so endearing.

As he had emigrated before they were born, it was rewarding for Traian to meet sisters he had never known, sisters his grandparents had cared for while Josif and Anna were wandering abroad. Traian's last visit to Rumania was short. By now he was thoroughly Americanized and homesick for Omaha. His older sister, Eva, agreed to go back with him. But America was not for her. By the time they had reached Italy, homesickness caused her return to Rumania.

Almost broke, Traian traveled to Omaha by way of Indianapolis where a loan of thirty dollars from Uncle Stephan allowed him to complete the trip. He was now twenty-six, but as before, he arrived penniless.

A job with Swift kept him alive until a winter strike; friends took care of him after that. They loaned him money until he could again find work with the Union Pacific and Missouri Pacific Railroads where he worked until 1923.

March 17, 1923 was an important date. St. Patrick's Day marked a new job with Updike Lumber and Coal Company. Except for a few lulls, he was to work for Updike for the next thirty-seven years, Nels

Updike found him to be a faithful employee. Beginning wages were twenty-five dollars per week. From these he paid ten dollars for board and room at 4432 Davenport Street.

Despite being laid off during several weeks of the following year, during which he found temporary work with the Omaha Water Works in Florence, by carefully saving his money he was able to ladle out four hundred and eight dollars in cash for a 1924 Ford Roadster. This really made him an American.

It was time to get married. On December 23, 1926, he wedded Gerda Oakeson, a lovely girl of Swedish descent from Mead, Nebraska, who soon blessed him with a daughter, Virginia.

Like most couples, Traian and Gerda struggled to get ahead. By 1930, their frugality allowed them to pay down five hundred dollars of the fifteen hundred dollar purchase price for their lifetime home: a small frame house at 3919 Miami. They were convinced that the low monthly mortgage payment of ten dollars would allow them to hold on to the house during the depression they saw coming down the road. In this they were right.

More children came to them: Robert Joseph Posa in 1930, John Lee Posa in 1932 and Donna Ann Posa in 1934.

Most people who lived in Omaha during the 1930s will never forget the period. The Depression winters were as bad as the summers. During the twenty-nine days of February 1936, the temperature never rose above zero. The summers brought day after day of one hundred degrees or better, with little rain.

When Traian developed a severe case of arthritis that threatened his job and tested the compassion of his friends, Gerda's family and fellow employees never forsook him. One winter, when his disease left him helpless in every joint, a kind Updike salesman drove him to daily steam baths in the Hill Hotel until remission came.

Be it winter or summer, rationing of gasoline during World War II required Traian to walk the mile and one half from his home to work and back again. This was his contribution to the war effort. During World War I he had been too young to enlist; now he was too old. In later years, his sons would serve their country proudly: Robert on a naval destroyer in the Pacific and John in the postwar military police in Okinawa.

In January 1960 Gerda died; in February Traian retired from Updike. Without Gerda, he found retirement a bore. A job with Samardick's Armored Car Service afforded him work for the following six years.

Even though he didn't mingle much with the Omaha Rumanian community, Traian's background remained a part of him. Loving to garden, he annually planted his Miami Street lot with the same vegetables his parents had put in their small plot of land in Sebescu de Jos. He had strawberry and rhubarb patches, as well as a vineyard for the grapes needed for wine making. He enjoyed swapping wine with his neighbors who had vines of their own.

Over the course of the years, he and Gerda planted and maintained an orchard that provided them with apples, peaches, pears and apricots for their table. In true Rumanian tradition, he kept the lower four or five feet of the trunks of these fruit trees painted with whitewash to protect against disease and insects.

After a few years of correspondence, Traian broke all ties with his Rumanian family. Their letters came less and less frequently and finally ceased altogether in 1971. Years following his last word from Rumania, a television program on his native land prompted him to reestablish contact. Few members of his family were left, and they had moved, yet he was able to find them.

His sister, Eva, told him that both his parents and four of his brothers and sisters had died after the Communist regime had forced them to move to Albino, a small town near the Rumanian-Yugoslavian border. Despite her invitation to visit, Traian opted not to return to his homeland. By now he was too much an American. Until his death he lived alone in his little house in Omaha, never to return to where his Old World family had slowly faded away.

Like most Omaha immigrants he was happy with his own American children, all with a good education and useful lives. These were his family. They were not Rumanians, but Omahans of Rumanian descent, and like Alex Morar, and each of those who came from his Old World country, Traian Posa enriched his chosen city by painting part of it with the distinctive color of his life.

Each of the newcomers added a hint of the special color of the land the ancient Romans had named, making Omaha the better for it.

REFERENCES

BOOKS
Larsen, Lawrence H. and Barbara J. Cottrell. **The Gate City: A History of Omaha**. Boulder, CO: Pruett Publishing, 1982.

INTERVIEWS
Covalciuc, Mary. Tape recorded interview by Harry B. Otis. February 8, 1996.
Posa, John. Tape recorded interview by Harry B. Otis. July 10, 1995.

MISCELLANEOUS
Traian Posa's Family History. A brochure.

THE GREEKS

A shriek of joy went up among the parishioners. At the church's general assembly meeting, president Nicholas Payne had just announced that the Jewish congregation of Temple Israel of Omaha would sell their synagogue. This Park Avenue house of worship was exactly what the members of St. John the Baptist Greek Orthodox Church had been looking for.

Not that the Greeks' building at Sixteenth and Martha was so bad. They had simply outgrown it. It had served them well since 1908, despite its tiny sanctuary. But now, in 1951, the more than a thousand parishioners were overflowing its brick walls.

Its Gothic windows belied the fact that the church housed Christians who were Orthodox, not Roman Catholic or Protestant. And it did not yet sport the intriguing golden onion dome later installed by Ukrainian Catholics to denote an Eastern rite of Christianity.

St. John the Baptist Greek Orthodox Church, 604 Park Avenue

Greeks

The Park Avenue edifice, on the other hand, had Greek Orthodox written all over it. Created in a Byzantine style by one of Omaha's leading architects, John Latenser, it had served Temple Israel well since 1908. But now this Reformed Jewish congregation wanted to build a larger temple of worship at Sixty-ninth and Cass, closer to their homes. They were most happy to sell it to the Greeks.

Orthodox religious service is lost without a building possessing a certain stylized architecture and interior design. After the fall of the Western Roman Empire to barbarian hordes in 476 A.D., the Eastern Empire flourished for a thousand years. So, too, did Christianity under the Byzantine patriarch of Constantinople, a patriarch that exists to this day as the spiritual head of all Orthodox Christians.

Over the centuries certain features, peculiarly Byzantine, have become identified with Orthodox church buildings wherever the Eastern patriarch sent missionaries to establish Christianity: Russia, Serbia, Bulgaria, Rumania, the Ukraine, Syria and especially, Greece. The dome of the Park Avenue structure, like that of Emperor Justinian's sixth century marvel, Hagia Sophia, in Constantinople (now Istanbul), contains windows piercing its bases. Four pendentives, triangular segments resting on four heavy columns, support the dome, producing a building with a huge unbroken space for its sanctuary and superior acoustics.

The excited assembly members could just picture the traditional image of Christ, surrounded by angels, looking down on them from above. They yearned to see the stylized icons of saints mounted on a wooden iconostasis that would shield the altar in front of them. These images would be of the Virgin Mary, the Angel Gabriel and many saints, especially John the Baptist, their patron. All of this would come in time, after plenty of sacrifice and hard work.

The negotiating committee of the synagogue had offered the building at a fair price. Led by their priests, Spyridon Zoys and Nicholas Velis, Nicholas Payne and his fellow parishioners would come up with the money. By 1953, having sold their Martha Street church to the Ukrainians, the synagogue was theirs. Later, after an extensive renovation that included the installation of an ornately carved oak iconostasis, they were ready for the elaborate liturgy of their Orthodox form of worship.

Although they placed on each of the four pendentives an icon for each of the four Evangelists, they symbolically blended the Old and New Testaments by retaining the large stained glass images of Moses and King David that the Jews had found appropriate for the north and south windows of their temple.

There was even more symbolic blending. While Temple Israel was completing its synagogue out west, it was most practical and fitting that for six months both Orthodox Christians and Jews share the remodeled Park Avenue building for their services: the Jews under Rabbi Sidney Brooks on Saturday, the Greeks under Fr. Nicholas Velis on Sundays. Nobody seemed to mind. Indeed, every Christian and Jew seemed to revel in this display of ecumenicism.

Most of the St. John's Greeks were immigrants from a land unsurpassed in beauty, but deficient in soil. Mountains cover most of it; what is left is rocky.

A Greek legend tells that God sifted the earth through a strainer while making the world. Making one country after another with the good soil that sifted through, He threw away the stones left in the strainer. According to the legend, these stones became Greece.

Yet during the twenty-five hundred years of their history, the Greeks have made good use of this rock. From marble and limestone they fashioned shrines and temples without equal in beauty. At the same time, from the few arable patches God afforded them, they grew enough olives, fruit, wheat and other grains to sustain themselves, the abundant fish in the surrounding seas supplementing their diet.

Poor soil produces exceptional people. In ancient times, Greeks established the traditions of justice and individual freedom that are basic to democracy. Their arts, philosophy and science have become the foundations of Western thought and culture. Architects

Greeks

Nicholas Payne

throughout the world return again and again for inspiration to the simplicity of the Parthenon and the Athenian Acropolis.

Nicholas Payne was born and christened Nicholas Papadopoulos in 1895. His birthplace was Aigion, Greece, a lovely, white Peleponnesian town situated on the beautiful bay of Corinth. The bay, like all Aegean waters, is as blue as Iowa's Okoboji, one of the bluest lakes in the world.

Nicholas's father, Spiro, had been a native of the village of Kalavrita, fifteen miles to the south. The 1821 Greek war of independence had its beginning in Kalavrita. After four hundred years of Turkish subjugation, the Greeks won their freedom, although in the process the retiring Turks had burned some of the buildings of Kalavrita's monastery. Later, during World War II, the Germans massacred many Kalavritans in the same monastery.

Spiro had moved to Aigion upon marrying the socially prominent Georgia Michalopoulos. On a nearby sixty-acre fruit and olive orchard, the couple reared Nicholas and his three brothers and two sisters, who thrived in the warm sunshine and happy existence of Greek family life.

The time came, however, when Nicholas's parents recommended that he emigrate to America. Not only would the relatively small acreage be unable to support all the Papadopoulos children, who undoubtedly soon would have families of their own, but at age eighteen Nicholas would face two years of compulsory military service. Rumors of an impending Balkan war quickened Spiro and Georgia's resolve to get their son to American relatives.

In 1910, at age fifteen, Nicholas left his homeland for Boston.

helped him find a job making candy.

It wasn't easy for either of them to adapt to the strange customs and utterly different language of a new country, but they found comfort in knowing they had an uncle, John Birbilis, in Lincoln, Nebraska. This Greek had immigrated there at the turn of the century and by now was a well-established confectioner.

For two years Nicholas worked with his cousin in a Boston confectionery, learning the art of candy and ice cream making. At the end of the apprenticeship, their uncle invited them to work for him in Lincoln. John's assistance was pivotal. He not only perfected their knowledge of making candy and ice cream, but taught them the nuts and bolts of running a business.

During this Lincoln period, Nicholas met and married a lovely girl of German descent, Clara Hoffman. Although of German Lutheran heritage, she readily embraced Orthodox Christianity. Within a year she presented Nicholas with a son, George, and six years later a daughter, Pearl.

By 1918, the family Payne and cousin Fred were ready for a new venture. Uncle John found them a business to buy: a confectionery in Council Bluffs, Iowa, located precisely where the streetcar terminated, at the intersection of Broadway and Pearl streets, before connecting with another line taking passengers to Lake Manawa. Their uncle helped them buy the shop and even made the first few rental payments on the leased premises.

After finding a Council Bluffs apartment for Nicholas's family and a room for cousin Fred, the two candymakers went to work in their new store. Typical of the time, it boasted a white tile floor, a metal ceiling from which large fans dropped down, a marble-covered soda fountain with a heavy mahogany back bar and matching candy cases on the sides. Embossed in gold on the boxes of candy in these cases was the company's name: Palace of Sweets.

Through their contact with the public, the young Greek immigrants quickly learned American customs and improved their English. Fortunately, both were willing to study hard and work long

Greeks

hours. Like many immigrants, Nicholas showed his affection for America by adopting an anglicized name.

The store's perfect location and good merchandise produced a thriving business, especially during holidays. At Christmas they rolled their own candy canes; on Valentine's Day they covered their candy boxes with satin; and for St. Patrick's Day they presented their customers with plenty of green candy.

Nicholas and Fred were typical of many Greeks who came to the Omaha area early in the twentieth century. Dr. John M. Bitzes, a member of St. John's Church, provides an outline of Omaha's Greek-American history.

Most of the early Greeks began to arrive in Omaha and surrounding cities in 1904 to work in the meat packing plants and on the railroads. Some came to establish their own businesses. The year 1907 found two thousand Greeks in the area, mostly in South Omaha.

In 1909 South Omaha was a small, independent municipality, yet the Greeks already had established thirty-two businesses there, including shoe-shine parlors, travel agencies, coffee houses, groceries and confectioneries such as Nicholas and his cousin established in Council Bluffs.

In general, Greek immigrants got along well with most locals. A few of the earlier settlers, nevertheless, hated the newcomers, especially Greek railroad workers. When winter conditions forced them to be idle from railroad work, some of these, mostly single men, would sit around all day in taverns drinking coffee or Greek wine and making little effort to learn English, or to identify with the native population or other immigrants. Little by little, contempt, and probably envy, of this lifestyle increased a hostility that was soon leveled at all Greeks. The language barrier also played a role in the matter.

A shameful series of events occurred. On February 19, 1909, a transient worker and gambler, who happened to be of Greek origin, shot and killed a police officer, Edward Lowery. The killer was

154

arrested and taken to Lincoln for incarceration.

Two days later a riot erupted. A mob, inflamed by irresponsible leaders and unable to get at the killer, used clubs, arson, pistols and fists to physically injure all Greeks they could find in the vicinity, as well as a few immigrant Poles. Homes and businesses were destroyed. Many Greeks fled the South Omaha area for good. To make matters worse, the following year the police arbitrarily singled out and shot a young Greek immigrant, Nicholas Jimikas.

While Lowery's death obviously triggered the riot, Dr. Bitzes attributes its underlying cause to economic competition, a lack of education, greed, cultural and ethnic differences as well as poor behavior on the part of both Greeks and non-Greeks before the riot.

Fortunately, the ruckus did not directly affect the smaller Greek business community in Omaha itself. The stands and shops of fruit and candy merchants and of other businesses on various downtown streets were undisturbed.

One Omaha shop was that of Stephan Abariotis, who had come in 1900 at a time when the census figures listed only twelve persons of Greek origin. Setting up a fruit stand, he later expanded it to a fruit and candy business, naming it Olympia Candy Kitchen after his famous home region in Greece. Another store, AB Sweet Shop, came later.

In a 1961 **Omaha World-Herald** article, Robert McMorris reports an interview with Abariotis. Although they started with fruit, eventually most of the vendors, as a sideline, made candy on the first floor of their places of business while occupying the upstairs of their premises as living quarters. Abariotis's early fruit stand was at Sixteenth and Douglas, his later fruit and candy business at 1518 Harney. When, after a few years, the fruit stands disappeared, their proprietors opened stores dealing only in candy and ice cream. At one time there were twenty such stores. During the Depression, many of these evolved into restaurants.

Together with his younger brothers, George and Constantine, Abariotis was one of the founders of St. John Greek Orthodox

Greeks

The Virginia Café, 1411-1413 Douglas Street

Church and supported it all his days. It was through the church Nicholas Payne would meet Stephan Abariotis and his brothers and become their lifelong friend.

After seven years of success in Council Bluffs, it was inevitable that Nicholas and Fred would try their luck in a business across the river. In 1920 they bought the Calumet, an Omaha restaurant at 1411-13 Douglas Street. Its owners were ready to sell, having done business on the site since 1893 for three hundred and sixty-five days a year, twenty-four hours a day.

Continuing to operate the Palace of Sweets, the cousins completely remodeled the double storefront of the Calumet and renamed it the Virginia Café. Until it burned down in 1969, Nicholas would continue the Calumet's tradition of never closing, even on

Christmas Day.

Again the young cousins had chosen wisely the location for their new enterprise. It was directly on the streetcar line from Council Bluffs; it was close to the principal office buildings of Omaha, the Union Pacific Building and the city's large department stores; it was very near all of the downtown theaters. In those days everybody came downtown to work, shop and play.

In time, the Virginia would become the largest all-hour restaurant west of Chicago and have a staff of eighty-five employees, serving a whopping average of three thousand rations a day.

Yet it had to grow slowly. For a few years Nicholas, continuing to operate the Palace of Sweets, kept his residence in Council Bluffs, but as the restaurant business expanded, he decided, along with Fred, to sell the candy store. The Paynes moved to Omaha.

During the first two decades of operation, Nicholas daily drove his own car to the open-air market at Twelfth and Jackson to buy the fresh fruits and vegetables needed by the hungry customers.

The Virginia's menu consisted of a wide variety of American dishes with a new luncheon and dinner every day of the week. According to Nicholas, they served so many different crowds so many different times a day, they had to have a wide variety of menus. Even at lunch time they offered thirteen to fifteen different selections that changed every day.

It is little wonder that during World War II, the Korean conflict and the Vietnam War, when the recruiting office up the street was actively recruiting personnel for the armed services, the government awarded the Virginia coveted contracts for the feeding of these new enlistees.

Business was steady and profitable. All hours of the day and night, the restaurant served meals to these recruits, yet weekly surprise quality inspections by the military meant that Nicholas and his employees had to stay on their toes to keep the contract. For three days during the 1930s, the restaurant likewise served more than a thousand National Guard soldiers three meals a day. These guardsmen had been called out by the governor of Nebraska to protect the public during a nasty streetcar strike.

To make this full-time operation go, Nicholas and Fred spent long hours. Moreover, Nicholas's hours grew even longer when, in 1930, Fred decided to start a restaurant of his own. However, Payne had other help. Earlier he had brought his brother, Peter, to the Omaha area to handle the Palace of Sweets and later work for him at the Virginia.

Young Nicholas Payne was handsome: five feet, nine inches tall, black hair, blue eyes and a fair complexion. Unlike most Greeks, who in general are of a darker makeup, he was subject to sunburn. Not necessarily classed as athletic, he nonetheless possessed the stamina and staying power necessary for the long hours of managing a twenty-four-hour restaurant. He would appear at work at seven-thirty A.M. and, after a two-hour recess in the afternoon, return to stay well into the evening.

As an older man, whether at work or at church, he dressed conservatively. Always wearing a suit with shirt and tie, he exhibited a sense of propriety and good breeding.

With a natural love of people and readiness to greet his many customers on a daily basis, it wasn't long before a speaking acquaintanceship developed with most of the city's leading citizens, who grew to admire and respect both the man and his business.

The public seemed to love the ambiance of the Virginia as much as its food. Handsome mahogany, clean table cloths and efficient waitresses were as important as the fact that one could order a hamburger as readily as a full meal. Nicholas genuinely wanted his customers to feel comfortable. They learned to count on his greeting and taking time to chat with them.

This attention to detail paid off. The restaurant began to attract national and international celebrities visiting Omaha who were directed there by others at the various hotels and theaters. Yet it was the local businessman who was the café's backbone. In addition to furnishing regular meals, the public used it more and more for

daily coffee hours and happy
hours and parties in a newly
created Redwood Room set
apart for this purpose.

Nominated by a friendly
competitor, Raymond C.
Matson, Nicholas entered
American Restaurant
Magazine's Hall of Fame in
1956. One of the founding
members of the Omaha
Restaurant Association, he
received that organization's
highest award in 1967,
Nebraska Restauranteur of
the Year.

Nicholas Payne pouring coffee

Despite his attention to the Virginia, Nicholas found time to
devote to the community, especially his church. St. John fast became
the cultural, especially religious, activity for the Greek family.
Nicholas was there to help when the first Greek play was cast from
local talent and when the first Greek language school was started
for the community's children.

He was a charter member when the Fraternal Order of AHEPA
(American Hellenic Educational and Progressive Association) took
root in Omaha. He later helped sponsor AHEPA's ladies' auxiliary,
the Daughters of Penelope and the youth organizations, the Sons of
Pericles and the Maids of Athena.

All of these groups soothed the Greek immigrant's transition
into American life while he retained the important aspects of his
cultural heritage. One characteristic, peculiarly Greek, is *philotimo*,
an unwritten value system or code governing one's behavior. Based
on a sense of honor, a self-restrained pride and an education acquired
at home, church, school and community, it is the root of the Greek
individualism, self-respect, patriotism and love of liberty.

Greeks

Nicholas's *philotimo* led him to many activities on behalf of his church, his community and his adopted country. While faithful to his church in both attendance and activity and to his Greek friends, he was ever faithful to the United States, supporting it in many ways. For example, he took time during World War II to sell over three million dollars in government bonds.

His reputation was such that in 1983 the ecumenical patriarch, Archbishop Iakovos, made him an archon of the Order of the Knights of St. Andrew, the highest lay recognition of the Greek Orthodox Church. In the Omaha community, only he and Dr. P. E. Papadakis have been so blessed with the honor.

The value of *philotimo* to the Greek community and to America as a whole is reflected in the patriotism of Omaha's Greek citizens who served their country in all of America's twentieth century wars. In World War I, twenty-two men enlisted; in World War II, thirty-seven (including Babe Petrow, killed in action); in the Korean conflict, eight; and in the Vietnam War, four. George Payne, Nicholas's son, served in both World War II and the Korean War.

On November 20, 1969, a stubborn, smoky fire burned down the Virginia. Omaha's oldest downtown restaurant was destroyed beyond repair. Neither Nicholas nor his son, George, opted to rebuild; its day downtown had passed. The land eventually would be part of the site of the W. Dale Clark Library.

Around the time of Nicholas's death, there were some fourteen hundred persons in Douglas County who identified themselves as being of Greek descent. Many represented the descendants of the immigrants who came to Omaha earlier in the century, many having illustrious careers in business, government and the professions.

A goodly portion of these citizens continue to give healthy support to St. John the Baptist Church and, by establishing Greek language schools, they encourage their children to do the same. As further motivation for succeeding generations to participate, the priests of the church now more frequently conduct the liturgy in both Greek and English. So it was that in 1989 an ample congregation of Greek-Americans of Omaha, dear friends of Nicholas, were in attendance at the church service to mourn his passing. In a memorial the board of directors of the church chose to praise him with words used by Dr. Samuel Johnson of England in describing his own friend: "Sir, he was a great, good man."

Greeks

REFERENCES

BOOKS

Greece. In **World Book Multimedia Encyclopedia**, Chicago: World Book, 1995.

Larsen, James H. and Barbara J. Cottrell. **The Gate City: A History of Omaha**. Boulder, CO: Pruett Publishing, 1982.

INTERVIEWS

Brooks, Rabbi Sidney. Interview by Harry B. Otis. April 16, 1997.

Payne, George. Interview by Harry B. Otis. February 10, 1997.

MISCELLANEOUS

Bitzes, John G. *Our History*. 1983.

Bitzes, John G. *St. John the Baptist Greek Orthodox Church, 1908-1997*.1997.

Payne, George. Notes on the story of Omaha Greeks. February 1997.

NEWSPAPERS

Big Murals Are Finished. **The Omaha World-Herald**. January 24, 1954.

Matson, Raymond C. *Nicholas S. Payne of the Virginia Restaurant Omaha, Nebraska*. **American Restaurant Magazine**. October 1956.

McMorris, Robert. *Single Men from the Balkans Often Sought Fortunes Here*. **The Omaha World-Herald**. December 17, 1961.

New Chapter Added to Horatio Alger Tale. **West Omaha Sun**. January 18, 1964.

Nicholas S. Payne. **The Hellenic Chronicle**. July 13, 1989.

Peyser, Verne. *Oldest Omaha Café Destroyed by Fire*. **The Omaha World-Herald**. November 10, 1969.

Renovated Church Ready for Visitors. **The Omaha World-Herald**. November 5, 1994.

THE CZECHS

Stand on the southeast corner of Thirteenth and William in Omaha and look to the west. You will see the remains of a once-proud, century-old, three-story red brick hotel, one time host to hundreds of Bohemians and Moravians. Over its lower windows are the words "Restaurant" and "Sample Room." On the pane of one of the windows are the words "Established in 1898." Under the building's cornice is the large word "Prague."

Turn your imagination to the turn of the century. In front of the hotel and on adjacent sidewalks you see milling immigrants dressed in Old World clothing, shopping the Czech stores in the neighborhood. They converse in their native Bohemian with gestures alien to American ones. All of a sudden, you are in middle Europe.

At that time, Omaha was the final destination for many such Czechs. They had heard of the city through relatives' letters, Czech newspapers and railroad posters luring pioneers to Nebraska farms. They had come in droves. Thirteenth and William was the heart of Little Bohemia, the principal Czech section of the city.

Typical immigrants were Anton Duda and Anna Franta, his future wife, both born in Nova Kdyne, Bohemia. Anton emigrated to the United States in 1879 at age seventeen; Franta a few years later. Their families, Old World friends, arranged their marriage. The wedding took place in Omaha.

*Danita and Doreen McKenney
at Czech Festival, 1989*

163

Czechs

Anton worked for the Cudahy Packing Company where he was electrocuted later in life by a faulty wiring of the company's elevator. Until this sad occurrence, his wages allowed him to rent a small house, tucked, like similar ones, on the alley behind a larger house on William Street east of Thirteenth Street. Thus, Anton and Franta's children, including their son Walter, grew up in a thoroughly Czech neighborhood where the Bohemian language reigned and was spoken exclusively in their home, at least at first.

One day Walter's public school teacher came to his home to see his parents. His schooling demanded a knowledge of English. They would have to start speaking English in the home. This launched the Duda family into the hard struggle for a new language. They continued to live in Little Bohemia, moving in a few years to 1405 William, directly west of Tesar's Market, and the Duda children successfully attended Omaha public schools.

After one year of high school at what is now Central High, Walter went on to become an innovative and successful businessman and farm manager. In later years he acquired a parcel of land on the Missouri River north of Dodge Park, where his grandson still actively farms while serving on the Douglas County Board of Commissioners.

A part of Bohemian culture is a love of wild mushrooms. For Walter Duda, hunting the spring morel was a passion. It is still a passion for his progeny. Walter would postpone out-of-town trips, business or pleasure alike, if the morel mushroom, one of nature's most succulent, yet elusive and ephemeral fungi, suddenly popped up on his Missouri River lands after an early May rain.

Some such mushrooms must have been used by the owners of Bohemian restaurants in Little Bohemia. Our imagination lets us smell the delicious cooking odors wafting from Joe Pivonka's restaurant in the Prague Hotel. His pork, roast duck, beef with dill gravy, sauerkraut and dumplings attracted customers, both Czech and non-Czech, for miles around. A myriad of neighborhood Bohemian shops provisioned him: rolls and *kolaches* from bakeries, and pork and beef from meat markets, such as Tesar's on William Street around the corner.

Twenty-three years later, one-half block north, Louie Maclan carried on Pivonka's culinary tradition by opening the Bohemian Café. Although he remained its chef until 1959, he sold the restaurant to newly arrived Bohemians, Joseph Libor and his wife, Ann Kapoun Libor, in 1947. Libor, a noted Prague concert pianist, composer and conductor, left his country in advance of the Communist takeover.

In 1959, the Libors moved the café to a new location abutting the Prague Hotel on the south where a Bohemian bank and grocery store once stood. To Omaha's great benefit, generations of Libor and Kapoun progeny continue to charm an admiring public with middle-European food served in a festive Bohemian atmosphere.

Love of their culture still lives in the hearts of these people. All during the 1970s and 1980s, a sign on the door of the restaurant echoed the relentless cry of all Czechs to invaders of their homeland: "Russians, get out of Czechoslovakia!"

In 1989, the Russians finally did.

The vast majority of the Czechs who came to Omaha were from that part of pre-World War II Czechoslovakia that now forms the Czech Republic. This nation, essentially all of what was once Bohemia and Moravia, lies on an elevated tableland, the Bohemian Plateau, which, like Nebraska, has hot summers and cold winters.

Mountains, a place of heavy rainfall, form its northern and eastern border with Poland. On the northwest, as well as the southwest, the Bohemian Forest forms the German border. Austria lies to the south; Slovakia to the east.

Over the centuries, most of these neighbors have taken turns muscling in on this feisty little ethnic area. Most recently it was Russia; before that, Germany. And earlier, for three hundred years, Austria-Hungary, under the Hapsburg Holy Roman Emperors.

The Czechs always have fought hard to shrug off these invaders. A proud, free people, they have kept their culture intact under

Czechs

tremendous pressure. Especially have they struggled to preserve and protect their language. According to the late, former U.S. Senator Roman Hruska, who spoke Czech fluently, it is formal, elegant and gracious. Yet in all matters, cultural and governmental, the Hapsburg monarchy deliberately made the Czech language subservient to the German.

Old grudges die hard. Evidence of Czech resentment of Hapsburg rule can be found in a 1906 **Omaha Bee** article reporting a meeting in Omaha's Bohemian Turners Hall, where Czech-Americans met to celebrate the occasion of the death of Karel Havlicek Borovsky, an anti-Hapsburg journalist and patriot, who had died fifty years earlier at the age of thirty-four.

Despite Hapsburg humiliations, Bohemians and Moravians remain proud. They are happy to have a heritage of King Wenceslaus, a Catholic saint, and Jan Hus, one of Europe's first Protestants. Burned at the stake for his beliefs in 1417, Hus became a martyr nearly a century before Martin Luther.

Czechs, also rightfully, are proud of Prague's Charles University, founded in 1348 and one of Europe's earliest. They boast, too, of many world-renowned artists and composers. Americans, especially, love the music of Antonin Dvorak, who wrote his Ninth Symphony, to a New World, following a long visit to Spillville, Iowa, where the presence of Czechs made him less homesick.

In 1620, when the Hapsburg Holy Roman emperors overcame the Bohemians and Moravians, they squelched a rising Protestantism and killed, or drove into exile, those who refused to embrace Catholicism.

Thus, the majority of the Czechs entering the United States during the nineteenth century, having come from part of the Hapsburg Empire, were identified by American immigration officials as Austrian-Germans and as Catholics. Despite such listing, upon reaching America nearly half of them chose to become Freethinkers or to join run-of-the-mill American Protestant churches of Calvinistic derivation, such as the Presbyterian Church.

American citizenship class at Brown Park School, 1925

This change in church affiliation, essentially anti-Hapsburg, was divisive. It weakened the movement among American Czechs for a postwar Bohemia/Moravia free of Austrian-Hungarian domination since the Catholic immigrants only weakly supported such a move.

Freedom did come, however. The efforts of Tomas Masaryk, strengthened by his friend, President Woodrow Wilson, gave birth to the Republic of Czechoslovakia following the World War I. For a time, no foreign power dominated Bohemia.

From 1870 forward, Czechs have formed a huge part of Omaha's population. This was in large part the result of the efforts of Edward Rosewater, a Bohemian Jew, who came to Omaha in 1871 to publish two newspapers, ***Pokrok Zapadu*** (**Progress of the West**) in the Czech language and ***Beobachter am Missouri*** in German. Widely circulated both in America and Europe, these weeklies helped cause a flood of Czech and German immigration

Czechs

to the United States, especially to Nebraska.

Other Czechs assisted Rosewater, among them U.L.Vondicka, a railroad land agent, and John Rosicky, the editor of the *Pokrok* newspaper. Their efforts helped make Omaha as famous as New York City. Witnessing only a few wooden buildings and a wooden railroad station when his train arrived in Omaha, one newcomer, Simon Rokusek, refused to believe the conductor who shouted out the city's name. This wasn't Omaha. Omaha was a city at least as large as New York! Only after much persuasion by Joe Mik the stationmaster, himself a Czech, did Rokusek get off the train.

The Union Pacific and Burlington Railroads also beat the immigration drum. Interested in attracting immigrants to virgin land bordering their Nebraska rails, they used colorful posters and brochures to entice Czechs and other Europeans to opt for farm life on cheap Nebraska land.

Many Czechs jumped at the opportunity. Up to 1880, three-fourths of all Czech immigrants to the United States came to Nebraska. By 1920, when European emigration markedly dropped, there were more Czech farmers in Nebraska than in any other state—one-fifth of all in the United States.

The experience wasn't easy for these newcomers. Many immigrants had a hard time adjusting to new customs, a new way of life and, especially, a new language. Some, such as the fictional Mr. Shimerda in Willa Cather's **My Antonia**, couldn't make it. After the beauties of Bohemia, life on a cold Nebraska prairie was not worth living. He committed suicide.

Some historians attribute the high suicide rate among such immigrants to Slavic fatalism; others, to a general lack of religion. Whatever the cause, the harsh life of the pioneer on the plains proved unacceptable for some, coupled as it was with a remoteness from customary music, dance and beer.

Nevertheless, the dogged determination of most of these farmers caused them to stick it out. They were helped by occasional visits to Czech neighbors both on the farm and in the growing number of villages nearby, such as Clarkson, Wilber, Schuyler, Verdigre and Crete, where many Czechs were starting to reside. There were few significant social disparities among them, and their sharing of difficulties in making a new home in America enhanced their sense of solidarity.

Czech-Americans in Nebraska organized their social life either around churches or within numerous fraternal benevolent associations. The latter offered death and health insurance with affordable premiums. The best known were the Czech-Slavonic Benevolent Society and its offshoot, the Western Bohemian

Sokol dancers performing at Sokol Hall, circa 1925

Fraternal Association, created in Omaha in 1897. Without them, many Czech immigrants could not have afforded life and health insurance.

Next to benevolent associations, the Czechs formed social interest groups such as reading societies, dramatic clubs, singing circles and gymnastic associations. Most prominent among the latter was *Sokol* (Falcon), a group that still promotes gymnastic and cultural activities. It often participates in annual festivals featuring

Czechs

folk dances performed by the young people of many Omaha ethnic groups.

An anti-Catholic bias in many of these groups encouraged Catholic Czechs to organize themselves into similar, separate groups such as *Katoliky Delnik* (Catholic Workman), usually centered around the local church.

During the final twenty years of the nineteenth century, an increasing number of Bohemians moved into both Omaha and South Omaha. Some came directly from abroad; others, who had failed on the farm or in other out-state enterprises, sought work in smelters and slaughterhouses. While a majority of immigrants to South Omaha found the packinghouse work difficult and not too remunerative, fully three-fourths of them eventually owned homes, and a few rose in business and professional fields.

An example of a Bohemian who remained out-state was Vaclav Tomek, who was only six years old when his family emigrated in 1867. In 1870, following an adventurous trip by boat from Sioux City, Iowa, to Niobrara, Nebraska, his family traveled by ox-drawn wagon over unmarked prairie to break the virgin sod of a one-hundred-and-sixty-acre homestead two-and-one-half miles north of Verdigre.

Despite the rigors of climate and isolation and the hardship of bobcats, coyotes, wolves, grasshoppers and flash floods that sometimes took out their corn and squash, Tomek and his family eked out an existence. With few material goods to show for his trials, he ended his days in Boyd County. Yet one of his grandsons did retire in Omaha, Robert Tomek, as a vice president of Peter Kiewit Sons', Inc.

The 1930 census figures show three thousand, nine hundred and forty-six foreign-born Czechs in Omaha, which by then included South Omaha, and a 1940 population study reveals twenty-three thousand Douglas County residents classed as Czech immigrants or first or second generation descendants of Czech immigrants.

In Omaha, early settlers found homes and places of business in three principal areas. We have seen a portion of Praha, or Prague, also called Bohemia Town or Little Bohemia, which was the largest. It extended roughly from Mason Street on the north to Cedar Street on the south and from the Missouri River to Twentieth Street on the east and west, respectively. Many Bohemians of the Catholic faith settled around St. Adalbert Church at Thirty-first and Arbor streets.

Another heavy Czech area was located north of Riverview Park between Tenth, Thirteenth and Atlas streets. This was called Brno, the name of the capital of Moravia. A third principal Czech colony was in South Omaha, north and west of Brown Park, extending to W Street and from Fifteenth to Twenty-third Street.

Not until after World War I, when a new American immigration law put an end to the flight, did Czech immigration slow to any extent. Yet in the early 1950s, another wave of immigrants arrived, driven from their homeland by the Soviets. In addition to Joseph Libor, there were others.

Jan and Ludmila Matys, for example. With their daughter, Lida, they escaped from Bratislava, Slovakia to Canada in 1951 and finally to Omaha. Bratislava, the largest city in Slovakia, lies on the east side of the Danube River, about forty miles from Vienna, Austria. Regardless of the fact that the Matys' business and home were in Slovakia, they were ethnic Bohemians who also had spent many of their years in Vienna.

The Matys successfully survived the awful fire and storm of Nazi oppression and the bombings of World War II inflicted by Nazis, Russians and Americans alike. Ludmila and Lida successfully avoided being raped and attacked by Russian soldiers entering Czechoslovakia as liberators. Finally, the Matys had to suffer the takeover of their country by the communists in 1948 and the subsequent confiscation of their business, home and personal possessions.

During a period of incredible hardship, involving icy river crossings, sprained ankles, false identification cards and close calls

171

with border inspectors, they finally escaped from Bratislava to the protection of American forces in Salzburg, Austria and to the sponsorship of a Canadian. They ended up in Toronto.

The death of a fellow immigrant, whose chocolate candy factory also had been confiscated by the communists, brought them in contact with the deceased's brother, Charles Koukol, minister of the Bohemian and Moravian Brethren Presbyterian Church of South Omaha. He and his son Dan, a member of the Omaha Bar, had come to Toronto for the funeral where Dan met and married Lida Matys. The couple moved to Omaha where the senior Matys later joined them.

The Bohemian-American most familiar to most Omahans is Roman Hruska. His illustrious career in the United States government, both in the House and the Senate, amply supports the honor of having a new Omaha federal office building bear his name. Born in 1904, the fifth of eleven children of Bohemian-American parents, Roman spent his first thirteen years in David City and other Butler County, Nebraska towns where for twenty years Joseph, his father, was a public school teacher for children mainly of Bohemian heritage. Joseph often taught them lessons in Bohemian, as well as in English. When not teaching, he served as County Superintendent of Butler County Schools.

Joseph was only six months old when his own parents brought him to America from Tabor, Bohemia, an anti-Hapsburg headquarters city sixty miles south of Prague. They came to Spillville, Iowa, then almost entirely populated by Bohemians. Although he had left the Catholic Church, his father helped to build the Spillville Catholic sanctuary that became renowned for Antonin Dvorak having once practiced on its pipe organ. On a summer day, while standing outside the church, Joseph's father loved to listen to the great composer play during the period of his nostalgic escape from New York City.

Roman's mother, Caroline, herself a Dvorak although not related to the composer, was a Spillville girl whose Bohemian family arrived there in 1850 in time to participate in the Civil War. It was natural that the Czech language would be a central part of their marriage. It also was natural that Roman, raised to read, write and speak it, would be at ease with it all his life. It remained a joy to him and a definite asset to his Nebraska political career.

Senator Roman Hruska

When in 1917 the Hruskas moved to Omaha from David City, Roman finished primary schooling in Farnam School (now gone) at Park Avenue and Farnam Street and thereafter attended Commerce High School (the predecessor of Technical High School), located in vacant store buildings near Seventeenth and Leavenworth streets.

Fellow classmates and lifelong friends were Richard Robinson, later a U.S. District Court judge, and Jerome Kutak, later the father of Robert Kutak, the head of one of Omaha's largest law firms. The Commerce High Debate Team, the high school's first, consisted of Hruska, Robinson and Kutak. It won many debates.

All three graduated in 1920; all three chose to attend college. Even though Roman had worked odd jobs all of his high school days, carrying papers and doing other tasks, he now needed to earn his college tuition. Two years in the bookkeeping department of Fairmont Creamery Company provided the seventy-five dollars necessary to enroll at the University of Omaha, then situated at Twenty-fourth and Pratt streets.

Two years of undergraduate study allowed him to attend Creighton Law College. After his first year with Creighton, he took

173

his second year at the University of Chicago (where he worked nights in a hospital) and his third year back at Creighton, thus qualifying for admission to the bar without an examination. To pay for his education, he also worked as a truck driver and as a bookkeeper for the Sokol Auditorium.

In 1930, right out of law school, Roman married a girl of Bohemian descent, Victoria Kuncl. In time, Victoria would deliver their three children: Roman Jr., Quentin and Jana Lynn and remain his faithful wife for more than sixty years.

Since the debates of high school days, Roman knew where his career was headed. He was born to be a lawyer; his personality fitted the role. The subtle use of logic and common sense to analyze a client's recital of facts and then the search for and consideration of the law governing them—this excited him. He loved the law all the way from the United States Constitution to the most recent city ordinance. He was destined to be a United States senator, and a most effective one.

But first, he would have to play a humbler role. Once out of law school, he entered the private practice of law. On an independent basis he associated with the firm of his old friend, Dick Robinson, and did all the things a young lawyer does: draft wills and contracts, read abstracts of titles and bloody himself in court fights. It prepared him for congressional arguments ahead.

Every American lawyer engages in some political activity; Roman was no exception. He joined the Republican Party, attended sessions of the Douglas County Republican convention and made speeches to any group that would listen. In 1944 came his first political break. He accepted a post on the Douglas County Board of Commissioners vacated by an incumbent called to military service. Over the next few years, he worked into the acknowledged leadership of the board, was elevated to its chairmanship and reelected twice.

Most importantly from a political standpoint, when it came time for him to run for the Senate, it did him no harm that he had become secretary and, later, president of the Nebraska County Officials Association and friend of many county commissioners in the state by traveling to their respective county seats. Furthermore, he was serving as first vice president of the National Association of County Officials Association at the time of his election to Congress.

All this time he continued to be active in Czech fraternal work and in his church. He served as president of the Iowa-Nebraska Unitarian Conference and for three years on the board of the American Unitarian Association. Named a regent of the University of Omaha in 1950, he held the post for many years. One wonders when he found time to practice law.

Then came national office. Successfully defeating a Democratic challenger, Roman was elected in 1952 to the House of Representatives. An appointment to the Appropriations Committee helped satisfy his lifelong yearning to put a dent in fiscal appropriations. He was overjoyed to be called a fiscal conservative.

Following one short term in the House, a successful campaign led to a short, four-year term in the Senate, the forerunner of three more terms. By the time he reached the end of his career, he had achieved national recognition, barely failing to become the Senate's Republican leader. He was long the protégé and close friend of the minority leader, Everett Dirksen, who once uttered the memorable words: "A billion here and a billion there, and pretty soon it adds up to real money."

In his retirement, Roman was most proud of the efforts he took to help revise the federal appellate court system and to help write the Criminal Justice Act of 1964. The appellate court revision was vital in relieving the Supreme Court of the time-consuming final disposition of patent cases. The Criminal Justice Act allowed federal judges to appoint adequately compensated defense counsel for indigent defendants in federal courts.

In all his doings, Roman never forgot his Czech heritage. In his distinctive Bohemian accent he willingly made speeches to whatever towns people summoned him, addressing all matters Bohemian or

Czechs

American. Like all his Czech neighbors, he reveled in his heritage.

Omahans, Nebraskans and citizens everywhere owe him a great debt. By reflecting the Bohemian spirit of freedom in his public service to the state and the nation, he has made us increasingly grateful for the liberties we enjoy and ever more fervent in our love of America.

Americans of Czech descent still form a large part of the city's population; Hruska can be said to have represented them all. Whether they came to Omaha early or late, whether they became famous or, like most, remained obscure, these descendants of immigrants from Bohemia have made a profound imprint on their adopted city.

REFERENCES

BOOKS

The Czech-American Experience. **Nebraska History**. Vol. 74, No. 3 & 4, Fall/Winter, 1993.

Larsen, James H. and Barbara J. Cottrell. **The Gate City: A History of Omaha**. Boulder, CO: Pruett Publishing, 1982.

Rosicky, Rose, compiler. **History of Czechs (Bohemians) in Nebraska**. 1929. Reprint. Evansville, IN: Unigraphic Inc., 1977.

INTERVIEWS

Hruska, Roman. Taped interview by Donald H. Erickson and Harry B. Otis. January 8, 1998.

Matys, Ludmila. Taped interview by Harry B. Otis. January 22, 1997.

MISCELLANEOUS

Duda, Walter J. Letter relating facts concerning Duda family. February 3, 1998.

Tomek, Vaclav Wenceslaus Bolaslav. Monograph containing memories, submitted by his grandson, Robert Tomek.

Matys, Ludmila. Monograph containing memories of World War II experiences and escape from Europe. January 22, 1997.

NEWSPAPERS

Landale, Ted. *The Meteoric Roman*. **The Omaha World-Herald**. October 25, 1953.

McMorris, Robert. *Czechs Corralled by Editor Rosewater's Pen*. **The Omaha World-Herald**. October 20, 1961.

Rosewater, Edward. *A Recent Visit to Bohemia*. **Omaha Bee**. July 27, 1906.

Rosicky, Rose. *Foreign Settlers in Nebraska*. **The Omaha World-Herald**. October 27, 1929.

Ter Horst, J. F. *Hruska Groomed for Leader Job*. **The Omaha World-Herald**. May 20, 1965.

THE BRITISH

A typical Scottish bagpiper

The British inhabit the United Kingdom, i.e., the islands comprising England, Scotland, Wales and, at least to the present day, Northern Ireland. From Omaha's very beginning, immigrants from such lands have come to it, not in great numbers, but steadily. Unlike those from Middle European countries, they didn't choose to reside in clusters around a church but scattered apart to live near English-speaking people from eastern states. After all, that English was their mother tongue, was to their great advantage.

Descendants of pre-Revolutionary immigrants from Northern Ireland helped to found Omaha; later on, few Ulsterites chose to live here. Those from Britain who did were principally of Scottish descent and most of them Presbyterians, the American name for members of the Church of Scotland.

Some Welsh immigrated to Nebraska, as witnessed by the existence of the St. David's Society in Lincoln. Relatively few came to Omaha, but the descendants of those that did still reside here.

Scotland, on the other hand, has been well represented. In addition to the many Scots of colonial descent who formed Omaha in its early years, at the turn of the century many came directly from the country itself. The First Presbyterian Church at Thirty-fourth and Farnam streets was the spiritual home for a number of them. During the 1930s and 1940s, the church even boasted a minister who preached his sermons with a Scottish burr, the

British

Reverend Dr. Thomas Niven.

Many of Scottish descent built the Dundee Presbyterian Church, first at Fiftieth and Underwood Avenue and later at Underwood Avenue and Happy Hollow Boulevard. Oddly enough, the name "Dundee," although Scottish, was not given to the church by these Presbyterian Scots, but by land developers from Kansas City who founded the village in which it was located and later annexed by Omaha.

Some examples of immigrants from Scotland are John Malcolm Dow, who came at the turn of the century, and Alexander James Young, who, sponsored by Dow, arrived a few years later in 1912. Both hailed from Edinburgh. Dow became the first mayor of the village of Dundee. Young, after graduating from the College of Medicine of the University of Nebraska in 1916, became a medical doctor.

Post-World War II residents were David Wallace and his wife, Janet, who arrived from Paisley, a few miles west of Glasgow. Alexander Murray and his wife, Joanna, sponsored by Omahan Dr. Allister Findlayson of Scottish descent, immigrated in 1955. Both Alex and Joanna were born in Glasgow. Joanna's father was of the clan MacLeod, based in the Isle of Skye in the Highlands. In 1973, Alex made the acquaintance of Edwin Range, whose father, a Canadian, loved all things Scottish—bagpipes especially. These two joined others of a common Scottish heritage to form the Scottish Society of Nebraska. Over the years its ranks have swelled.

Early on, the society members met monthly, in later years not so frequently. However, the group has always managed to meet at least twice a year, once to celebrate the November 30 Feast of St. Andrew with a banquet at some Omaha private club and once to observe the January 25 birthday of Robert Burns. A typical banquet menu offers Dornoch crab, Aberdeen Angus beef with meat sauce, oven-browned Ayrshire tatties, broccoli in *crowdie bree* (cream sauce), *baps* and *butteery rowies* (butter rolls) and claret.

At the Burns gathering a traditional Scottish dish of *haggis* is ceremoniously piped in from the kitchen by kilted pipers and set before the chief, who in the early days, more often than not, was Alexander Murray. The *haggis* in place, the chief solemnly recites to the assembled diners Burns's poem, *Address to the Haggis*. Customarily in attendance are eighty to a hundred Scots and descendants of Scots eager to give homage to their national bard.

The present chief of the Scottish Society of Nebraska is Dennis Neff. In addition to banquets, his society is affiliated with a bagpipe band, the Pipes of Bannockburn and dancing groups, Highland Dancers and Country Dancers. Independent of the Scottish Society of Nebraska is an even larger marching band, Omaha Pipes and Drums. All of these groups gather annually to participate in a Celtic festival.

Those of English descent also have gathered fraternally in the past. One such organization was the British Commonwealth Society, which was active in the postwar era of the Strategic Air Command (SAC) when many Royal Air Force personnel, both officers and enlisted men, resided in the Omaha community. The society had its own banquets and other activities for the benefit of all British persons in the community. However, with the demise of SAC and the return of British military personnel to duties elsewhere, it has faded away.

One Englishman, who shortly after the turn of the century made Omaha his home and who did not fade away, was Edward Lewis Holland. After a few years his mother and sister also arrived to spend the rest of their lives here.

The Oxford English Dictionary defines a cockney as an Englishman born within the sound of the church bells of London's St. Mary-le-Bow. His speech is characterized by an extreme gliding mixture of original vowels, the loss of an initial *H* and the use of an intrusive *R*. Holland fitted the definition; he was something of a cockney.

Born in 1886 a few blocks from the Tate Gallery in London's East End, he was as true to the tradition as *My Fair Lady*'s dustman, Doolittle. Years in Omaha softened its edge, and his accent became a bit more Oxfordian in time, yet his colloquialisms endured. To the delight of his family and friends, he would ask a restauranteur for "two cuts of kike" and would direct attention to his mother with: "Ark ye to marm barterin' with the tradesman."

Edward Lewis Holland (E.L., as his son Dick would later call him) was born to Benjamin, a musician of limited means, and Ada, whose dressmaking and millinery skills would keep the family together upon his father's death. Pursuing a career as soloist in one of London's largest churches, St. George of Hanover Square, Benjamin developed into a fine singer, only to face an early demise from tuberculosis and alcoholism. He left a wife and two very young children.

Late nineteenth century London was a city of constant smog created by thousands of separate coal-burning hearths. This smoke soiled not only its buildings and streets but also the lungs of its people, leaving many to die from complications of the disease that took Benjamin.

The Sherlock-Holmesian era of horse-drawn hacks moving through fog-filled cobblestone streets may seem romantic to us today, but the era had its obvious drawbacks. E.L. and his younger sister Dora grew up with few physical comforts in a society that supported a rigid caste system that labeled them lower middle class. Very few broke out of the strata into which they had been born. Although Dora, helped by more affluent relatives, did attend a private school in Sherwood Forest.

Circumstances allowed E.L. to attend London Technical Institute, a trade school, where he received the equivalent of an American high school education, yet the rigorous social system effectively blocked him from a career other than that of artisan. Not that he scorned such a career, he merely wanted something more. Nevertheless, his class prevented competition with those young men whose families could send them to private and elite schools like Eton and Harrow and, later, Oxford and Cambridge, virtually permitting them alone to attain positions in government or the professions. E.L. had the drive of a Winston Churchill, but not the prerogatives.

Frustrations aside, he developed into an excellent artist, artisan and writer. His training at the Institute and his extracurricular studies of art at the Tate Gallery honed his natural talents, so that by the time he came of age he could paint a picture as readily as make a fine piece of furniture. Most important, he worked very hard at what he did, later passing this virtue on to his children.

All his life he was a phenomenal reader, a book a week or even more. He was a person who in later life loved to talk about literature and the world of ideas. If he got onto the subject of Charles Dickens's books, he would tell you about whole novels—"Hold you with his glittering eye, so to speak," says his son. He was to continue his education through the years, even taking Hamilton Institute business courses.

E.L. Holland

Many of his talents he must have inherited from his mother. As a widow, her own abilities as a seamstress and maker of hats permitted her to provide a respectable living for her family. Elaborate women's hats were very much the thing at the end of the nineteenth century, and Ada made the most of it. Catering to the carriage trade, she even made a hat or two for Queen Alexandra, the consort of King Edward VII.

Hardworking and determined, Ada's sharp tongue often got her what she wanted. Once, in later years in Omaha, her grandson bought a hat from the Nebraska Clothing Company that in no way pleased her. Marching Bill to the store by the ear, she told the clerk that she

British

Ada Holland

was returning the item. "But Madam, he has worn the hat," said the clerk. "I'll sit right here until you take it back," she replied. The hat went back. E.L.'s response: "I guess they didn't want Marm for a permanent fixture."

In 1910, when twenty-four years of age, E.L. stood about five feet, eight and one-third inches tall and weighed about one hundred and fifty pounds, or about eleven stone, as the English would say. A thick head of hair covered a large forehead; his build was stocky and athletic. People considered him handsome.

He much engaged in sports of the time, soccer and cricket in England, tennis and golf in America. Later, vacations, often to Colorado, allowed him to ride horseback, a sport he loved.

In his early twenties, finding no real economic future for himself in England, E.L. decided to emigrate. His choice was Canada since it was a part of the British Empire and easy to enter. With little in his pocket and no job prospects, he sailed for Halifax, Nova Scotia.

Arriving in Canada, he found a call from far away Saskatchewan where workers were needed for the wheat fields. A promise of certain wages and working conditions prompted a trip to the Western Canadian province where he learned only too soon that he had been hoodwinked. A miserly farmer-employer, failing to fulfill his bargain, cheated the young immigrant out of promised wages.

Under such circumstances, one season of farm work was enough.

A letter from an uncle, his mother's brother whom he had never met but who had emigrated to Omaha in 1870, assured him of a better life there and promised him sponsorship until work might be found. Thus, early in 1911 he arrived in his uncle's adopted town with high hopes and few funds. In fact, he was practically penniless. Though his uncle sponsored him, he gave him little financial help. E.L. was on his own in a strange city.

He quickly found work in the Union Pacific shops, the mecca of so many immigrants. He was hired to break up obsolete passenger and freight cars, hard, exhausting, dirty work that paid but little. He often wondered whether his decision to come to the New World had been a wise one. Yet during the ensuing months, cheap lodging in a boardinghouse with other workers let him save most of his money for a better life and a better job that soon were to come.

Omaha had very few immigrants from England at the time, and those who had come were scattered; they declined to live as a distinct group and almost at once assimilated with the native-born Americans. They were specially privileged, for none had to suffer the ill will that some of the natives exhibited toward non-English-speaking newcomers.

Early arrivals were the Reverend Joseph Barker and his wife and children, a family who came by way of Salem, Ohio in 1856. Barker was a Methodist minister in England who had three years earlier emigrated to America. An outspoken enemy of both slavery, as practiced in the Southern American states, and landowner greed, as practiced in England where he was once jailed for excessive zeal, he and his family were to invest well in Omaha real estate. Many of his descendants remain residents of Omaha. One, J. Scott Barker, is an Episcopal priest.

There is no record that E.L. formed any close friendships with Omahans of English descent. He was often homesick. One day, however, he found great comfort in the voice of a fellow U.P. worker who, pulling out a Victoria Cross, Britain's highest medal for valour, said to him in pure cockney: "Gov'nor, 'ave ye ever seen one of these? I got it in the Boer War."

With his engaging accent and personality, Holland was a man people enjoyed. Late in 1912, a job with a dry goods company allowed him to leave the U.P. yards. Benson and Thorne found use for his artistic talents, asking him to trim their store windows and assemble their stock in trade, the better to attract customers. This he did so successfully that he soon was handling their advertising. He became a jack-of-all-trades for the store, and his income rose with his responsibilities.

Soon he accepted an even better job with the Eldridge Gift Shop, a fine old company carrying a high quality line of china, silver, bric-a-brac and some oil paintings. His talents blossomed as he began to charm the store's customers, the more affluent of Omaha. Eldridge promised him a role as a future partner. On the strength of this, E.L. decided to marry.

Alas, a business recession intervened. The gift shop went broke, and E.L. went to Orchard and Wilhelm. He had to take some merchandise as his final pay from Eldridge, a part of which included belated wedding gifts for Ellen, his wife.

Like his sister Dora, E.L. had been reared in the Church of England, the mother church for the Episcopal church of the United States. Somehow or other in Omaha he was lured away from this brand of Christianity. During his early weeks, one of his friends invited him to attend services at the Unitarian Church, located then, as now, at Turner Boulevard and Harney. Even though the Unitarian form of service differed dramatically from the church he had known, he felt comfort in it. It better identified with his humanistic view of the world.

About the same time, his future wife Ellen Walsh Dean, born and raised a Roman Catholic by her mother, found her own way to the same church. The Unitarian Church was more in tune with the philosophy of her father, a "free thinker" in the parlance of the day. Here Ellen met E.L. Here the two were married and remained members all their lives.

One of their new acquaintances in the church was Dr. Harold Gifford, Omaha's leading opthamologist. It may have been he who encouraged them to stay with the Unitarians. At least for E.L., a new country and a new American friend may have led to a new outlet for his social thought.

E.L. hated Hitler and all he stood for. He was almost violent in his rejection of anti-Semitic remarks or behavior, and he reacted the same way to any racial slur. His whole background led him to believe in fair play for the little guy and for those who were poor.

He was extraordinarily polite to people. He always bowed upon being introduced and addressed the new acquaintance with quite Old World, formal words. Circumspect in his speech, he rarely, if ever, swore or used gutter language. The closest he came to the latter was when he one time told a man: "You are the first person I've met who reminds me of the south end of a horse heading north."

Yet he lacked any pretension, liking jokes, particularly of the kind where words played a part. He was a lover of puns and composed many; e.g., "It's not the heat, it's the humility." His wonderful demeanor and accent let him get away with these.

What drew Gifford and Holland together was the doctrine of socialism. They both called themselves socialists. Radical as the Socialist party may have seemed to turn-of-the-century citizens in both England and America, it attracted many people. In England, Sydney and Beatrice Webb led a cult called the Fabians that preached a gradual, non-confrontational achievement of socialism and counted as members many prominent Londoners, among them George Bernard Shaw. The Fabian Society eventually became the British Labor party.

The dictionary defines socialism as a social system in which the producers possess both political power and the means of producing and distributing goods. It defines a socialist party as one advocating socialism to be achieved by democratic means.

As an idealistic teenager in England, E.L. was thrilled to attend lectures on the subject delivered by both Shaw and the Webbs. He

British

may have found in this political doctrine a partial answer to his resentment of the rigid English class structure. He and Gifford noted that the Socialist party slowly was gaining strength both in the United States and England.

Nevertheless, socialism was then, and remains today, anathema to a majority of Americans. Most of today's citizens find, in the tyrannical and unsuccessful handling of production and distribution of goods by the authoritarian Soviet Union, enough to make them leery both of the word itself and of government control of economic enterprise, in particular. Curiously, for many years all electric power in Nebraska and much of its water and gas have been produced and distributed by legislatively-created, publicly-owned and controlled districts.

In many ways E.L. remained an Englishman. He was a man of integrity. Thus it was that when he applied for United States citizenship in 1918 and his papers asked for his politics, he truthfully responded "Fabian Socialist." Not a little upset by this response, which in later years had a ring similar to the word "communist," the federal judge conferring citizenship asked E.L. whether anyone would vouch for him.

"No problem, your honor," replied Holland. No less than the town's leading eye specialist came down to the court and testified that E.L. was a good person and one deserving of naturalization. After all, despite being socialists, both E.L. and Gifford were Unitarians in good standing. The judge made the Englishman an American.

Before he was naturalized, as one ready to enlist in England's army when war was declared against Germany in 1914, E.L. registered with the British consulate but was never called. Following the war, he headed the Omaha branch of Near East Relief aimed at helping the Armenians who were undergoing genocide at the hand of the Turks.

Despite being an announced socialist, E.L. found himself so greatly attracted to Herbert Hoover, who had headed America's postwar relief efforts in Europe, that, despite his wife's objections, he voted for him in 1928. With the Depression, however, he became an avid follower of Franklin Roosevelt and after the war, Harry Truman. He greatly admired both men.

E.L. so loved Omaha that soon after his arrival he wrote to his mother and sister inviting them to come and live with him. Early in 1912 Ada and Dora agreed. They would come, if only on a "trial basis." Scheduled to sail on the doomed *Titanic*, lucky circumstances caused them to miss its horrible fate. They sailed a month later on *The Empress of Scotland* and arrived safely in Omaha in July. E.L. found them lodging near his own apartment at Twenty-fourth and Lothrop streets.

*Dora Holland,
sister of E.L. Holland*

His sister Dora, two years his junior, in no way resembled him. Short in stature and attractive, she was blessed with blue eyes and the coveted fair skin of an English female. She also was very bright. She took little time finding a business college there to learn enough of how American business is conducted to launch a career of her own.

Having anticipated Ada and Dora's arrival, their son and brother respectively, this person of enormous energy and drive, in his off-hours, and with his own hands, commenced to build two adjoining houses in the vicinity of Thirty-fifth and Decatur streets. For these he used much of the material purchased from the remains of homes wrecked by the tornado of Easter Sunday, April 1913. For the first of these houses he laid a fortress-like foundation and in both he installed beautiful stained glass windows salvaged from someone's old mansion. His London school training paid off.

British

Not long after their arrival, Ada and Dora moved into the house first completed. E.L. was just finishing up the second one the day he and Ellen were married. In later years his bride confided that having worked like a horse all day long, he came home, took a bath, put on his clothes, and traveled to the Unitarian church for their wedding. There would be no loitering around for him while waiting for the ceremony.

Ellen Holland must have inherited her fair features from her Irish ancestors. And perhaps she inherited her high intelligence from a distinguished line of American forebears descending from Silas Dean, an early American patriot. Whatever the fact, she proved to be an enduring mate for E.L. and an enormous source of strength for him and their children as the years went on.

Following the wedding, the young couple moved into the house just completed and stayed there until 1917. Commencing that year, they made a series of household moves: first to a home in Bemis Park, then to one in the Field Club district, and in 1921 to one near Windsor School, each house bigger and better than the previous.

Schools became necessary. In 1916 Ellen had borne a son, Bill; in 1919 another, Jack, and in 1921, still another, Dick. It was not until 1923 that Ellen delivered a daughter, Jean. Now the family had to make yet another household move, a final one, to an acreage at 5851 Pine Street in then far West Omaha. Sixtieth Street marked the city limits.

After the couple moved out of their honeymoon house, it provided a home for Ellen's father and mother. The second house was sold when Ada and Dora moved to an apartment. Both of the houses were razed after World War II to provide more land for Franklin School.

From the base of her home, Ada was able to help support her daughter and herself by reentering the seamstress and millinery business. Her hats were much in demand. How proud E.L. was of his mother, who, having once made chapeaux for the Queen of England, now applied her talent for the good ladies of Omaha.

190

London's loss was Omaha's gain.

Sometime in 1917, with the failure of the Eldridge firm, E.L. happily accepted a job with Omaha's leading furniture store located on the northwest corner of Sixteenth and Howard streets, Orchard and Wilhelm. It hired him to handle all its advertising. Recognizing this as real opportunity for an immigrant who had appeared penniless at the city's gates only a few years earlier, he resolved to make the most of it.

In a period when almost every man worked six days a week, E.L. sometimes worked seven. Orchard and Wilhelm's business was both wholesale and retail, covering six Midwestern and Rocky Mountain states. Customers located throughout this region made an annual catalog a necessity. In addition to all his other advertising duties, he faithfully bore the burden of the catalog's huge annual publication and revision. It was up to him to get the thing out on time, a matter of constant deadlines, even if it meant taking the streetcar downtown early in the morning and returning home late in the evening. It paid off. Until the Depression of the early 1930s, as the store prospered, so did Holland.

Even in his few spare hours, E.L.'s nature forced him to keep busy. His hobbies were making furniture and painting pictures. He also pursued many interests connected with his business, such as the Omaha Retailers Association where he was president for two terms and the Ad-Sell League, which he helped found. Somehow, he even found time to be active in the YMCA Chess Club, where he once became Omaha's champion.

In 1927, the circumstance of the extension of a streetcar line south on Sixtieth Street to the east entrance of Ak-Sar-Ben made it possible for him to move his now large family to the edge of the city. He bought the north side of the whole block on the south side of Pine Street between Fifty-eighth and Sixtieth and positioned his new house close to the center. The acreage permitted all sorts of activities for the Holland children: a football field, a miniature golf course, a baseball diamond and, best of all, a fruit orchard with all kinds of fruit: cherries, pears, damson plums, apricots and apples.

In this happy environment of Coolidge and early Hoover prosperity, things went well for E.L. and his family. Clad in a white shirt, tie and very nicely pressed suit, he would ride the streetcar each morning to Sixteenth and Howard. (He hated automobiles and when later forced to buy one became, despite his other motor skills, a terribly jerky driver.) E.L. was always nattily dressed. Even later, during the Depression years, he would sponge his suit daily and press it himself to save dry cleaning bills.

Once at the store, he would work the long hours necessary to help Orchard and Wilhelm prosper. C.M. Wilhelm and Ephraim Dixon recognized his talents. They touted E.L. as their heir apparent, the firm's future chief operating officer.

It was not to be. The Depression came. Retail trade collapsed. E.L.'s salary was cut in half. With a growing family and bills to pay, life became hard. Yet the whole country had it tough; sometimes the Hollands found their neighbors without food. Even though in time Orchard's business grew better, it was Mr. Wilhelm's son-in-law who became CEO of the company.

In 1944 Holland decided, with Orchard's blessing, to start his own advertising company. Happily, the furniture company insisted that he maintain his new office on the premises and that the store be his primary client. More importantly, it granted him a retainer for his services greater than the amount of his previous salary. Gradually his new firm took off.

Following the war, his son Dick joined him. Deciding to expand, while retaining his office in the store, he found larger quarters in the Aquila Court Building directly across the street. It was there he worked until his death in 1954. Dick carried on and enhanced the business, acquiring in time many prominent business clients.

E.L.'s sister, Dora Holland, had her own career. Very shortly after coming to Omaha, she met Dr. and Mrs. C.C. Criss, the founders of two preeminent American insurance companies, Mutual of Omaha and United Benefit. Dora and Mrs. Criss became fast friends. Dora was hired to administer the company's ever-growing stenographic services, a job she held for over forty years, authoring books on letter writing for hundreds of secretaries and company executives. In 1963, the company finally convinced her to retire. Beloved by both the Mutual family and her own kin, she died in 1981.

Each graduating from Central High School and the University of Omaha, the Holland children pursued illustrious careers: Bill as a chemical engineer, leading to CEO of a large chemical manufacturing corporation; Dick in advertising; Jack in research psychology; and Jean in pathology with emphasis on genetics. Jack became world-renowned in his field of career testing and counseling.

Even in the year of his death, E.L.'s Old World courtliness survived. His daughter-in-law, Mary, cites an example. Although heart problems had brought him to the Medical Arts Building where he was waiting to be picked up after seeing the doctor, he acted as the doorman. She found him patiently standing outside on a cold January day opening the door for people entering the building.

It would be hard to deny that the cockney Englishman from the East Side of London and his little sister, no less than those who came from other countries, more than repaid to their adopted land, and especially to their adopted city, any debt they may have felt was owed. Omaha freed them from the bonds of England's class structure. Their response was a love for Omaha that shone through their industry and good citizenship. Everybody benefitted.

British

REFERENCES

BOOKS

Larsen, James H. and Barbara J. Cottrell. **The Gate City: A History of Omaha**. Boulder, CO: Pruett Publishing Company, 1982.

INTERVIEWS

Holland, Richard D. Interview by Harry B. Otis. September 8, 1995.

Murray, Alexander and Joanna Murray. Interview by Harry B. Otis. April 25, 1999.

MISCELLANEOUS

Holland, Jean Dean. Letter suggesting draft revisions. October 12, 1995.

NEWSPAPERS

Taylor, John. *Ordination Returns Omahan to Family Roots*. **The Omaha World-Herald.** January 3, 1993.

Zelenka, Julie. *History Lives in Letters*. **The Omaha World-Herald**. September 14, 1986.

THE ITALIANS

Warm and sleepy, Salvatore Seminara dozes off in his church pew. Sam (as everyone calls him) is eighty-three. It is January 23, 1972, and the very important occasion of his great granddaughter's baptism at St. Robert Bellarmine Catholic Church. Rose, Sam's loving wife for fifty-six years, sits beside him. Godparents reverently stand near the priest. Family and friends witness the ceremony.

Four generations of Seminaras have gathered. The baby belongs to Sam's grandson, John, and the baby's proud mother, Theresa. A dentist, John is the younger son of Louis Seminara, Sam's eldest. Louis and his wife Camilla sit quietly next to Rose, all smiles. The baby's aunt and uncle are there, too: Cathy Seminara and her brother, Ron, a Jesuit priest in training.

St. Philomena, now St. Frances Cabrini Church in Little Italy

The baby doesn't make a sound when the parish priest washes her head with the holy water and, with his thumb, rubs her forehead in the sign of the cross. Except for the intonation of the baptismal service, the church is silent.

No doubt about it, Sam muses, Bellarmine is a beautiful church. It should be, situated as it is in a wealthy West Omaha suburb. But, it isn't as solemn and grand as his own parish church, Sacred Heart, down in a humbler part of Omaha, or as warm and comfortable as St. Philomena (now St. Frances Cabrini) in Little Italy, where Rose and he

195

Italians

were married. And he wishes it were more like his centuries-old Sicilian church in Calascibetta, where he worshiped as a boy. New churches these days are too slick and clean, too modern. He misses the mustiness; the smell of the residue of years of burnt candles; the sound of the Mass said in Latin.

Calascibetta, what memories he has of it.

Some ancient Greeks had perched the town on a high hill smack dab in the middle of Sicily. Over the centuries, its size increased some, but even when Sam was young it housed scarcely two thousand people. Its reddish brown stone buildings, piled on top of one another, clung to the side of the hill in tiers, like honeybees on a hive.

On a similar hill to the southwest stood the much larger city of Enna. Separating the two, eight hundred feet below rambled a dusty road (now a paved *autostrada*) connecting Catania on the East Coast of Sicily to Palermo on the northwest. Some said that from their positions on the separate hills, Enna the husband kept watch on Calascibetta the wife, and she on him.

Although Sam had never seen it, there was a large black lake, Pergusa, lying close to Enna. When he was a small boy, his mother had told him the story of the rape of Persephone by the Greek god, Pluto. After abducting Persephone, the daughter of Demeter, the goddess of the harvest, he had dragged her down through this lake to the underworld. Yet each spring she had come back to earth to scatter flower and fruit for man, to return to Pluto only when winter came. Of course the Seminaras were solid Christians and didn't believe such outlandish tales; yet the fable, together with the ruins of the Greek temples near his home, lay deep in his memory and were a part of him.

After a paltry eighteen months of schooling, Sam had worked for several years in his father's orange grove on the town's outskirts. He still could smell the orange blossoms and the fragrant odor of the maturing fruit. During this time his father had suffered from exposure to the chemicals of a nearby sulphur mine where he had worked as a young man. Having ruined his lungs breathing the mine's noxious fumes, he had been forced to sell his grove to fund efforts to find a cure, exhausting his meager estate in the process. After his father sold the orange grove, Sam found the only work then available to a thirteen year old in the same detestable mine. He worked as water boy. It was a nasty place. He remembered how the fumes would make him cough and cause his head to ache.

After a few years, his father insisted that he quit such labor and leave Calascibetta for good. He and his brother Tom should go to America where they could find good healthy jobs. Sicily offered no future. He would finance their trips from the small amount left in the paternal purse.

In 1906, with little money in his pocket and a few clothes in his satchel, Sam left his beautiful Sicily—his fatherland of flowers, grape vines, olive groves and citrus orchards—to travel in steerage from Palermo to New York. The trip was a three-week nightmare of crowded humans in a fetid atmosphere. Food and drinking water were at best inadequate.

At length Sam and his fellow passengers were allowed on deck to view the famous Statue of Liberty and Ellis Island where the ship docked and where earlier Italian immigrants welcomed them. One of these people provided Sam with temporary board and lodging.

However, there was no work in New York City for a common Italian laborer. How crestfallen he had been. What work there was the Irish kept for their own kind, treating the newer immigrants as they themselves had been dealt with in earlier years by settlers of English descent. Instead of "No Irish need apply," it was now "No Italians need apply."

Yet fortune favored Sam. His friendly benefactor steered him to a one dollar and twenty-five cents a day job completing a new football stadium at the West Point Military Academy. Eager for cheap labor, the contractor had even agreed to house and feed the workers. Since Sam and most of the others spoke no English, their

Italians

Italian straw boss translated for them the orders issued in English by the main boss, a circular yet successful operation.

One of Sam's fondest memories was being allowed with his coworkers to witness the first football game played in the completed stadium, but only if they would don their best bib and tucker for the event. In Sam's case this was a worn jacket and frayed tie.

While Sam was so engaged, his older brother also had immigrated to America, all the way to Omaha where he had found a job with the Burlington Railroad. Tom sent word to him that there was plenty of railroad work in that city and that Sam should come at once. With no second thoughts and enough savings from his West Point job, Sam bought a rail ticket to a strange new city on the Missouri River.

Those of us who have never left the land of our birth for good can ever fully put ourselves in Sam's shoes. Nineteen years old, an Italian immigrant without friends, unfamiliar with the customs of a strange country, unable to speak, read or write a totally different language, or even to read or write his own, and with little money in his pocket and few possessions, he had traveled across the Atlantic Ocean, thence west more than a thousand miles to a city with a strange Indian name. And he had come with only a hope of finding work on a railroad.

Comfortable now in his St. Robert Bellarmine pew, he remembers how frightened he had been.

God had taken care of him. Everything his son, Louis, had said to him that morning was true.

> *Dad,* he had said, *when you came to America you couldn't speak English, let alone read it or write it, and you couldn't even read and write Italian. And you still can't. But I want to tell you something. You reared a son who is a successful lawyer, you have a grandson who is a specialist in dentistry, and another grandson, soon to be a priest, who teaches English*

Sam and Rose Seminara, married in 1916

in one of the finest universities in the United States. What do you think of that?

It hadn't been easy, but what truly had saved Sam and hordes of other Italian immigrants was the host of earlier Italians ready and able and, more importantly, willing to help him adjust to his new home. In 1908, Omaha boasted an Italian population of no fewer than two thousand persons, most of whom had come recently either from Sicily or from the toe of the Italian boot, Calabria. Those from Sicily were overwhelmingly from Carlentini, which lies in

Italians

the hills some twenty miles south of Catania, about eight hundred feet above the larger town of Lentini.

Carlentini was so named around 1525 when the Hapsburg Charles V dominated the island. Before that time, the site had been a haven for robbers and thieves. The Carlentinesi had looked down upon the housetops of the Lentinesi with scorn, and the latter had pointed up to the heights and shouted, *"Ladri di Carlentini!"* (Robbers of Carlentini!) Years later, transplanted to Omaha, the citizens of both communities became one. Their descendants would one day join hands in providing great financial help to a Carlentini racked with earthquake damage.

In Omaha Sam happily found not only his brother but others from Calascibetta who had come at Tom's urging. He immediately bonded with these fellow immigrants. In fact, the place his brother located for him to stay was owned by a Roxas family from his hometown, earlier arrivals in Omaha. With them he would find room and board for the next seven years, sharing their four-bedroom house near Seventeenth and Nicholas streets with three or four other men, who from time to time arrived in Omaha from Sicily.

Like many other immigrants from the Old World in this period, the Roxas enhanced their fortunes by providing these newcomers a place to survive. Roxas's wife was the mainspring of this effort, while Roxas found work in a packinghouse.

The Sicilian and Calabresi immigrants chose to live in three distinct colonies: one, a haven for the Carlentinesi, known as Little Italy, centered around Santa Lucia Hall at Sixth and Pierce streets and St. Philomena Cathedral at Tenth and William streets; another, consisting mainly of persons from Calabria, centered around St. Ann Church at Twenty-fourth Street and Poppleton Avenue; and the last clustered around Holy Family Church at Eighteenth and Izard streets and St. Alfio Hall at Seventeenth and Clark streets.

Sam had come directly to the Holy Family colony. The Roxas boardinghouse was near the Nicholas Street viaduct over railroad tracks to the Union Pacific shops where Sam soon found a job.

Upon arrival, he had been directed to Joseph Santa Luca, one of the labor foremen in the U.P. car shops. His son one day would be an Omaha lawyer contemporary with Sam's son, Louis. Santa Luca interviewed him, hired him and assigned him to work with Primo Marchello, a car carpenter ten years his senior. Primo became his best friend.

Sitting quietly in his church pew, Sam feels his heart swell with gratitude for the gift of his now-departed mentor. Primo not only had taken this poor immigrant under his wing and eased him into a steady job with the railroad, but he had shielded him from those, in and out of the company, who might otherwise have taken advantage of his illiteracy. Those of us who take reading and writing for granted can hardly understand what it meant for Sam never to do either in any language, be it his native tongue or English.

Primo's first act was to assist him in applying for American citizenship. Both men knew that this goal would be attainable only if Sam were able to learn by rote the answers to the hard test questions Primo would ask him. That's what Sam did. He had labored to pass the tests for more than the five years minimum residency required for U.S. citizenship. But the day came when the federal judge swore him in. He became a citizen of the United States. What a day that had been!

Having lived in Omaha for some time before Sam's arrival, and having worked for some years for the Union Pacific as a finish carpenter, Primo, himself, had climbed the success ladder. He lived in a brick house near Forty-second and Dodge streets, a far cry from Sam's own humble lodgings. What a splendid example to Sam of what hard work could produce. As the years went on, with Primo's help, he learned more and more about his new city and his new job; moreover, he came to feel for his adopted country a love far greater than the affection he had ever had for his native one.

Sam was aware that his experience in America was little different from that of the most other Omaha Italian immigrants. They came scared, had to cope with a new culture and had to learn a new

Italians

language. Fortunately, all had the joy of the same immense resource, each other.

In Sam's case, his fellow boarders at home and his fellow workers at the U.P. shops gave him courage. Daily he ate his brown-bag lunch over small talk with these companions. Every Sunday he worshiped with Holy Family Church members, mostly Sicilians and a good many from Calascibetta, and joined them in social doings. Goodbye to nostalgia.

During the seven years he boarded with the Roxas, Sam had many opportunities to visit the Italian colony in Little Italy. His U.P. coworkers, mostly Carlentinesi, welcomed him into their homes. Sixth and Pierce wasn't that far; he could walk. In later years, he would take the streetcar. He went there often to drink his friends' wine, listen to their music, play cards with them and banter with them in Italian. Later on, while his sons were growing up, he would insist that his family speak nothing but English in his home, yet in those early years, the one thing that had soothed his homesickness was to hear the dialect of his birth. And there had been many to talk to him in Sicilian.

Sam learned that although a scattering of his fellow countrymen had come to Omaha as early as 1863, including George Giacomini from Lombardy who had started a successful bar and restaurant, as late as 1890 there were only five hundred and thirty-eight foreign-born Italians in his adopted city. And in 1900, only four hundred and sixty-six. Many of these were Calabresi who ultimately had settled around Twenty-fourth and Poppleton. The economic depression of the 1890s had inhibited immigration during that decade. But with the Trans-Mississippi and International Exposition of 1898, prosperity returned to Omaha, and with it came an immense Italian immigration.

Sam became acquainted with the Salerno brothers, Joseph and Sebastiano, who brought hundreds of Carlentinesi to Omaha after 1900. Joseph Salerno had come in 1895 due to urging by his brother-in-law, Antonio Marfisi, South Omaha's first Italian fruit merchant.

Two years later Sebastiano arrived to establish a shoe shop and second-hand clothing business and later became a steamship agent charged with selling Omaha to Sicilians.

The new immigrants clustered in Little Italy around these Salernos who, having prospered in their early trades, now acted a benevolent *padrones* and provided the newcomers with everything from apartments to banking services. Luckily, Sam kept his own meager funds in a U.S. postal savings account and thus avoided their losses when the Salerno bank failed, due to a Florida land bust in 1926.

Others of Sam's acquaintance were Angelo Rosso, a prosperous wholesale fruit dealer, and Augustino Minardi, the manager of a Fourteenth and Leavenworth rooming house and business center for arriving immigrants. Later, a close friend was Alfio Garrotto, a native of Carlentini who ran a grocery store at 504 North Sixteenth. His daughter, Annunciata, became a famous diva, singing operatic arias at the Met, La Scala and throughout the world. Other later friends were Filippo Pattavina, from Carlentini, who dealt in groceries, dry goods and real estate and whose family later would figure in law enforcement; Guilio Cantoni from the Piedmont, owner of the Roma Hotel whose family would establish a leading Omaha restaurant; Louis Finocchiaro, who would become Omaha's largest wine distributor; and Alessandro Rotella, who, together with Alphonso and Raphaelle Orsi, would later provide Omaha with most of its Italian bread.

From these Italian immigrants came many professional people. The families Caniglia, Carnazzo, Garrotto, Inserra, Troia, Raneri, Turco, Pattavina and Panebianco have produced attorneys-at-law, and from these, some, such as Sam Caniglia and Paul Garrotto, became outstanding judges. Subby Anzaldo served on Omaha's city council for many years. The families Menolascino, Longo, Tribulato, Bolamperti, Buda, Trenisi, Catania, Mangiamelli, Carnazzo, Sophio, Campagna and Manganaro have enriched the community with doctors, dentists and pharmacists. Priests, too, have

Italians

emerged: Salinitro, Faso, Monzu and others.

The sons and daughters of the Italian immigrants permanently affected the Omaha cuisine, presenting the public with a treat few cities enjoy: the true Italian steak house. Here are served luscious charcoal-broiled steaks, always with side orders of pasta and, in early days, a gratuitous glass of wine. Omaha owes much to the families Salerno, Caniglia, Firmature, Marchio, Lorello, Piccolo and others.

Italian cuisine became a trademark of Omaha dining

The Little Italy Sam found in 1908 was exactly as described by the Works Progress Administration authors of **The Italians of Omaha**, who wrote in 1941:

> *Today with immigration at a practical standstill for nearly two decades, Little Italy has much of the color of Old World life. The people, dark haired and dark eyed, represent the best of the peasantry which has come out of Italy. Their virtue of frugality has been taught them by years of poverty. A fusion of many races throughout the centuries, their character has many facets. They have a sunny disposition, They are theatrical, clannish, hardworking, courteous and vindictive. Omaha, a melting pot city, assumes color and life from its various nationality centers and Little Italy is most generous in its contribution to the general scene.*

The streets of Little Italy resound with the noise and laughter of little children. The stores display foods dear to the hearts of this people—salamis, cheeses, olive oil, macaroni, spaghetti, braided lengths of garlic and strings of gleaming red peppers drying in the sun. In season the Italians make pasta pomo d'oro, *a highly seasoned tomato sauce, and the appetite-teasing odor of it pervades the entire neighborhood. Autumn is the joyous time of wine making. From native Nebraska grapes the people make the best red wine—*vino nero, *the much sought* dago red *of the dry era. From California grapes they make* vino blanco, *a sweeter, lighter wine. On warm days the women talk volubly and gesticulate across backyard fences. The atmosphere of the colony is one of vast neighborliness.*

Through the years Sam became a skilled carpenter. His native intelligence overcame his illiteracy. Primo Marchello taught him how to read blueprints and translate their contents into finished products with saw and hammer. His early work was exclusively in the repair and rebuilding of old, rough, wooden railroad freight cars, but the day came soon when he could help build such cars from scratch.

He moved from laborer to helper, and finally to carman. In later years, he became a finish carpenter and wore white gloves while repairing the fine mahogany veneer of the wainscoting and furniture of the railroad's business cars.

Indoors or outdoors, often too hot or too cold, he found the hard work a joy. Omaha was not balmy Sicily, but what advantages! Here one could live in freedom, enjoy life among his friends, save his money against the day he could buy a piece of real estate of his own, and find a wife to go with it.

That day came soon enough. About the time he had his eye on

Italians

Rose Arceri, a Holy Family parishioner and the daughter of Sebastiano (Yano) Arceri, Yano had his eye on him. He would be a suitable son-in-law. In those days, marriages among Omaha Italians were made, not in heaven, but by the families of the prospective brides and grooms. Even though Sam didn't hail from Lentini, Yano found much about him to like. At five feet, eight inches he was taller than the average Sicilian and had a fairer complexion. Besides, he held himself splendidly erect. In 1916, after a correctly chaperoned courtship, Sam and Rose were married.

It turned out to be the perfect match for Sam. Rose eased his burden of illiteracy and reared three sons with the frugality expected of an Italian wife. Yano himself had worked in the Union Pacific shops and was proud that his son-in-law had a good job there. After a few years of railroad employment, Yano had accumulated sufficient money to buy a row of flats on Seventeenth Street, plus a house for himself next door. In 1916, the newlyweds moved into one of the flats. There, two years later, Rose delivered her first-born, Louis.

Sam had started work in 1908 at one dollar and seventy-five cents a day. Moving up the ladder to carman, he soon was earning thirty cents more an hour and stashing away a good part of this in his U.S. postal savings account. In time, this frugality allowed him to fulfill a big dream. In 1919, Rose and he bought a house at 2518 North Nineteenth Street. They paid twenty five hundred and fifty dollars, seventeen hundred and fifty dollars in cash plus a promise to pay the eight hundred dollars still owing on the seller's mortgage, the only major obligation they ever incurred. Eleven years after coming to Omaha Sam had a stake in America. It made him very proud.

Immigrant housing history repeated itself, for his own house soon provided a place for his cousin to live. This man, also named Sam Seminara, arrived from Calascibetta in 1922. To avoid confusion and because he was only five feet, three inches tall, the family called him Little Sam. He lived with the Seminaras for twenty-five years and was a second father to their sons. He was more than this to Sam, himself, for he became his eyes, ears and hands. Having been blessed with four years of schooling in Sicily, Little Sam could read the news to his cousin from the Italian newspapers and later from the **Omaha World-Herald**, and he could help him in a hundred different ways where reading and writing were essential.

Little Sam also became Sam's wine-making buddy. After having bought a press and a grinder from a fellow Italian, the two annually turned out the two hundred gallons of wine permitted the head of a household by federal law. Unlike many Italians, Sam turned his back on the cheaper local Concord grapes requiring sugar for sufficient fermentation and made his wine from the white Tokay grapes mixed with ten percent Zinfandel, both varietals coming

The Santa Lucia Festival became an annual event after 1924

from California. Even if they were more expensive, their natural sugar made them better for wine making.

Being very price conscious, the frugal winemakers, along with many others from Little Italy, always carefully shopped the fruit and vegetable market at Eleventh and Jackson streets for the grapes that flowed from the Union Pacific boxcars. While Rose was not a wine drinker, both Sams loved a glass or two at the end of the working day.

One of Sam's favorite Omaha memories was that of the festival honoring Santa Lucia, the patron saint of Carlentini. Copied from similar festivals in Carlentini, this was an annual event in Little Italy after 1924. Each year, on a Friday at the beginning

Italians

of July, members of the Santa Lucia Festival Committee and members of Italian lodges, clubs and societies formed a procession preceded by American and Italian flags and a banner bearing a picture of the saint.

Starting at St. Philomena Cathedral, they moved north on Tenth Street to Pierce and east on Pierce to Sixth Street where the banner was placed upon a triumphal arch. A huge throng accompanied the parade, laughing, singing and shouting "Santa Lucia!"

The next day, following a Mass said in her honor, a richly dressed, life-sized image of the saint was removed from the church, placed on a flower-bedecked float, and, in the company of the same noisy procession of the day before, carried by manpower to Sixth and Pierce on the same route used to carry her picture. There she was placed beneath the elevated Santa Lucia arch. During the procession the revelers threw gifts at her feet and pinned money on her gown. In more recent times the ceremony has been repeated at Rosenblatt Stadium.

Each year, coming to the area by streetcar on a Saturday afternoon, Sam would sing and laugh with the rest of the Italian community, eat good Italian sausages, and, over Sicilian small talk, sip a glass or two of homemade wine with friends. It was just like being home in Calascibetta.

The years went by. More sons arrived, Arnold in 1923 and Lawrence in 1928. The great day came in 1929 when the whole family, including Little Sam, walked haughtily from their home at Ninteenth and Lake streets to the old post office at Sixteenth Street and Capitol Avenue. After Sam withdrew six hundred and twenty-nine dollars and fifty cents of his postal savings, they proceeded to a car dealer where Sam bought his first car, a new Model A Ford. A few weeks later, after the dealer had given him a lesson or two, he drove the family all over his adopted city, even out West where the "richa people" lived.

In Sam's block there were three Italian families in addition to a Scot named Burns, who lived next door, and a Swedish real estate salesmen named Larson, who lived across the street. The rest of the block's residents were Irish or Jewish. All of them were the best of neighbors. From time to time, they would pitch in to help each other in any way they could. Burns and Sam even built a fence together.

With the 1930s came some changes. At Sam's urging, Louis was in Central High School preparing for college. Although many of his friends had chosen to attend Tech High to study for a trade, Louis and his pal, Harold Zelinski, opted to enroll at Central for college-oriented courses. Louis's friendship with Harold had blossomed during the early years at Lake Grade School after the two had beat up a bully for calling Harold a "kike." While Sam didn't approve of Louis's fighting, he admired his loyalty to a friend.

Despite ethnic diversity, there was very little friction among the neighborhood teenagers. Louis and Harold regularly played ball in Kountze Park with boys of various backgrounds, principally Irish, Swedish and Jewish. One of their friends, Louis Blumkin, was the son of Rose Blumkin who would later become the renowned "Mrs. B" of the Nebraska Furniture Mart.

In 1932, the Depression was in full swing. Along with many others, Sam lost his Union Pacific job indefinitely. They were out of work with virtually no hope for finding new jobs. Many friends found relief in the New Deal's Works Project Administration. In vain, they urged Sam to join them. He never did. He would not accept the thirty-five cents an hour WPA paid for doing little or nothing. It was charity, he insisted.

Instead he chose the twenty cents an hour offered to him by his close friends, the Rindonis, who were masonry subcontractors. His work involved toting fresh concrete in wheelbarrows, a strenuous job for a man in his forties accustomed to lighter labor. He came home so exhausted he would drop into bed.

During these burdensome years, Rose kept things together. She handled the finances, making the most of the meager sums Sam was able to give her. The Seminaras always ate pasta of one kind or another: one day with beans, another with ricotta, and another with broccoli. They also had soups but seldom any meat. Sometimes Rose would serve her family sardines on pieces of bread soaked in olive oil.

A little male rebellion occurred. One day during the Depression, while he and Lou were cutting wood, Sam said: "Don't tell your mother, but this afternoon we'll sneak downtown, buy twenty-five cents worth of steak and cook it while your mother is visiting."

While daydreaming during the baptism in his St. Robert Bellarmine pew, Sam thinks of a conversation he had with Rose in their living room when he first learned of his Union Pacific job layoff. "The boys are going to get an education," he had said, "even if we hafta sella the house." Although the thought of losing his home had been devastating, he had meant what he said. And Rose had instantly agreed. They never knew that Louis, with watering eyes, had, half asleep in his adjoining bedroom, overheard this expression of his parents' love.

But the house wasn't sold. God had seen to that. Louis had been able to finish both college and law school. Furthermore, before launching a successful law practice, he had served Sam's adopted country as a World War II army intelligence officer. Nor did Sam's other sons fail to receive all the education they had wanted. After military service, they, too, followed useful careers.

In 1935, Sam had been rehired by the Union Pacific. Now Primo Marchello could help him become a finish carpenter. At the time of his retirement in 1954, Sam was working almost exclusively on the interior repair of the railroad's business cars, earning, of course, a great deal more than the daily 1908 wage of one dollar and seventy-five cents.

As the priest finishes the baptism, all these memories overwhelm him. His life in Omaha had been so full. Looking around the sanctuary, he sees his whole blessed family and all his close friends, most of whom are immigrants or the children of immigrants. He is proud of them and of himself. They represent the nation and the city he has grown to love.

He is especially pleased with his answer given to Louis that morning when asked what he thought about an illiterate immigrant from Sicily having a lawyer son, a dentist grandson and another grandson who sometimes taught English in one of the finest universities in the United States.

"Atsa pitty good," he had said.

REFERENCES
BOOKS
Larsen, James H. and Barbara J. Cottrell. **The Gate City: A History of Omaha**. Boulder, CO: Pruett Publishing Company, 1982.
WPA Writers' Program. **The Italians of Omaha.** New York: Arno Press, 1975.

INTERVIEWS
Lynch, Patrick W. Interview by Harry B. Otis. September 1995.
McMahon, Father Aloysius, Rector of St. Peter Catholic Church. Interview by Harry B. Otis. June 1996.
Seminara, Louis. Interviews by Harry B. Otis. January 20 and 23, and March 9, 1995.

THE CROATS/SLOVENES

Since 1991, Croatia and Slovenia have existed as sister republics; since the seventh century they have stood as ethnic clusters, Slovenia north of Croatia in the northern tier of the Balkans. Croatia (no larger than Pennsylvania) and Slovenia (no larger than New Jersey) have populations of less than ten million and two million, respectively, and are ethnically much the same. Their people speak similar forms of the Slavic language.

As Christianity was introduced by the monks Cyril and Methodius during the ninth century, almost every Croat and Slovene today embraces Roman Catholicism and fiercely defends his faith against all comers.

Croatia was an independent kingdom during the Middle Ages. Slovenes elected their leaders by a vote of their citizens as early as 700 A.D. (A democratic movement which Thomas Jefferson studied while helping to create the American republic.) Over the centuries, however, outsiders have dominated both of them: Turkish and Germanic neighbors until World War I, Serbia until World War II and Russian-sponsored communists under Tito until 1991. Despite this pressure, they have retained their language, customs and form of religion.

At the turn of the century, along with those of other Middle European countries, Croatian and Slovenian farmers eagerly sought the cheap lands and ready employment of America. Settling first on the East Coast, they gradually moved to Chicago, St. Louis and thence to Omaha where the meat packing industry promised good jobs and steady work. When the impending World War I affected their lives in Europe, other fellow countrymen joined them.

Their settlement in Omaha was in Goose Hollow, an area between V, W, Thirty-first and Thirty-fifth streets, along a small creek. It was so named from the residents' continuation of an Old Country habit of keeping geese. Most settled in rental houses formerly occupied by earlier immigrants. Until they got a church

Croats/Slovenes

of their own, they worshiped at St. Agnes Church at Twenty-third and Q streets along with other European newcomers.

Father John Zaplotnik

Then along came Father John Zaplotnik. Born in Krantz, Slovenia, in the foothills of the Alps, his family had brought him to America. He studied for the priesthood, was ordained in 1908 at age twenty-five and immediately came to Omaha to minister to the Croats and Slovenes as assistant pastor of St. Agnes. By that time they numbered one hundred and twenty families.

During the succeeding ten years, while handling the spiritual affairs of people of all the ethnic groups comprising his church, he worked toward his flock's dream, the creation of a new, separate Croat/Slovene ethnic church. It was a struggle. None of these parishioners was affluent; indeed, all were stockyard workers earning common labor wages. Yet the quarters, half-dollars and occasional dollar bills added up. The raffles, bake sales and roast lamb dinners paid off.

By 1911 they were able to buy three lots at Thirty-sixth and X streets. By 1917 they had acquired another lot and had secured Archbishop Jeremiah Harty's permission to build a church under the patronage of Saints Peter and Paul. Fr. Zaplotnik held its first service on Easter Sunday, 1918. Each Sunday, thereafter, he preached his sermon in three languages: Croatian, Slovenian and English.

He did much more than preach. During his tenure, which ended in 1925, he helped many of his flock apply for and earn their citizenship papers. Then he urged them to vote, a privilege they never before had possessed.

Zaplotnik profoundly influenced their lives in another way. Realizing that owning a home was a concept foreign to people who were poor and had lived under the iron rule of the Austrian-Hungarian Empire, he was concerned about the role communism was playing in the world and its possible effect on them. After all, communism had just overwhelmed czarist Russia. Most of his flock were laborers, sitting ducks for propaganda. At that time the American Communist party was recruiting new members and was actively targeting the Croats and Slovenes. Zaplotnik devised a plan.

Finding that most of his people rented their homes from landlords willing to sell them at reasonable prices, he persuaded some Omaha bankers to provide low-interest loans to allow their purchase by the tenants. Finally, when it was necessary to do so, he personally co-signed the immigrants' mortgage notes.

His plan worked. When the Communist organizers approached these immigrants to join the party, they were sent away. Father Zaplotnik, who everyone considered "a real saint," had won the day. The newcomers now had a stake in their new land. No more would agitators stand in the back of his church, shouting, *"Pope laze!"* ("The pope lies!") in Croatian. In gratitude, the parishioners built him a new rectory, completely paid for by the time of his departure.

Among the more than fifty families who built the new church were Paul Bizal, Nicholas Mihalic (later Mickells), Paul Goricki, Joseph Lesac, Peter Greguric and Nikola Babic. They and others visited all the Croatian and Slovenian families in the area to solicit funds. Among them was Blaz Cupich, who recorded all the gifts paid to him in his little notebook. There were many donations of hard-to-come-by quarters.

Born in Slavonia, Croatia in 1887, Blaz emigrated to Omaha in 1913 to find work with Cudahy Packing Company. There he became a first-class sausage maker. His wife, born Rose Gradicek, near Varazdin, Croatia in 1897, was sent by her family to the protection

Croats/Slovenes

of Croatian friends in Omaha during World War I.

Neither Blaz nor Rose ever returned to Croatia. They found each other, married and reared a huge family in the then tiny Croatian community. As did all their fellow countrymen, the couple became devoted members of Saints Peter and Paul.

The Cupichs are typical of the Croatians and Slovenians who came to America to escape tyranny and war and to live free of fear

Rose and Blaz Cupich

and want. In their new country's fertile soil, Rose bore thirteen children, losing only two in early infancy. The remainder, eight girls and three boys, were reared in a modest house at 5605 South Thirty-first Street.

They didn't have much to help them, only Blaz's wages of twenty to thirty dollars a week as a sausage stuffer and Rose's skill as a housekeeper. Friends among their fellow immigrants would be there to lend them a helping hand. Until the 1930s, there was no government aid to count on. Like all the others in Goose Hollow, the family relied on themselves, their friends and their church.

Blaz's wages took care of the bare necessities, the monthly mortgage payment and the other items requiring cash. Without his salary the family couldn't have functioned. But it was Rose's magical running of the household that pulled them through.

Their house was indeed a modest one considering the size of the family. With only two bedrooms (each with two beds) and a living room and dining room (each with two hide-a-beds), the house just barely could sleep all the family members. The little boys were sometimes three to a bed.

Early on a potbellied stove in the dining room, fired with wood or coal, provided their heat. This was supplemented by a kitchen stove that burned coal in one end and wood in the other. A gas stove later replaced this practical item when the house received central heating some time before World War II.

Vital to the family's survival were Rose's vegetable gardens that, together with fruit trees, provided food for thirteen hungry people. She planted gardens and fruit trees on vacant lots on either side of the house, near enough for ready Cupich care. Rose was proud that nearly every passerby remarked on their beauty—how orderly they were and how well attended.

This attention was not by chance. Every summer morning Rose gave all the Cupich children a five A.M. wake-up call, so that they could weed the gardens in the cool dawn. These gardens were the family's grocery store. Apples, plums, pears, apricots, peaches and

*Susan Cupich, Robert Cupich and Marilyn Zalovich from Kolo Kids of the
Croatian Fraternal Union*

cherries came from the orchard, with a separate area for a strawberry
patch, and beds of potatoes, beans, peas, beets, carrots, turnips and
squash. All these provided the substance of endless canning for
Rose and her older daughters. When winter came, the fruit and
vegetable cellar was full.

Rose had livestock, too. In addition to geese (a must), she raised
a few ducks and many chickens. There always would be a chicken
or two for the Sunday dinner and especially for holidays, such as
Christmas or saints' days. There was no frozen meat in those days.
To preserve the fowl, Blaz smoked them in his smokehouse together
with other inexpensive cuts of meat from Cudahy. After slaughtering
a pig on the premises, he made certain the family had an adequate
supply of homemade smoked sausage made with his own expert
hand.

Rose and her daughters served the family dinner at a long table

218

that stretched for each sit-down meal from the living room into the dining room. Blaz would preside, a switch ready at hand to discipline any young Cupich inattentive to the blessing being offered before dinner. Other meals were informal. The Cupichs regularly breakfasted on corn meal mush.

Except for the luxury of running water and electric power in the house, Rose's lot was not much different from that of any farm wife. There was constant work for her, and for her daughters as they grew older. So many things to do. In addition to dusting and cleaning the house, tending gardens and feeding fowl, to say nothing of caring for little children, bread must be baked and meals prepared. Rose baked ten loaves of bread every other day.

The daughters had their own chores. One of them was sweeping the fowls' yard every day. Another sometimes was washing the family clothes in a large oval brass tub, to be hung on clotheslines in the yard. The hanging was tolerable in nice weather, but when the temperature dropped and the wind blew it was hard on their fingers. Later, after the clothes were washed and hung, they had to take the tub of hot, soapy water to the outhouse for the scrubbing of seats. There were no indoor toilets until the late 1920s.

Like most Depression families, immigrant or not, the Cupichs didn't think of themselves as poor. Blaz had his job. True, no one ever had any money to speak of, but they enjoyed life's simple pleasures like working jigsaw puzzles together on a winter night or reading to one another.

The girls and their friends sometimes pooled what pennies they had to buy a chunk of chocolate to slice and share. And when only one dime was available for the movie at the Roseland Theater on Twenty-fourth Street, the oldest girl would go, telling the others afterwards what she had seen. The girls appreciated simple gifts. They thought it wonderful when one time someone gave them head scarves made of cheap, shining rayon.

The Cupich boys made ready friends with the other lads in the neighborhood: Lithuanians, Serbs, Poles, Czechs and Rumanians.

Croats/Slovenes

Together they visited each other's churches and ethnic festivals; together they hung out and played baseball and football. During this period before World War II, a love of sports generated a distinct camaraderie among the youth of South Omaha, regardless of their national origin.

For all Christian people, Christmas ranks as one of the two holiest seasons. The Croats, and the Cupichs in particular, were no exception.

They were slow to accept the standard American form of the holiday. During the 1920s and 1930s, the Croatian lore prevailed. The stocking you hung on St. Nicholas Eve, December 6, would receive a toy if you had been good and a lump of coal, if otherwise. (One trusts there were few lumps of coal.) On St. Nicholas Day itself, one of the children's relatives would dress up like the devil and enter the house dragging chains. If you had been bad, you would seek refuge under a bed. Christmas Eve morning was a time for the children to greet Croatian neighbors at their homes, much like English wassailing. Every household looked forward to blessing them with candy and fruit.

For Christmas and all the big holidays, Rose set a lavish table spread with plenty of Croatian strudel, nut bread, cookies, candy and fruit. Traditionally, she would present a garlic-permeated pork loin roast together with superbly baked chickens from her yard and vegetables from her larder. Only in later years were gifts exchanged among family members in the American fashion.

Like their Polish neighbors, Croats early on held wedding feasts in their homes. To announce the wedding date and to issue invitations, the young couple, or the groom and the best man, would personally go to the door of each prospective guest with a glass and a bottle of cheer. No engraved invitation nonsense for them.

Following the church wedding, all of the guests would repair to the bride's home for refreshments and dancing. Unlike the Poles, they usually danced in the living room of the bride's home, not out in the backyard. A real Croatian *tamburitza* orchestra provided the music. This is how Mary Cupich was married.

As the Cupich family grew, so did Saints Peter and Paul. When Fr. Zaplotnik left, Fr. John Juricek arrived to find a parish free of debt, but in need of a parochial school. More than two hundred children were ready for religious instruction. By late 1926, the parish had built an eight-room school ready for the services of the Ursuline nuns of York, Nebraska.

Early church of Saints Peter and Paul

These sisters used two rooms of the schoolhouse as their convent. In 1941, the Benedictine sisters of Atchison, Kansas, took charge, an event calling for the erection of a completely new convent for their housing.

Just before World War II, the parish received an assistant rector, and just after the war, Fr. Juricek was elevated to the rank of Monsignor. The stage was set for further expansion. Plans for a new rectory led to the erection in 1954 of a four-unit brick rectory to house three priests and a housekeeper.

Then came the postwar baby boom. The schoolhouse had to be enlarged two times to accommodate the population explosion. The congregation found funds for additional schoolrooms plus a new auditorium. By 1961 these were a reality.

By now, however, the congregation had completely outgrown its church. A new building was a must. By June 29, 1967, the fiftieth anniversary of the parish, this, too, was a reality—a half-million-dollar building seating six hundred communicants and containing a chapel dedicated to Our Lady of Bistrica, patroness of Croatia.

The church's artwork was the creation of Charles B. Vukovich,

Croats/Slovenes

a Croatian artist from Maywood, New Jersey. Furthermore, the congregation got to enjoy the music of a pipe organ of unsurpassed quality of tone, a Cassavant.

Most of the social life of the Cupich family, and of all Balkan people, still centers around their church. From the time of their early arrival, it was in the parish hall of St. Agnes Church that these immigrants held dances, with the Croatian *tamburitza* orchestras providing the music. The people sang and danced *kolos*, Croatian folk dances.

Every year on June 27 the parishioners of Saints Peter and Paul celebrate their patron saints' day. Two of their organizations, the Croatian Fraternal Union and the Croatian Catholic Union serve as catalysts for these affairs.

Following the dedication of the Saints Peter and Paul parish, the church activities increased. Fr. Juricek taught youngsters the Croatian language; church members performed Croatian dramas; the musically inclined formed choral groups to sing Croatian music at concerts and Masses; and the Ursuline nuns taught the children Croatian songs for Christmas and Easter plays.

Dear to everyone's heart were the church picnics featuring barbecued lamb and suckling pigs served with Croatian delicacies produced by the women: *sarma* (cabbage rolls), sausage, *crahnaca* and *povitica* (nut bread). The parishioners still dine on this fare, entertained by the songs and dances of fellow countrymen garbed in costumes from the various regions of Croatia.

From the very start, various groups have carried on the nitty-gritty work, fund solicitation, food preparation, booth manning and such, required in sponsoring Croatian festivals and sporting events for charitable purposes. Through the Croatian Club of Omaha, Sacred Heart of Jesus, Lodge Sixteen of the Croatian Catholic Union, The Triple C Club (organized by Rosa Greguric, a tireless church worker) and many others, the men and women of the parish have faithfully discharged these tasks.

Organized during the early years by many of the parish founders,

Saints Peter and Paul Lodge One Hundred and One of the Croatian Fraternal Union, and later its sister lodges, have played a heavy role in these religious and patriotic activities. Recently it supplied clothing and medicine for Croatian relief and raised and forwarded over ten thousand dollars to St. Theresa's Orphanage in Zagreb to help care for children, otherwise bereft, whose parents lost their lives in recent Balkan conflicts.

In 1966, Fr. Anthony Petrusic, who had joined the church as its pastor in 1969, formed the Croatian Cultural Society to promote and encourage the country's literature, music and folklore through

Bishop Blase Cupich and his parents, Mrs. and Mr. Blase Cupich

presentation and distribution of Croatian arts to libraries, universities, schools and museums. Blaz's son, Joseph, helped in its creation and another son, Blase, later helped acquire a headquarters at 8711 South Thirty-sixth Street.

Most of Blaz and Rose's children received diplomas from South High School, after having attended the parochial school at Saints Peter and Paul for most of their primary training. Only Joe Cupich, and later his sister, Madeline, graduated with college degrees. Joe graduated from the University of Omaha and Madeline received a degree from Omaha's College of St. Mary and took holy vows to become Sister Blaise, R.S.M. Four Cupichs served the military with distinction during World War II, all in the Navy: Blase, Joe, John and their sister, Eva.

Most of the Cupich grandchildren have pursued successfully the American dream of a higher education leading to success in business, education and research. Had they lived to see it, Blaz and Rose would be especially proud of the elevation of one grandson, Monsignor Blase Cupich. Like his own father, Blase had inherited the now anglicized name. At age forty-nine he was the pastor of Omaha's St. Robert Bellarmine Church. On June 22, 1998, Omaha Archbishop Elden Curtiss announced that the Vatican had made Monsignor Blase the bishop of South Dakota at Rapid City.

"I felt like a ton of bricks fell on me," he said, when the word was passed. Despite this weight felt by their beloved brother, the appointment thrilled and honored all the Cupichs, all his hometown Croatian-American friends and, indeed, everyone in the community of Omaha.

REFERENCES

BOOKS
Larsen, James H. and Barbara J. Cottrell. **The Gate City: A History of Omaha**. Boulder, CO: Pruett Publishing, 1982.

INTERVIEWS
Cupich, Joseph. Taped interview by Harry B. Otis. August 5, 1998.

MONOGRAPHS
1917-1992 Saints Peter and Paul Parish: 75th Anniversary.
Zaplotnik, Rev. J. L. *Saints Peter and Paul Church a Reality.*

NEWSPAPERS
McCord, Julia. *Omaha Surprised at S.D. Bishop Appointment.* **The Omaha World-Herald**. June 30, 1998.

THE SERBS

Father Vojislav Dosenovich looks out from his Omaha rectory at his new St. Nicholas Serbian Orthodox Church. He is so very proud of it and so grateful to the Serbian-American flock that built it. "If only some of my childhood family were here to share in its consecration," he mourns.

Gazing at a few old family photographs, he reflects on his years in Bosnia and on the book he is about to write. His eyes water a little as he thinks about his lost loved ones. "How can I get people to believe what happened to them?"

His thoughts turn to the millions of innocent Jews who perished in the Holocaust.

> *Everyone knows about these unfortunates, but they don't know that at the same time the Nazis, and Communists too, tortured and murdered nearly one million Orthodox Bosnian Serbs. Maybe they'll believe this when they read how they butchered my father, brother and sister.*

Father Vojin Dosenovich inside St. Nicholas Serbian Orthodox Church

Serbs

Maybe when people learn how God carried me through four years of Bosnian bloodshed to this wonderful city of Omaha, they will understand and believe me.

He was baptized Vojislav, but his mother called him Vojin. Although only thirty-two when he arrived in Omaha in 1949, he felt as if he already had lived a lifetime. He thanked God for providing him with a new start in America. Here he had found and married his beloved Nadine. Here he had been ordained to the Orthodox priesthood for which six pre-war years in a Sarajevo seminary had prepared him. By 1950 he was pastor of St. Nicholas.

In 1988, he held services in a shiny Serbian-Byzantine building, at Fiftieth and Harrison, laden with beautiful icons which his parishioners had provided. Many of them had been fellow sufferers during the war. Surely God had blessed them all.

As though five hundred years of Turkish tyranny and forty years of Hapsburg hatred were not enough, beginning in 1941, especially in Bosnia Herzegovina, Serbs were to suffer not only four years of brutal genocide at the hands of Nazi-sponsored Croatian terrorists and Soviet partisans, but forty additional years of oppression under a Soviet-imposed communism, permitted, if not approved, by the Western powers.

Following World War I, the victorious Allies had sponsored the formation of Yugoslavia, encouraging Serbs, Croats, Slovenians, Bosnians, Herzegovians and others to produce a loose federation under King Alexander, a Serb. Belgrade was its capital.

Although most of these ethnic Slavs possess similar physical attributes and write and speak what is basically the same language, they hold strikingly different religious beliefs. The Croats and Slovenians are militant Roman Catholics, while the Serbians, who received their brand of Christianity from the patriarch of Constantinople, are devout Orthodox Christians. In contrast, the Bosnian Muslims follow the God of Islam, just as their Turkish conqueror from the year 1389 had led them to do.

While Croatia and Slovenia in the northwest were settled mainly by people so named, many Serbs also lived there. Serbia in the southeast, although basically populated by Serbs, also housed many Croats and Slovenians. The Muslims lived everywhere. Especially in Bosnia Herzegovina, in central Yugoslavia, these bodies mingled together. Many villages contained all of these varieties of Slavs plus a few Jewish families.

Until 1941, such religiously disparate peoples, albeit maintaining a cool distance, lived together without friction. They traded with each other and sometimes even socialized together. For example, once a year on the Day of Unity they and their respective clergy would unite to celebrate the 1920 creation of their new country.

Despite the fact that King Alexander had been assassinated in 1934 by a Croat terrorist, during the twenty-two years that Vojin grew to manhood, Yugoslavia enjoyed peace. It seemed that almost everyone, Croats, Slovenians, Serbs, Muslims and Jews alike, wanted their young country to succeed.

It was not to be. Like the unseen lava of a dormant volcano waiting to erupt, human emotions seethed beneath the surface. Then, as now, Yugoslavians were cursed with deep, festering, religious differences.

Born in 1916, Vojin grew up in the village of Oraslja near Sanski Most, a central Bosnian town thirty miles west of Banja Luka and some two hundred miles west of Sarajevo. He was the third of seven children; a sister, Radojka, and five brothers, Branko, Bosko, Mirko, Kolta and Petar, who died of diphtheria when four years old.

Their father, Pero, a retired civil servant pensioner, and their mother, Mara, a successful general store operator, reared them on an acreage of hay fields and plum orchards that expanded in size as the frugal handling of money permitted. Increasing prosperity allowed them to send their children to schools away from home.

Vojin attended grammar school in Sanski Most, eight kilometers east of his village, and graduated from a *gymnasija* in Priedor, forty kilometers north. From the time he was seven, except for vacations, he boarded away from a home and family that he sorely missed.

But when summers came, and school was out, what a blessing he found in returning to the lovely acres that stretched south on a

Serbs

wide plateau to the foot of a hill where a river meandered like a silver ribbon. In the golden sunshine of childhood and peace, Vojin, a handsome, husky, athletic boy, found a paradise in the scent of breezes that were cool and crisp and smelled like the air he would later encounter in Colorado.

As for the river, really a creek but it seemed like a river to him and his brothers, its waters were ideal for a swim on a hot summer day following hay making on the family farm. As they grew older, their father would teach them to fish the creek for the family's dinner.

All of Bosnia is lovely, hilly and tree covered, and the Dosenovich homesite was one of the most beautiful. In the morning the rising sun would paint the sometimes snowy top of Mount Gmech lying to the west, just as it would, upon setting, silhouette

the mountain. To the east Vojin's little river flowed between steep hills and under woods, continuing further eastward until it plunged some three hundred feet over a cliff to a canyon below. Memories of these scenes would comfort him during the troubled days ahead.

Waterfall near the Dosenvich home in Bosnia

Immediately to the north of the farm lay the village Oraslje (Walnut Place), about forty-two homes. It was divided into halves: the Eastern part mostly Serbian-related and Orthodox; the Western part Muslim, with the exception of two Roman Catholic Croatian families.

In dress, food and general behavior, each group had its own distinct way of life. For example, each claimed its own cemetery and, curiously, had a separate pronunciation and spelling for the word, grave. The Christian cemeteries were considered semisacred by all groups despite the fact that Muslim cemeteries were not so

230

honored by the Christians. Of course each sect had its own church or mosque, and in spite of the sometimes close and friendly relationships between Christian and Muslim families, intermarriage was strictly taboo.

The Dosenovich family devoutly followed the Orthodox Christianity of its ancestors. Vojin's father felt deeply that one of his sons should study for the priesthood. During World War I, priests had appeared like visiting angels to minister to him and his fellow Serbian soldiers. He considered the priesthood a noble profession and chose it for Vojin.

Like most Serbs, the family devotedly celebrated all the holy days of the Orthodox church, most especially the *Slava* (Glorification). A Christian holiday found only among Serbs, it is the occasion that commemorates the saint's day on which one's ancestors were baptized into Christianity. It is celebrated formally with festivity and food, especially a special bread, *slava kolac*, that is blessed by the priest to symbolize Christ as the Bread of Life.

In 1932, at age sixteen, Vojin entered the Sarajevo seminary. For six delightful years he studied the religion of his forefathers and discussed the world's problems with fellow seminarians. With them and other university students, both male and female, he enjoyed the wonderful world of Bosnia's principal city, walking its tree-lined streets while eating roasted chestnuts and *baklava* pastries. Some of his fellow students later would serve with him as *Chetniks*, Mihajlovich guerrillas, supporting the Allies during World War II.

While a seminary student, Vojin visited Kosovo in South Serbia where the Turks had conquered the Serbs in 1389 to hold them in slavery until the end of the ninteenth century. During these five hundred years, the victors had forced thousands of them to convert to Islam and, far worse, had torn thousands of male babies from their Serbian mothers' arms to be reared in Istanbul as Muslim *janizaries* in the Sultan's army.

Not until the latter half of the nineteenth century did the Serbs and Croats succeed in throwing the Turks out of the Balkans. Then they were obliged to look on while Austria moved in to fill the void, dominating Croatia and Bosnia Herzogovina and threatening

Serbs

Serbia itself. A few years later, defeat in World War I would remove Austria as a master, but at the price of thousands of Slavic lives.

In 1938, following his seminary training, Vojin entered the Yugoslavian army for six months of compulsory service. In his camp in Bitola, not far from the Greek border, he and a fellow seminarian shared barracks with two Croatian Roman Catholics. Between the two types of Christians there was no animosity, only indifference on the part of the Croats who regarded Orthodox Christians as heretics.

Once discharged from the military, Vojin found work in the diocesan office in Banja Luka situated in a beautiful Serbian Orthodox cathedral, soon to be destroyed. Then, in 1939, he was overjoyed to return to Sanski Most to teach religion in the same grammar school that he had attended earlier. He was thus occupied when the hurricane of murder blew in from the northwest.

In the late 1930s, ever restless under the Yugoslavian mantle and inspired by the Nazis, Croatia broke free and established an autonomous territory called Hrvatska Banovina. It immediately started harassing the Serbs living there, principally by excluding them from government service. It even forced some to abandon their homes, announcing that its mission was to convert whatever number of Serbs it could to Roman Catholicism or drive them from the country.

Eventually this new Croatia grew larger, creeping southeast to encompass Vojin's Bosnia Herzegovina. The expansion was made easy by the steady wartime German occupation of every country surrounding Yugoslavia and by its enlistment of a militant Croatian terrorist group called *Ustashi,* which was charged with the dirty work of subduing or eliminating Bosnian Serbs.

With the help of the Muslims, it did its work well. In 1941, approximately two and a half million Serbs lived in the Bosnian portion of this expanded Croatia. During the next four years nearly one million of them—men, women and children—were liquidated, mainly by the *Ustashi* and the Muslims, but also by Tito's partisans. By the end of 1941, Germany's army had beaten Yugoslavia's and had forced its government into exile.

Nevertheless, the Serbian people refused to roll over and play dead. Until finally driven out of their mountain lairs, guerrilla *Chetniks* under Mihajlovic remained loyal to the cause of the Allies. Historians assert that such stubbornness fatally delayed Hitler's drive to Moscow; however, the fact remains that thousands of Slavic people, mostly Serbs, died as a consequence.

Sadly, the Yugoslav guerrillas found themselves fighting Communist partisans as well as fascists. The partisans had sprung up to counter the *Ustashis*, yet disloyally saw fit to further their own cause by eliminating any Serb who refused to enter their fold. Such was the political chaos of the day.

In the end, the vastly outnumbered *Chetniks*, loyal to Yugoslavia and the Allied cause, could not prevent the merciless torture and slaughter of Serbs by both totalitarian factions. Mihajlovic, himself, finally met death at the hands of the Communists after the Allies sided with Tito and his partisans against the legitimate government of Yugoslavia and failed to protect him.

Early in 1941, the Dosenovich family had a foretaste of what was to come. A German colonel rolled into their farm with his cohorts, took whatever he wanted from the shelves of Mara's store, giving a receipt for the merchandise "to be paid later."

In the summer of 1941, so-called friends gave both Vojin and his father written word that the family was in danger and that their only safety lay in conversion to Roman Catholicism. One evening a crestfallen Pero came to the kitchen to show his family a message from an acquaintance: "Sign the enclosed conversion form or die." Upon seeing this, Mara dropped the dish she was carrying to the stone floor, slumped on her stool, and bowed her head. "It would be better for us to die than to live under the shame of this kind," she cried. Pero threw the form into the fire and left the room.

Soon the Axis powers, acting through the *Ustashi* and the Muslims, embarked on a program of outlawing all things Serbian and Orthodox. In addition to direct physical threats, they began deporting Bosnian Orthodox bishops and priests and destroying Bosnian churches and cathedrals. They also forbade writing in the Cyrillic alphabet, which was time-honored by Serbians.

Serbs

Vojin learned that the populations of whole villages had been wiped out. Such had been the fate of the Serbs in nearby Tominaa and Tramoshnja while preparing their *Slava*, the date of the Feast of St. George. What would be the fate of his own village and of Sanski Most?

A few days later he learned it. The *Ustashi* impact was direct. Rounding up all male Sanski Most Serbs between the ages of sixteen and sixty-five, including Vojin, they crammed them into the basement of his school. There they remained for hours, nearly suffocating, before being conducted, one by one, to be tried by a Muslim judge as accused *Chetniks* opposed to the Nazi invasion.

Later, twenty-seven of the prisoners were led away to be shot. Returning the dead to Sanski Most, the *Utashis* forced the Serbs to suspend the bodies by ropes from the town's trees. This was the beginning. By the end of 1941, three thousand of the town's Serbs were dead; by 1945, eight thousand.

Vojin's father was designated a hostage for the good behavior of Sanski Most citizens. On a July evening two brothers, acquaintances of Pero, came to the farm armed with revolvers and

The Dosenovich home in Sanski Most, Bosnia

bright letter *U*s sewn to their caps. They were to escort him, they said, to the Sanski Most city hall for his own protection. They would guarantee his safety.

Indicating to his anxious family that he departed willingly and would be safe, Pero left with his escort. His family never would see him again. His captors tortured and killed him and dumped his body, along with many others, in a common Sanski Most grave.

Late in August, the hammer fell on the rest of the family. Armed *Ustashi* soldiers invaded Vojin's little village, pillaging and burning. Mara was alone in her home at the time. God intervened to save Vojin and his brothers who were working in the fields of a neighboring farm. When Mara refused to disclose their whereabouts to a neighbor named Stifan, he pushed her out of the house and knocked her down with the butt of his gun.

Stifan and the other soldiers then stole whatever they wanted of the family's possessions, scattering the rest, including precious photographs, around the barnyard. Then they attempted, unsuccessfully, to burn down the house. When they finally all went away, Mara sought safety in nearby woods where her sons found her.

Of the four sons left to protect their mother, the youngest, Kolta, insisted on joining his sister, Radojka, who lived alone in Prijedor with two tiny children. The *Ustashi* had eliminated her husband and his father. Kolta's trip was a fatal mistake. On his way to Prijedor he disappeared and never was seen by his family again. Nor was Radojka's own life to be spared. Her hostile mother-in-law accused her of being an enemy of the people. Communist partisans separated her from her children and then murdered her.

Years later, one of Radojka's sons, Ranko, had a tearful reunion with his uncle Vojin in Omaha. He would tell how Mara had rescued him and his brother from an orphanage and had taken them to live with her in the unburnable Oraslje farm home to which she had returned.

The day after the raid on their home, Branko, Mirko and Vojin joined their mother in the woods. From there they escaped southwest to Bosanski Milanovac to the home of relatives and then south to the larger village of Davar. Wherever they went, they found people unable to believe the horrible things they had experienced. In the mountainous terrain news traveled slowly.

Yet, many years later Mirko told of worse happenings. After many months, his mother and he finally returned home to find the charred bones of many elderly and children, some of them the Dosenoviches' close relatives. The *Ustashi* and Muslims had driven them into the family's barn to be burned alive. They also discovered the remains of many other bodies burned alive in the family's large plum fermentation vats.

Seeking the relative security of villages with greater Serbian population, Vojin and his family moved southwest to Palanka and finally Jelanovce. There they stayed while the men assisted in the military operations of commander Petar of the Jelanovce *odred*, a loosely cast military body. There they were to cheer when Petar, later killed in a skirmish, mined the railroad tracks and blew up an *Ustashi* train.

While in Jelanovce, Vojin was invited to a meeting of *odreds* of neighboring districts. God intervened a second time to save him. A severe head cold prevented him from attending a conference that had been initiated by the Communists. Friends who did attend informed him that not only was partisan Tito at the meeting but also that a Zagreb woman had inquired whether any one there knew a "Vojo Dosenovich" who, she had been told, was "a reactionary, beyond any hope of reeducation, who must be liquidated."

With Communists in the vicinity, Vojin wanted his family to continue its journey southwestward, yet his mother insisted on remaining in Jelanovce. Feeling secure with Branko and Mirko to protect her, she insisted that Vojin move on in an attempt to establish some contact with the outside world.

So with the hoard of three gold coins his mother had given him the day they had left their home, Vojin started walking. He was to wear out his shoes hiking the many kilometers west to Drvar, to Smolana, to Strmica and finally to Knin in Dalmatia, eluding both *Ustashi* and Communist partisans by sleeping under haystacks and in the woods. For two years he remained in Knin, identifying with the *Chetniks* and even becoming an informal paymaster for Mihajlovic.

Then in midsummer 1943, following a series of military adventures, he obtained papers allowing him to travel to Belgrade where he joyfully reunited with his brother Bosko, who was hospitalized there after being freed from a German prisoner of war camp.

In 1944, with fascist fortunes declining, the Communists were definitely taking over Yugoslavia. Convinced that Yugoslavia had been betrayed and that he had no future there, Vojin opted to abandon his country for good. Even though Austria was the eye of the tornado, he chose it as the most practical escape haven.

Fortune favored him. Without effort he bought a train ticket to Vienna. As a parting gift, Bosko gave Vojin a present of his most prized possession, the new shoes the Red Cross had given him as a returned prisoner of war.

Although the train was strafed en route, Vojin arrived in Vienna safely enough, yet bereft of any identification papers. God again intervened. It may have been that the war had so disrupted their lives that the Austrians were too busy to question his right to be there. At first no one challenged him, but eventually he was discovered and put to work tending horses and laboring in the fields as a prisoner of war.

By the end of 1945, with the war over, Vojin felt lucky being in a displaced persons camp in Rosenheim, Germany. There he was able to attend classes in English and enjoy the contents of CARE packages provided by the American public. He could not return to his native country; the Communists were in charge, and there was a price on his head.

He decided to emigrate to the United States. Along with a Russian professor from Ljublljana University, he soon found himself in charge of two hundred Jewish refugees aboard the *S.S. Fletcher* bound for America.

Upon his arrival, the Church World Service, a Protestant church group, found him a rooming house and gave him a bit of money with which he bought some oranges, milk and raisin bread. After eating these good things, he fell into twenty hours of unbroken sleep in his new country. Welcome to America!

The Church World Service soon directed him to St. Sava Monastery in Libertyville, Illinois. Here Vojin was employed as a traveling secretary finding sponsors for other displaced persons. He was thus engaged in St. Louis, Missouri when he met his future wife, Nadine, a child of Serbian parents. Born in the United States, but taken to Serbia as a little girl, Nadine was fluent in both English and Serbian. Because she was an American, the Serbs had denied her permission to study in a Yugoslavian university. As a consequence, her family had brought her back to America before the European war had started.

The year 1949 proved to be very important to Vojin's new life and career. First, on May 1 he and Nadine were married. Later in the year Serbian Bishop Nicholay, who also had fled Yugoslavia, ordained him as an Orthodox priest. During the war the Nazis had interned the Bishop in the Dachau concentration camp. Like Vojin, Communist rule prevented him from returning to his homeland.

Finally in 1949, Vojin was to answer a call from St. Nicholas Serbian Orthodox Church in Omaha. The Chicago-based Bishop Dionisiye sent him to a meeting with twenty-nine St. Nicholas parishioner-members who, after a secret caucus, unanimously elected him their priest. He was here to stay.

Shortly before the turn of the century, along with other Balkan peoples, Serbs came to Omaha. Their objective: jobs with the meat packing companies. The prosperity that Omaha was beginning to enjoy after a decade of recession meant they were welcomed, not only by the meat packers, but by the railroads and other heavy industries.

Some Serbs brought their wives; others remained bachelors until they could meet and wed a local girl or find one by mail order from their native land. The exchange of photographs and references from their friends and acquaintances helped in this regard.

They also brought with them their church, Serbian Orthodox, establishing it in a building they constructed at Thirtieth and S streets. Naming it St. Nicholas Serbian Orthodox Church, they built and bought homes in its neighborhood and remained loyal to it. They were relatively few in number. Only seventy families celebrated the Serbian Christmas in 1928, but they observed well the Old Country traditions.

Since Serbs follow the Julian calendar, Serbian Christmas lands on January 7 instead of December 25, but it is no less revered and enjoyed. First, there is a church service from which very few Serbs are absent by choice. This is followed by the giving of presents amid shouts of *Hristos se Rodi!* (Christ is born!) The first neighbor to enter the house on this day receives gifts from the family.

Then comes a family feast of roasted pig and other delicacies in homes where the floors have been strewn with straw as a reminder of Christ's manger and under tablecloths have been placed straw crosses as a symbol of Christ's love. In the midst of all this some Serbs doubtless have a nip or two of *slivovitz*, the plum brandy so popular with Balkan people.

During the Depression, the lack of meat packing jobs caused many Serbs to leave Omaha for Chicago, Detroit and other Eastern cities. Yet, as late as World War II, St. Nicholas still boasted about one hundred and fifty members with one hundred and nineteen of them fighting for Uncle Sam. Pete Plechas, president of the church, had three sons in the war, one a lieutenant colonel, who later became a doctor, and two in the merchant marine.

After the war many Serbs continued to leave Omaha. Vojin arrived in 1949 to find only forty-seven families in his parish, yet 1961 saw an increase to one hundred and fifty families when new Serbs, refugees like himself, came to escape Tito's communism. Since then, despite its ethnic nature, membership at the church has diminished only a little, and although some families opt to live in other parts of Omaha, many continue to reside close to their early roots around Thirtieth and S streets. They like being together.

Over the years, Serbs organized social clubs. Newspaper accounts reported their activities. For example, in 1936 Nick Shuput, who bore the name of an early Omaha Serbian family, was elected president of the Serbian Sokol club, while members of other families, Churchich, Mandich, Drakulich and Legino served the club in other capacities. In 1968, a particular Nebraska type of fame came to the community when Robert Churchich starred as a quarterback on the University of Nebraska football team.

Perhaps the most colorful St. Nicholas parishioner was Robert Samardick, an immigrant from Montenegro, who served as a federal agent enforcing liquor laws in the 1920s and as Omaha's police chief in the 1930s. As honest as he was indiscreet, Samardick was admired greatly by the community. He lost his police chief job after calling Mayor Dan Butler "a plain four-flusher, and a bulldozer, and public enemy No. 1," when the mayor had found him too tough a law enforcer.

The aftermath of World War II affected each Omaha Serb personally, as most had relatives and friends still residing in Yugoslavia. All somehow believed that Serbia would win out in the end. One of these was Dmitrije Despotovich, who was decorated for heroism while serving in the Serbian army against Austria during World War I. Though many were too old to serve, like grocer Louis Churchich, they were eager to enlist anyway.

Fr. Dan Milakov, the pastor of St. Nicholas who had come from Belgrade only two years earlier, predicted his country's resistance to the Axis invasion and never faltered in this belief despite news reports that his country might join the Axis powers.

Thus, when Germany and Italy invaded Yugoslavia in 1941, all Omaha Serbs were elated to see her team up with the Allies. Gathering in living rooms, their ears tuned to their radios, old-time Serbian emigres and new ones alike grabbed onto every bit of news. They knew that their little homeland would not lie down before Hitler as so many others had done. The Axis might take Belgrade, but not Yugoslavia. The Serbs knew how to fight from their country's hills that now were heavily fortified. Hadn't they licked Austria in World War I?

Alas, Yugoslavia prevailed against the Axis only to lose their country to Tito's Communist partisans.

The number one hero for Omaha Serbs is General Draja Mihajlovich who, with five armies of twenty thousand men each, fought for the Allies against both Nazis and Communists. Sadly, neither the prayers of free Serbs, including the parishioners of St. Nicholas, nor the intercession of Congressman Howard Buffett with Secretary of State Edward Stettinius could save the general. After a mock trial on trumped-up evidence, he was executed by Tito in July 1946.

But Serbs have not forgotten him. Nearly every year since his death, he is remembered in memorial services. In 1951, soon after Vojin arrived, General Momcile Djujich, second-in-command of the *Chetniks*, arrived in Omaha to speak at the church in his honor. Many Serbs, locals as well as from surrounding states, attended a Mass in his memory and heard Djujich praise him.

Nor did the American government forget the general. The government was well aware that many American pilots parachuting into Bosnia after bombing Polesti oil fields were rescued by Mihajlovich and returned to fly again. In 1952, America awarded him the Legion of Merit, posthumously, of course.

Just as Vojin built his parish, so also did he and Nadine augment their family with three children: Gordana, Petar and Miraslava (Mira). In turn, these children have rewarded them with grandchildren, Anna, Mark and Andrea.

In 1954, following study at the University of Omaha, where he also taught evening adult education classes in Russian and German, Vojin received a master of arts degree in sociology and psychology and later became a full professor there. Still later he studied for his doctor of philosophy degree at the University of Kansas.

In addition to the theses for his graduate degrees, Vojin has written four books, three on religious subjects and a fourth, **So Help Me God**, that describes his years before and during World War II.

But his dream was to build a new St. Nicholas Church. He cites several miracles that caused this dream to come true. The first was a bequest from an elderly parishioner which formed the nucleus of a fund, soon enriched by other donations, for the purchase in 1969 of land at Fiftieth and Harrison.

After several more miracles in the form of a load of parishioner generosity, toil and sweat, a community center opened in 1976. During hours off from their regular jobs, the men would literally

Father Vojin and Nadine Dosenovich in front of the new St. Nicholas Serbian Orthodox Church

contribute their labor in the erection of the buildings, while the women organized bake sales, bazaars and bingo.

In 1986 the church building itself was completed. Its architectural style is Serbian Byzantine with the face of Christ, of course, looking down from the overhead dome. The builders have filled its sanctuary with beautiful icons, painted by a Greek artist, and have graced it with a lovely walnut iconostasis, the ornate screen that separates the nave from the altar.

Prominent among the parishioners who have helped build the new church and assembly hall is Joseph Bertich, a church member for eighty-eight years. Long an altar boy, he traveled to many a parishioner's home with the priest when called to bless it. Over the years he has witnessed the devotion of his fellows to St. Nicholas and has shared their trials and triumphs in creating the new buildings.

Another loyal church member, who sings in the choir, is Eli Vukas, born in Omaha of parents who immigrated from a section of Yugoslavia dominated by Hungary. Together with a host of other Serbian-Americans, including Vojin, he tells stories of the difficulties faced by his relatives who remained in Yugoslavia under Tito's rule.

Like many other dreams, a church, estimated at half a million dollars to build, ended up costing more than double that amount. But Vojin and his Serbian community find the new St. Nicholas worth all their toil and every penny they so diligently scraped together for it. They are proud that it is a credit to their city of Omaha.

After all, now they live in America, the land of dreams.

REFERENCES

BOOKS

Andric, Ivo. **The Bridge on the Drina**. Chicago: The University of Chicago Press, 1959.

Larsen, James H. and Barbara J. Cottrell. **The Gate City: A History of Omaha**. Boulder, CO: Pruett Publishing, 1982.

West, Rebecca. **Black Lamb and Grey Falcon: A Journey through Yugoslavia.** Penguin Books, 1941.

INTERVIEWS

Dosenovich, Fr. Vojislav. Taped interview by Harry B. Otis. April 26, 1986.

MAGAZINES

Hart, Philip D. *Omaha's Untouchable—Robert 'Raiding Bob' Samardick*. **Serb World USA**. November/December 1995, pp 52-9.

NEWSPAPERS

Billotte, Bill. *Omaha Serbs Sight Early Belgrade Fall, Long Battle*. April 2, 1941.

Gregg, Sucille. *Orthodox Church Keeps Tradition*. **Sun Newspapers**. December 20, 1979.

McMorris, Robert. *Dream of New Church Fulfilled After 35 Years*. **The Omaha World-Herald**. September 23, 1989.

Serbs

McMorris, Robert. *Single Men from Balkans Often Sought Fortunes Here*. **The Omaha World-Herald**. December 19, 1961.

Mihailovic's Death Stirs Omaha Serbs. **The Omaha World-Herald**. July 17, 1946.

Omaha Serbians Hail Coup as Turning Point in the War. **The Omaha World-Herald**. March 27, 1941.

350,000 Serbs Are Executed. **The Omaha World-Herald**. November 16, 1961.

THE POLES

Over the last thousand years Poland periodically has been devoured by invaders. Essentially a vast plain, her land is surrounded by three principal antagonists: Germany, Russia and Austria. The first two have bit into her from west and east while Austria has gobbled up her Southern Uplands. Only infrequently have these powers left some of her standing as a buffer between them; mostly she has entirely disappeared—at least politically—to pop back up again later like a reinflated balloon.

Thus in 1772 did Catherine the Great of Russia, Frederick the Great of Prussia and the Hapsburg emperor of Austria divide her completely, claiming dominion until the 1919 Versailles Treaty established a Polish republic and restored most of her lands—at least for twenty-two years. Then in 1941, Hitler and Stalin chopped her up again, this time the most mercilessly. Millions of Poles, Jews and non-Jews died in Nazi concentration camps or as slave laborers.

Poland already had been raped and pillaged from the east in 1241 by Genghis Khan's short, fast-riding Mongolian Tartars (to despoil the land); from the west in 1410 by Teutonic knights (to Christianize a country that already had received Christianity); from the north in 1655 by Swedes (to bring Protestantism to a Catholic country); and from the south in 1681 by Turks (to bring the blessings of Islam to infidel Christians).

To help oppose this threat to Christianity, Austria called upon a Polish king, Jan Sobieski, to lead an army of his Poles against these Turkish marauders. Sobieski's efforts proved critical in saving Vienna and all of Western Europe, especially when the Hapsburg emperor chose safety in the West to avoid the fight. The Poles and their king, despised by the Austrians, received little credit for stopping the Turks in their tracks.

Poland fiercely engaged all her adversaries, sometimes winning, sometimes losing. The only constant was the misery bestowed upon the Polish peasants who did the fighting. Their reward would be to

Polish

rebuild the nobles' castles despoiled by the battles and to continue to work the owners' lands. It was said that to each invasion the peasant came with a sword in one hand and a shovel in the other.

These conflicts helped produce a tough, resilient peasant population, from which would emerge in later years Karol Wojtyla, to become Pope John Paul II, and Lech Walesa, to become a labor leader. Both would help free Poland from Soviet domination.

Whether or not foreigners ruled, for centuries her lands were owned by Polish nobles who presided over vast inherited estates. When no foreign power held dominion, the nobility operated through a parliament called the *Seym* under an elected king who, curiously, often was a foreigner from France, Germany or elsewhere. Jealousy among the Polish aristocrats frequently blocked the election of one of their own, a character flaw that usually produced weak kings and ineffectual governments.

To make matters worse, the vote of only one disgruntled member of the *Seym* was enough to dissolve this legislative body and block any move desired by the majority, yet the nobles cherished this *liberum veto*, calling it their golden freedom. Designed to check abuse of political power, its main effect was to stifle valid efforts to defend and strengthen the country.

Thus Poland entered the nineteenth century in a semi-feudal state. Regardless of what neighboring countries held political dominion, the Polish nobles held sway over the people working it. It was almost impossible for a peasant to acquire title to even the small plot he and his ancestors had worked for centuries. In the latter half of the century, they felt an increasing impulse to emigrate, especially when they learned of opportunities open to them in America.

Emigrate they did. Beginning in 1870 they came in great numbers to provide labor for the steel mills in Pittsburgh, Pennsylvania and Gary, Indiana and the packinghouses and railroads in Chicago, Illinois and Omaha, Nebraska. Although their original attraction was the promise of rich farm land they could call their own, they soon found comfort in the steady wages of industry.

When they came to Omaha, they were certain to settle in Sheelytown or later in a smaller South Omaha settlement called Little Poland. Adopting its name from the Sheely Brothers Packing Company at Twenty-seventh and Martha streets, Sheelytown had borders roughly described by Hanscom Park on the north, Frederick Street on the south, Thirty-first Street on the west and Twenty-fourth Street on the east. Union Pacific Railroad tracks running through it were bridged later at Bancroft and Martha streets. Little Poland was bounded by Twenty-fifth, Twenty-ninth, F and L streets.

Mayor Jim Dahlman and Sheelytown "Mayor" Nick Dargaczewski
at a Sheelytown celebration

Many of these early immigrants would find shelter in temporary wooden shacks often erected on city property. Despite low wages, they somehow would find the funds, only a few years later, to build substantial frame houses on lots of their own. Like those of many

Polish

Immaculate Conception, Twenty-fourth and Bancroft streets

other European immigrants, their goals were to own homes free and clear of debt and build churches for the use of their own particular ethnic and religious groups.

Poles found special comfort in a universal love of the Roman Catholic Church. Their lives revolved around it. After worshiping for a time at St. Joseph Church, built by immigrants from Germany in 1891, early Sheelytown residents built St. Paul, a frame church at Twenty-ninth and Elm where they could hear sermons in Polish. When this church burned in 1895, they were back at St. Joseph until they could build another Polish church a few blocks east at Twenty-fourth and Bancroft streets, Immaculate Conception.

For themselves, Little Poland congregations built St. Francis of Assisi Church at Thirty-second and K streets in 1899. As the South Omaha Polish population grew, another South Omaha church arose in 1919, St. Stanislaus at Forty-first and J streets. For a time, sermons in all these churches were preached in Polish as well as English.

A number of societies bolstered the immigrants' morale, among them the Polish Roman Catholic Union, the Polish Union of the United States, the National Alliance, the Pulaski Club, the Polish

Welfare Club and the Polish Citizens' Club. In all these, immigrants found strength and comfort. Polish traditions, customs, folklore, dances and music, handed down from generation to generation, came across the Atlantic and were fostered by these institutions.

Outside of traveling to work, probably to the South Omaha meat packing plants that blossomed in the early days, a Pole needed no goods or services not provided in his immediate district. In Sheelytown, in the mid-1880s, the business district was strung along a five-block stretch of what later was called Twenty-seventh Street. After a few years the main businesses, including three saloons, assorted shops and three dance halls, shifted to Twenty-ninth Street. There also were stores and services to fit every need: drugstores, grocery stores, cobblers, cleaners, shoemakers and schools. Why leave the neighborhood?

Sheelytown even had its own unofficial mayor, Nicodemus (Nick) Dargaczewski, who came to Omaha from the German section of Poland in 1884. A blacksmith shoeing fire department horses, he later became a saloon operator, gaining the favor of the populace by cashing their paychecks. Whether as blacksmith or bartender, when not at work he dressed immaculately in a dark blue suit, white pleated shirt and a white bow tie. With a white flower, usually a carnation, for his buttonhole, his uniform was complete.

Nick Dargaczewski, unofficial mayor of Sheelytown

Nick became an intimate and loyal supporter of the real mayor of Omaha, James C.

249

Polish

Dahlman, a non-Pole who reigned perennially under Tom Dennison's political machine during the first thirty years of the century. Greatly admired by Sheelytown Poles, Dahlman considered the neighborhood his good luck talisman. Every campaign he waged ended up in the district with speeches and free beer.

Sheelytown became an institution. The Irish, who early had lived in the area, were slowly driven out by the Poles, resolute in making it their own turf. Much blood was shed in the fights between the two groups as more and more Poles moved in. Such brawls often enough resulted from Saturday night alcohol-inspired efforts of youthful Poles to block Irish lads from picking up Polish girls. It is said (by Polish spokesmen) that the Poles always prevailed.

Whatever the fact, for many years prior to World War I, no non-resident of Sheelytown, Irish, Pole or otherwise, was allowed to cross into the district through its invisible boundaries without a Sheelytown escort, unless he wanted to risk a loss of blood. The only exception was Mayor Dahlman.

These fights eventually lost their vigor after Officer John J. (Gentleman Jack) Pszanowski, a Polish immigrant, began walking his Sheelytown beat in 1908. He became known as gallant, fearless, tough and for bringing in drunks horizontally. He later served with distinction for twelve years as Omaha chief of police.

If any Sheelytown Polish family might be deemed typical, it would be that of Stanley and Anna Nykiel. Both were immigrants from separate parts of Poland: Stanley Nykiel from Siewertz in the north of Poland and Anna Juchka from Brzoster in the south. They met and married in Omaha.

Stanley had come in 1906 to live in a boardinghouse for young men run by a Kurtz family; Anna came in 1909 to board with Sheelytown's Skoczs. At age twenty-seven, Stanley had a steady sausage-making job with Cudahy; at age twenty, Anna worked in a laundry. Their respective landlords served as matchmakers. There was no prolonged courtship. They soon were wed.

Until their first child came, the couple lived with the Skoczs.

Anna worked fifty hours a week cleaning homes to earn ten dollars; Stanley worked at the packing plant fifty hours a week to earn twenty dollars. Anna worked in part to save money to bring her two sisters to Omaha from Poland. They eventually arrived, allowing Anna to quit her employment outside of the home.

A short while after their marriage, when their first child was on the way, the Nykiels found a suitable house right in the middle of Sheelytown at Twenty-ninth Street and Bancroft.

Stanley and Anna Nykiel

During the next eighteen years Anna would deliver nine children in this home, seven of them with only the aid of a midwife.

As with most Polish immigrants, the church played a most important part in Anna's life. Although her parish was Immaculate Conception at Twenty-fourth and Bancroft, five blocks east of her home, Anna never missed a day at church. It was virtually her only relief from the drudgery of child-rearing and housework, to walk over the Bancroft Street bridge crossing the railroad tracks to the haven of the church where she could worship God and chat a while with her friends.

As for Stanley, after a long day at the packing plant he felt it was his right to stop at a few taverns on his way home for several beers with his coworkers. No matter the weather and despite the availability of a streetcar, he always walked. He took the route of

Polish

Dahlman Avenue that, in the early days, was only a dirt trail leading from Sheelytown to the stockyards. It became dotted with bars. The carfare money saved could buy Stanley an extra beer or two. Such was his social life.

Ever a loyal factory worker and company man, Stanley was rewarded early by being moved from the sausage department to the casing branch. This paid a little more money but afforded working conditions not much better than the old ones. The fact that much salt was involved with the stuffing process eventually led to skin problems for both Stanley and his coworkers. Although the company provided gloves, the employees didn't use them. Gloves slowed the work. Salt began to eat away at Stanley's skin, and in 1938, after thirty years of service, the company gave him a disability retirement and a small pension.

In the meanwhile, the care of the home and children was left to Anna, to whom Stanley faithfully delivered his weekly paycheck. So also did the children. Until the day they left the home for good, the money they earned from various odd jobs went to her. To maintain the large family, especially during the periods of hard times such as the Depression days, it took everyone's contribution, plus a vegetable garden and a flock of chickens.

Although the Nykiel children were taught to be proud of their Polish heritage and Polish was the language spoken in the home, Anna encouraged their Americanization. With only a third grade education in Poland and having had to learn on her own how to read and write enough English and Polish to get by, she knew how important schooling was for her offspring. They all attended parochial school at Immaculate Conception. Most got through eighth grade; some through high school; and one, Anthony, went on to higher education in a seminary.

The children were keenly aware of their Polish heritage, not only through their family and church, but also through community contacts. All the shops, whatever their nature, were operated by Polish-speaking Poles. Thus there was little rubbing elbows with other ethnic groups, such as the Czechs, or with other Omahans.

Anthony Nykiel recalls his Polish youth. Regardless of St. Adalbert Catholic Church being located only one block from his home, for church or school he and his siblings had to walk the five blocks over the bridge to Immaculate Conception. This church was Polish, and St. Adalbert was for Czechs, his mother told him.

Anthony also attests to the integrity of Sheelytown. First, it was unthinkable that anyone not of Polish descent should date a Sheelytown girl. But even when Anthony's sister, Sophie, was being courted by her future husband, himself a Pole but from Little Poland and therefore a foreigner to Sheelytown, to assure his arrival at his girlfriend's house with an unbloodied nose, Anthony's father or brothers would have to meet him at the outskirts of the district and escort him to the Nykiel residence. In any event, the courtship was successful. The couple married.

Today Polish weddings have a reputation for being both joyous and long-lasting. In days before World War I, they often would last a very long time. To begin with, days before the wedding, menfolk in the bride's neighborhood would join forces to build a large dance floor in the backyard of her parents' home. At the same time, their wives would prepare all manner of foodstuffs for the wedding party.

Following the nuptial Mass, the guests slowly would arrive at the bride's home to be greeted at the front door, first by a small group of musicians with a song, and then by the bride and groom with a glass of wine or a shot of spirits. Then the guests would go into the dining room for a bite to eat before going down to the basement for something more to drink.

The wedding party would proceed in earnest when the invitees, now more comfortable, would begin to climb to the backyard to dance to the music of the orchestra assembled next to the dance floor. As the hours went by and the crowd grew merrier with polkas, *schottisches* and waltzes, neighbor children would show up, until bribed to disappear, to tease the bride and groom with a *chivaree*.

Polish

Polish dancers at St. Stanislaus Church, 1993

Everybody would continue to eat, drink and dance until the small hours of the morning. Nobody wanted to go home.

Some of these weddings would last for three or four days. Men would go to work while the women cooked some more food. Then the wedding party would start all over again the next evening.

When Prohibition came in the 1920s, it naturally took the edge off the exuberance of these affairs and, indeed, of much of Polish social life. Yet such was the public scorn of the Prohibition laws, that otherwise law-abiding persons began both manufacturing and consuming illicit liquor. Despite the strenuous still-smashing efforts of agents such as Robert Samardick, a zealous federal enforcer of the liquor laws, Omaha bootleggers everywhere began satisfying the public demand for the product. Anna Nykiel was one of them.

Anna was twice raided but never apprehended. Her loyal customers, all Poles, would tip her off as to any impending raid. She hid her still in a flour barrel which, when its top was removed, revealed flour but not the distilling apparatus lying below a false bottom. When the raiders left, production went on. Anna's husband and children would find the grain and the necessary empty bottles, and she would make the illicit fluid. All during the dark days of the

Depression, the Nykiel family eked out a living partly by selling her product at fifty cents a pint to thankful customers.

In the years following World War II, in order to insure its receipt, Anna similarly would hide American money in cans of flour and coffee she sent to impoverished relatives in Poland.

Like most children, the Nykiel youngsters loved Christmas the most of any season. It brought with it events such as the mysterious appearance of the Christmas tree on Christmas morning and the silent arrival of St. Nicholas the night before. It also brought traditions peculiarly Polish. Along with many other Polish families, the Nykiels celebrated a special one.

One of the younger children, going outdoors, returned to report the first star he saw shining in the night sky. At this point all the children knelt by a table where their father, also kneeling, led them in prayer. Arising, they proceeded to the dinner table for a meatless supper, which had been prepared by their mother, consisting always of nine, eleven or thirteen courses of simple dishes. There might be fish, peas, sauerkraut, bread and mushrooms.

Before eating, however, each one was handed, one after the other, a large, communion-like wafer from which he broke off three little pieces. As he received it, the passer wished him health, wealth and happiness and, further, anything else he wanted to. Anna often bid Anthony health, wealth and happiness and "to be a good boy."

In time Polish-Americans got to fight real battles. As reported by Robert McMorris in an October 22, 1961, article in the **Omaha World-Herald**, in 1940 there were about fifteen thousand persons of Polish extraction living in Douglas County, most of these in the two Polish districts referred to earlier. All of these proved to be true patriots, expressing their love for their adopted country by military service during World War II and by otherwise helping Uncle Sam in war-oriented jobs such as those provided by the Martin Bomber Plant at Fort Crook.

By 1960, the Polish population had increased to eighteen thousand, including two hundred who had immigrated since the

Polish

war as displaced persons. By then the intense concentration of Poles in Sheelytown and Little Poland had dissipated, leaving only the vestiges of what had been. The Sheelytown Tavern remained, its name visible to motorists on Interstate Highway 480 that was paved right through the district during the 1960s.

By 1960, Polish-Americans lived throughout the city and had careers in all businesses and professions.

Though now thoroughly Americanized, they are proud that their ancestors came from a country with a glorious history of world-famous heroes. Yet they are prouder still that their ancestors were incomparable survivors.

REFERENCES

BOOKS

Karnash, John Edward. *History of the Omaha Poles*. In **The Souvenir Book of the Grand Opening of the Polish Home**. Omaha: The Polish Home, 1937.

Larsen, Lawrence H. and Barbara J. Cottrell. **The Gate City: A History of Omaha**. Boulder, CO: Pruett Publishing, 1982.

Mitchner, James A. **Poland**. New York: Random House, 1983.

INTERVIEWS

Nykiel, Tony. Taped interview by Harry B. Otis. March 3, 1998.

NEWSPAPERS

McMorris, Robert. *Poles Introduce Three Day Weddings to Adopted City*. **The Omaha World-Herald**. October 22, 1961.

THE SWEDES

John stepped out of his office into the fresh air, the better to admire the red and white sign on his new brick building: ENGDAHL TOP AND BODY COMPANY. The backdrop of an azure sky stopped him in his tracks. "Red, white and blue," he said. "The good old USA!" How America had blessed him since he had come from his native Sweden, *"Det gamla landet."*

He remembered as a little boy starting his walk to school with his sister, Frieda, lingering down the old country lane on just such a March day back in Skane.

He could see his mother standing on the stone stoop of their yellow clapboard farm house, bidding her children goodbye. "Bundle, bundle, no colds tonight," she shouted, as her braided yellow hair and white smock waved in the fresh breeze.

Turning down the lane, the youngsters could see all the buildings of their little farm. The rays of the morning sun, glancing off the windows of their little home, shimmering like a lake, made it seem dearer than ever. As they passed the red barn by the road along the split wood fence, they could hear their father's horses whinny from their stalls.

As the wind picked up and blew dust and dirt along the way, John wrapped his scarf around his neck and took Frieda's hand. He started to run, an invitation to a footrace. Freeing her hand, Frieda pulled away, her gray bloomers flapping in the wind, and soon outdistanced him. The heavy, rough hide of John's leather boots chafed at his calves and slowed him down. "Anyway, Frieda could always beat me in a footrace," he said to himself.

Their one-room schoolhouse was only two kilometers away from home, very near the manor where their father worked as a groom in the Count Ingelstad's stables. John and his brother had done heavy labor there during the summer. Today he was glad to be going to school. He loved it much more than tending horses. He was eager to learn new things.

Swedes

As Frieda and he turned up a hill toward their schoolhouse, the honking of geese caused them to twist around and follow the flock in the blue sky. As they shouted, "Go! Go!" at their favorite birds, John remembered dropping his lunch bag of bread, cheese and milk that he luckily rescued from a ditch. A call from the schoolhouse ended the fun.

As his childhood dream faded, he entered his new building, thanking God for all his blessings.

* * * *

John Engdahl

John and Frieda were born John and Frieda Nelson, changing their name to Engdahl only when they came to America. There were many Johns and Friedas in Sweden in 1897, the day these two went to school. Thousands of them. And many were destined to travel to America where they could use this book-learning to their advantage. Thousands of others had preceded them to the New World, to work on the railroads and in the fields and factories, to provide the muscle a growing America needed.

In time, many came to Omaha. In 1900, out of thousands of foreign born, 3,968 came from Sweden. In contrast, 5,522 came from Germany, 2,430 from Denmark, 2,164 from Ireland and less than 2,000 from all other European countries.

By 1910, the year John Engdahl arrived in Omaha at the age of twenty, the Swedish population numbered 8,024, counting both foreign-born and those born in America of Swedish parents.

Good, early schooling in Sweden assured all Swedish immigrants a ready acceptance in America and put them a cut ahead of those coming from poorer countries with little or no literacy. Nevertheless, as unfamiliar with English as the others, the Swede almost always had to start with a common laboring job, perhaps working for a street or building contractor, a packinghouse or as a teamster. If he had a trade, as John Engdahl did, a shop or factory job often was available. Many Swedish men worked for the Union Pacific in its railroad shops; Swedish women ordinarily found jobs as domestics, where their services were gratefully received.

America would welcome John, but only after a series of experiences in Sweden that shaped his later career.

Together with one brother and three sisters, John was reared on a three-acre plot of ground in a place called Ingelstads Engar, whose post office was Smedsterup. This was near the city of Malmo in the province of Skane in Southern Sweden near the Baltic Sea. Despite cold winters, the area's climate was much more temperate than Northern Sweden. The gentle rolling coastal plains produced bountiful crops; the nearby coastal waters, plentiful fish.

While never hungry, the Nelsons were not well-to-do. To survive, everyone had to do his share, including the children, who even made their own toys to play with. In the summers all of them worked at the nearby Ingelstad Manor: John and his older brother, Nils, as stable hands, and their three sisters in the manor house as domestics.

Sunday, however, found all of them walking with their parents to the ancient Lutheran church located a half mile from the manor. From the sanctuary a flower-strewn cemetery stretched down to a pretty lake bordered with stands of beech trees sprinkled with ash and linden. Inside the church, the Nelson family found seats in the middle on worn wooden benches. The count and his family sat on the right front, close to the raised pulpit, in boxed pews decorated with golden trim and the Ingelstad family crest. Solemn decorum was always the order of the day.

Whenever possible during the summer, the Nelsons would swim on Baltic beaches near the coastal cities. Other joys were a mid-summer festival, one of the great annual Swedish events, and the annual raising of the maypole at the manor, celebrating the continuity of life.

When John was thirteen his mother developed a severe, incapacitating case of arthritis. Together with Frieda, he quit school to help care for her and support the household. He never returned to school.

A year or so later, John served a one-year apprenticeship with a shoemaker in the town of Loderup, followed by a three-year term with a harness maker. During this period, some friends enticed Frieda to join them in emigrating to the New World, specifically, Omaha.

Hohngren the harness maker, a bachelor who lived down by the sea with a cousin as caretaker, kept his shop in his home. John and another apprentice found lodging in the loft of a nearby barn and received excellent meals at one dollar a week from a woman whose husband had been lost at sea.

During their apprenticeship, the boys became experts in harness-making and the craft of upholstery and developed sufficient skills to be sent directly to farmers' homes for furniture work. The warm reception given them by their customers, who treated them as craftsmen, enhanced their self-confidence. Along the way, John's brother also gave them work. In his Loderup cabinet firm, Nils made all kinds of furniture, some needing their upholstery talents.

In 1909, proudly armed with a diploma of master of upholstery, John traveled to Jenarp, a short distance from Malmo. Frieda was home for a holiday after a five-year stay in America. The invitation to return with her to Omaha stimulated John's wanderlust. She would teach him all the English he needed. John decided for the New World.

A dismal and seasick trip across a rough North Sea brought them to Grimsby, England, and thence to Liverpool for a five-day trip to the United States. Their ocean ship was the *Mauritania,* and their voyage this time was pleasant and enjoyable. In New York they had to go through customs to be examined as to how much money they had. John had to have twenty-five dollars. He met the test.

It was here that Frieda convinced her brother to change his name. The family name of Nelson was too common, said she. Why not adopt Engdahl, the name of a well-known Swedish harness maker? John agreed. It was easy to convince the American immigration official to write his new name on his papers: John Sigfried Nelson Engdahl.

Twelve of his hard-earned hoard of dollars produced a three-day train trip to Omaha from New York City. John felt the usual amazement of Europeans at the utter immensity of the country. Taking nearly as long as their ocean voyage, the trip required changing trains five times. At last they were greeted by Frieda's Omaha friends, the Fritz Carlsons, who welcomed them into their own home.

During the trip John had practiced his English, learning phrases from Frieda. Later, with the help of new Swedish friends, his conversational English took off. Little by little he became comfortable with the new language.

Dreaming of one day founding his own business, he worked for a variety of employers. Following thirty days as an upholsterer with a fellow immigrant named Peterson, he labored three months for Keys Brothers Luggage Factory making luggage tops. Then he was hired by Omaha Auto Top Company at Fifteenth and Jones which, after a year, sent him to open a company branch in Sioux City, Iowa.

John Engdahl was a frugal man and regularly saved his money, but he was not yet willing to settle down. Despite his good work experience, his wanderlust compelled him to see as much of this new America as he could.

Inevitably he traveled to Los Angeles where his sister Frieda now had found work as a domestic for a family in Pasadena, California. A job John found with an automobile top firm lasted only six months. He was laid off when business slowed.

It was 1912. Now he had enough confidence and sufficient capital to start his own business: an auto top shop with a used car trade on the side. This he ran successfully for four years, waiting for his wanderlust to cool. It didn't. At age twenty-two he owned a business, a parcel of Los Angeles real estate and had a five thousand dollar bank account; yet he was dissatisfied. Selling out, he got ready to see more of America.

When his friend Fritz Carlson, Jr. summoned him to Kansas City to be the best man in his wedding, John was off and running. Following the wedding, he traveled again, this time to visit a friend in Chicago, then his sister Frieda, who was now married and living on a farm in Wisconsin, and finally, the city of Minneapolis.

While in Minnesota, a telegram from the owner of Omaha Auto Top Company summoned him for help. He was to take over running the company while the man convalesced from an illness. Although restless to start another business of his own, he stayed with this employer for several years.

Events now dispelled the wanderlust. He acquired a new car, a Model T Ford, and a new girl friend, Olga. Joining the recently organized Trinity Lutheran Church at Twenty-fifth and Ames, he became a member of the choir. Olga was the church organist. One thing led to another. After a few rides home from choir practice in John's Model T, Olga accepted his offer of marriage.

The wedding in Trinity Church took place in June 1917. After a brief honeymoon, the couple returned to Omaha to reside in Florence with Olga's parents, the Pearsons.

Now was definitely the time for John's own Omaha business to open. He set up a shop with a partner in a building at Eighteenth and Harney. They did quite well until construction of a building next door caused their own premises to develop cracks. A building inspector required them to move.

In any event, the business could not support two families. John's partner chose to sell out. So John opened a temporary shop at 1718 Cass and made ready to build his own building at Eighteenth and California.

In 1921, he proudly moved into his permanent business home, a new brick building housing Engdahl Top and Body Company

Olga Engdahl

with its red and white sign. Here he would operate for more than sixty years.

The auto repair business had changed dramatically since John first started installing inside upholstery and auto tops. Cars now came with totally enclosed metal bodies. When careless new drivers caused frequent collisions, the lack of availability of separate body parts meant that he often had to rebend, braise, sand and repaint the original. Nevertheless, his cars came out looking like new. This wholly different trade required investment in new tools and machinery, but frugal John was up to the challenge.

People from all walks of life became his customers. Dressed in a suit with a nice tie, he greeted upset car owners daily in his front office, his pleasant demeanor calming their distress. Throughout the years his ability to fix their damaged cars, always their pride and joy, made him hundreds of friends.

Only once did he lose his temper with a customer. A man appeared at the shop one day to pick up an estimate of accident

Swedes

Engdahl Top and Body Company, Eighteenth and California streets

damage for his insurance company. He complained that John had failed to list a certain item of damage. When John informed him that it didn't arise out of the accident, the customer said: "List it anyway. No one will ever know that." Furious, John threw the man out the door, telling him never to return.

His growing reputation for integrity had a positive effect on adjusters of insurance claims who never hesitated to recommend his company to their policy holders. His dependability brought him many loyal customers and lasting friendships.

John really was no different from hundreds of other persons of Swedish descent who came to Omaha to live and work and create businesses. Many of such companies, firmly established, that founders or descendants run today include: Olson Bros., sheet metal; Grunwald, plumbing; Bloom, sash and door; Bloom, monuments; Larson, cement stone; Swanson, clothing; Jerpe, produce; Swanson, produce; Swanson, blueprints; and Lindwall, construction. There are many more.

Swedes

In the 1935 edition of **The Swedish Element in Omaha**, the author, O.M. Nelson, after stating that Omaha persons of Swedish descent in that year numbered fifteen thousand, asserts:

The natural inclination and adaptability of the Swedes for acquiring the language and ways of the people with whom they comingle have enabled the Swedish immigrants to become Americanized more quickly than most foreigners, causing their outward racial characteristics to disappear more rapidly, while their moral and intellectual heritage is passed on to their descendants down several generations.

Despite such rapid Americanization, all Swedes, especially recent arrivals, were hungry for news printed in their native tongue. Almost from the beginning, in the 1860s, a Swedish press appeared to fill this need. For one hundred years many Swedish language newspapers circulated in Omaha and out-state, only to fade away as time passed and Swedes more and more adopted English.

Like most other Omaha ethnic groups, immigrant Swedes tended to band together. While some spread throughout the city, many resided near Twentieth on streets north of Cuming. There they lived along with many other ethnic groups: Irish, German, Jewish, Polish, black and Italian. Children of all such nationalities gathered in public schools or met in social and sporting events with those attending parochial schools. There was little friction.

Outside of their homes, Swedish social life centered in the church, usually Lutheran, but Methodist and Baptist as well. One of the first churches created to accommodate immigrants was Immanuel Swedish Evangelical Lutheran Church, incorporated in 1874. Salem Lutheran followed in 1883, Zion Lutheran in 1902 and Bethel Lutheran in 1915.

That same year, 1915, saw the newly organized Trinity Lutheran, the Engdahls' church, find a home in a building at Twenty-fifth and Ames. Then, in 1920, its members erected its present sanctuary

Swedes

at Thirtieth and Redick Avenue. Olga Engdahl played the organ at its first service.

Immigrant Swedes also established other solid institutions. One of these was the Immanuel Deaconess Institute. Patterned after similar societies of mercy in Sweden and Germany, the institute erected its first hospital during the 1920s north of Ames, building at the same time housing for the aged, nurses, children and invalids. More recently, its activities concern a new Immanuel Medical Center with ancillary functions at Seventy-second and Sorensen Parkway.

Swedish folk dancers

Swedes early formed other societies that have endured to this day. A notable example is the Noonday Scandinavian Club (originally the Noonday Club), that was created in 1909 and has ever remained "A Patriotic and Public-Spirited American Organization of Omaha Business and Professional Men of

Scandinavian Birth or Descent Dedicated to Public Service and the Promotion of Acquaintance and Good-Fellowship Among Its Members." Its membership is open to both men and women and even to loyal non-Scandinavian admirers.

Obviously the Noonday Club, as it continues to be called, embraces all Scandinavians: Danish, Norwegian, Finnish, as well as Swedish. These nationalities may disagree with each other from time to time, yet on one thing they do concur. It is fun to meet with other Scandinavians. Its members have even been known to toast one another with a glass or two of *aquavit* or *glüg*.

The Noonday Club is the oldest civic organization in Omaha. Many prominent Omahans have presided over it, including John Engdahl during the 1938-39 term. Two of his sons, Falton and Don, served later. During more than eighty years of monthly meetings, it has hosted diverse speakers, including Prince Bertil of Sweden and Charlie McCarthy, whose mentor was Edgar Bergen, Candice Bergen's father.

John and Olga didn't live with the Pearsons for long. Over the next ten years they moved from house to house, always in North Omaha where Olga bore baby after baby: Falton, Wallace, Donald, Beverly, Rodney, Herbert and Stewart. Only the last three were delivered in Immanuel Hospital.

Even if the family changed houses, it never changed its church. During the 1930s, Sunday would find Olga upstairs preparing each child for Sunday School, while downstairs John fed each descending child a sandwich made from a freshly baked *bolla* (a Swedish roll), a glass of juice and a cup of coffee. Then it was off to Trinity for Sunday School in a Packard with jump seats, where John taught and Olga played the piano. Formal church services followed, attended by all.

Home from church, the family ate a Sunday dinner that Olga had cooked in advance on Saturday and Sunday morning. Always invited were John's sister Frieda and her husband. Nellie Hughes, an Irish girl whose husband worked for the Engdahl company, served the assemblage. Over a period of sixteen years, Nellie virtually became a member of the family. Upon her death, the six Engdahl boys served as pallbearers.

On Sunday evenings John might take the family for a ride, six children in the back seats, John in the front with Olga holding Stewart. Any continuing noise from the rear would invite a sweep of John's right arm, which might or might not contact one of the offenders, but always accomplished its desired effect. Part of the ride involved a stop for treats, ice cream and root beer.

As every Depression family did, the Engdahls made their own fun. Of an evening, school homework done, the children would often pop corn or make fudge while John read his newspaper and Olga darned socks.

Then came Christmas. As with most people of Swedish heritage, Christmas was half religious, half secular. Without fail the whole family went to Trinity's midnight service on Christmas Eve, but not before consuming a hearty Christmas feast created by one great Swedish cook.

For weeks in advance, Olga had prepared the special Christmas Eve smorgasbord for her family. At the dinner hour the assembled Engdahls, their friends and relatives first were offered hor d'oeuvres of *marinerad stromming* (marinated sardines), *ansjovis gratin* (anchovies au gratin), *stekt svamp* (sauteed mushrooms) and *fylida agghalvor* (stuffed eggs). Next came *griljerad skinka* (baked ham) or *kokt lax* (boiled salmon), accompanied by *flask-och kalvsylta* (jellied pork and veal), *inlagda rodbetor* (pickled beets), *gronsalad* (mixed green salad) and *korv* (potato sausage). Sometimes they had *flaskkorv mit bruna boner* (pork sausage and brown beans). Always they had rye bread *bollas*, freshly baked.

All this must have challenged their attention during the following midnight church service.

Christmas morning was present-passing time. Like all children, the seven Engdahls reveled in the openings and were overjoyed when something special appeared, like a new bike.

As the years wore on, John and Olga saw to it that each of their children had the opportunity for advanced education. This led to admirable careers in medicine, accounting and business. In addition, as their sons reached manhood, those physically able to do so served in the military of their country, both in war and peace.

Although John never neglected his business, he devoted himself to Omaha in many time-consuming ways. Most important was his twenty-two-year service on the Omaha School Board, which he presided over for three years. When asked why he stayed for so long a time, he replied: "I've had seven children in the school system. I ought to do something in return for all that."

Along the way he received from the Swedish government The Royal Order of Oslo, the highest civilian award the King could deliver.

But his greatest thrill came in 1963 when Nebraska named his beloved Olga Mother of the Year and when, a few months later, she received the coveted title, National Mother of the Year. "He was one proud Swede," says son Donald.

What John really felt is perhaps reflected in a **New York Times** picture of Olga standing with John who holds a banner that reads: "He says she's the nicest girl in town."

Swedes

REFERENCES

BOOKS

Larsen, James H. and Barbara J. Cottrell. **The Gate City: A History of Omaha**. Boulder, CO: Pruett Publishing, 1982 .

Lund, L. Dale and Reuben T. Swanson, editors. **Swedish Omaha Past and Present**. Omaha: Swedish Cultural Committee, 1914.

Nelson, O. M. **The Swedish Element in Omaha**. Omaha: Morell Printers, 1935.

INTERVIEWS

Engdahl, Donald. Taped interview by Donald H. Erickson and Harry B. Otis. October 21, 1996.

MISCELLANEOUS

Engdahl, John Seigfried Nelson. Autobiographical sketch.

THE DANES

What young girl would *not* want to grow up in her parents' boardinghouse with twenty Danish uncles, even if they weren't real ones? Reared by such a family during the 1920s, Ruth Thorup reveled in it.

Even though the men were only her folks' immigrant roomers and boarders, their appearance and speech qualified them as uncles. Their rugged physiques, blonde hair and sky-blue eyes were just like those of her Danish mother, Mathilde, and most spoke only Danish around the house or, at best, uttered any English words with Danish accents. Most importantly, they adored Ruth and her brother, Roy, and tried to spoil them.

Thorup family cutout at the Durham Western Heritage Museum

Both of their parents had immigrated to America from Denmark after the turn of the century. Their father, Marinus Thorup, came in 1911 from Aalborg, Jutland; their mother, Mathilde Kirstine Jorgens Pedersen, in 1917 from Nyborg, Fyn. Like many fellow Danes, Marinus emigrated to escape peacetime conscription; Mathilde to earn cash necessary to open a confectioner's shop on a return home. Fate brought them together.

After living for a time in Mt. Hewitt, Pennsylvania, where aunts, uncles and cousins galore greeted him,

Danes

Marinus moved to Omaha to live with an older brother. There, in 1917, he found a military cause he did believe in, fighting Germany. Joining the American army, he trained for battle, and while so engaged, requested and received naturalization as a foreign-enlistee. He fought in France with the American Expeditionary Force as a proud new American citizen.

In the meantime, Mathilde arrived in Philadelphia to stay with a sister and work in the Edison Rifle Plant. One day she spotted a notice in the city's Danish newspaper placed there by Marinus and some of his overseas buddies. They sought penpals. Mathilde decided to be Marinus's correspondent.

Returning from the war, Marinus hied himself to Philadelphia to meet his writer friend. It didn't take him long to persuade her to return with him to Omaha. There she could find work as readily as in Philadelphia, he told her.

She found more than work, she found a husband. Amidst the dust and rubble of extensive remodeling of Our Savior's Danish Lutheran Church, where the delicately carved figure of Christ had to be covered with a drop cloth, Pastor V.S. Jessen married the couple in the presence of Danish friends.

There was little chance to celebrate after the ceremony. Weeks in the watery muck of France had severely damaged Marinus's health with swamp fever. His energy was sapped. How would they live while he was recovering? The couple found a rental home at Twenty-fifth and St. Mary's Avenue where they could establish a boardinghouse for Danish immigrants.

The house venture was successful; immigrants filled it most of the time. On *Julesaften*, Christmas Eve, 1920, Ruth was born. Exactly a year and one-half later, Roy blessed the family.

By 1923, a much larger house was called for. Marinus and Mathilde were able to buy one they found at 1117 Park Avenue. With the help of Danish artisans and with their own hands, they remodeled fireplaces and ripped out stained glass windows to make it functional for tenants.

Though the dwelling accommodating the Thorup family and fourteen roomers generally was fully occupied, sometimes hungry men showed up from other rooms in the neighborhood to eat at Mathilde's table. As many as twenty guests might sit down to a meal. The landlords and their children ate later.

When vacancies occurred, they were filled by the recommendations of friends, or the Danish owners of pool halls where young immigrants congregated. Most of the time there was a waiting list, those who roomed in the neighborhood having first chance at an empty bed.

Who were these guests of the Thorups, and where did they come from? Most of them were Danes around twenty-five years of age and hailing from all parts of their native land. They were the descendants of Scandinavians, the stocky rough-hewn Vikings who inhabited modern-day Denmark, Sweden and Norway and who, twelve centuries earlier with long boat and ax, had invaded and ravaged all the lands bordering the Baltic and North Seas and Northern France.

Eventually these pillagers became occupiers of the lands they had invaded. In time they melded with the native races to become part of new independent nations. A thousand years later, Scandinavians again set out for foreign lands, primarily for the United States of America. This time, however, they came as invitees, not conquerors, again to eventually merge with the existing populace as a part of a great new nation and the thriving city of Omaha, Nebraska.

Between 1850 and 1914, three hundred thousand Danes emigrated to the United States. The decade of the 1880s saw 88,132 enter. At least seventy percent of these immigrants were of the laboring class, mostly farm workers. The second largest group consisted of domestic and industrial workers, while the balance consisted of craftsmen such as smiths, joiners, bricklayers, carpenters and bakers. All of these groups provided the Thorups with tenants.

Danes

Earlier, during the 1860s after the Civil War, some Danes settled in Eastern Nebraska from the states of Iowa and Illinois. Those who chose to live in Omaha took jobs with the Union Pacific and related industries, while others grew grain, worked in dairies or raised cattle and swine for the Omaha packinghouses.

There was no Danish neighborhood in Omaha; the Danes lived everywhere. Although a Lutheran church had been organized as early as 1874, four years later it merged into Our Savior's Danish Lutheran Church, first at Nineteenth and St. Mary's Avenue and later at 819 South Twenty-second Street, to become the principal place of worship for those Danes who resided on the south side of Omaha. In 1886, the Synod headquartered in Blair organized Pella Lutheran at Thirtieth and Corby streets for north-side residents.

Some early Danes were prominent professional people. Dr. H.C. Jessen was one. Arriving in 1869, he built a fashionable residence at Twelfth and Jackson. His granddaughter, Rubie Jessen, later would live in Dundee and retire in 1961 as a Benson High School English teacher. Rubie was Danish on both sides. Her maternal grandfather, Hans Peter Sorensen, in 1867 chose to build a house for his wife and family "way out in the country" at Twenty-third and Cass, on Capitol Hill. One day, his wife came into her dining room to find an Omaha Indian sitting at her table drinking her soup. "Heap good!" he said as he left the house.

Another Danish doctor, who came to America in the 1860s and to Omaha in the 1880s, was James Borglum. His son, Gutzon, after attending Omaha High School and Creighton University, studied art in Paris. Lasting fame came to Gutzon Borglum with the creation of the four great stone faces of American presidents at the Mount Rushmore National Monument in South Dakota.

A Danish descendant who served Omaha with great distinction as its mayor during the turmoil of the 1960s was Al Sorensen. His firm leadership and quiet patience helped slake fiery unrest, while his vision inspired the erection of the new city-county building.

The most successful of Omaha's many Danish-born bakers, P.F.

A.V. Sorensen, Omaha mayor 1965-1969

Petersen, had a tough life when he came to America in 1882. After many jobs, he opened a one-man bakery at Twenty-fourth and Cuming. Following his marriage in 1891, his wife became his retail staff and his business prospered. Peter Pan bread became one of Omaha's favorite loaves.

Danes seem to love the dairy business. Frank Lawson, former Danish vice-counsel and secretary and counsel of the Danish Brotherhood, estimated that in 1908 when he came to Omaha, about seventy-five percent of the city's dairy industry was controlled by Danish-Americans. There were a lot of little ones; however, they proved too small to keep up with changes in the industry. By 1961 there remained only Joseph P. Moeller's Alamito Dairy, Grobeck Dairy in South Omaha and that of George E. Sorensen.

Like similar emigres from other European countries, the Danes left home for adventure, escape from economic hardship and desire for political and religious freedom. More specifically, it was Denmark's rapid population growth, the result of the Industrial Revolution of the nineteenth century, that caused them to move out. Denmark's population more than doubled during the nineteenth century. The rural economy was unable to accommodate such an explosion.

Furthermore, a Danish conflict with Germany played a clear role in fostering emigration. Until 1864, the provinces of Holstein and Schleswig, located south of mainland Denmark and bordering

Danes

Germany, held a mixed population of Danes and Germans, and were linked with Denmark through a personal union with the Danish crown. In that year Prussia and Austria jointly wrested away those ethnically and linguistically mixed areas.

The shadow of militant Prussia fell on the Danes who were ripe for conscription into the German army. This alone caused sixty thousand of them to leave North Schleswig (returned to Denmark after World War II) during the first forty years after the annexation, mostly to flee to the United States.

Census statistics note that in 1890 Iowa with 15,519 and Nebraska with 14,345 were the two largest largest Danish-born populations, Omaha claiming a large proportion of Nebraska's figure.

A front page box of the **Danish Pioneer,** published July 4, 1882, contained the opening words of the Declaration of Independence. Reading these, a young employee of a Copenhagen printing office, Sophus Neble, decided America was for him. He took off for Omaha where he eventually met Mark Hansen and bought the newspaper. Sophus and his family continued its publication until 1958, when it was moved to Chicago.

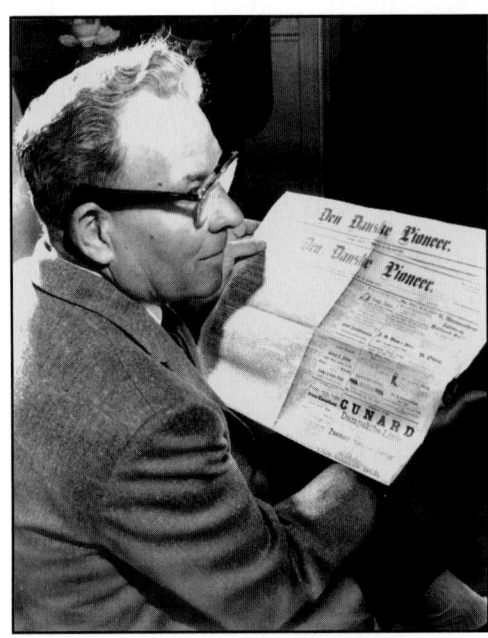

*Sophus Neble and the **Danish Pioneer***

In another first for Omaha, the Danish Brotherhood of America was created in 1882 from an immigrant insurance company. Originally a veterans' support group, it later was opened to all. Omaha was selected as national headquarters. It soon became the largest secular society for Danish immigrants and still is thriving today.

Danish immigrants of the 1880s had the opportunity to see plays performed in Danish at Washington Hall at Eighteenth and Harney, at the Swedish Auditorium on Sixteenth Street north of Dodge and at Bohemian Hall at Thirteenth and William. They also attended dances at these halls. When they ran out of things to do, they would run down to the depot and watch new Danes come in. Immigrants would appear on nearly every train. They could spot them immediately.

Omaha also saw the creation of small local and regional associations to serve musical, athletic, literary and other interests. The arts were not neglected. In 1869 from Denmark came Ernest Nordin who became one of Omaha's most influential musicians. At age sixteen he played the violin in a Copenhagen casino; at age twenty he arrived in Omaha to get a job in the pit orchestra of the Boyd Theater. Soon he became the orchestra's director. One of the two organizers of the Omaha Symphony in the 1920s, he was named its assistant conductor.

In the 1920s, the Danes created Vennelyst Park north of Florence, a twenty-one-acre site, for the eventual establishment of a Danish retirement home. They also founded the Danish American Club where every year they celebrate *Grunlobsdag* (Constitution Day). On May 20, 1976, Governor Exon proclaimed Danish American Day in honor of Queen Margarethe of Denmark, who was visiting Nebraska on the occasion of our nation's Bicentennial.

Thus, by the time the Thorups arrived, Danes were firmly established in Omaha. After regaining his health, Marinus eventually found work with the Union Pacific as a steamfitter's helper, while continuing to help Mathilde with their rooming house enterprise. The work was rigorous and unending.

Since the boarders took a Danish lunch to work with them, Mathilde rose at five A.M. to prepare *smorrebrod* (pumpernickel), *rullepolse* (roast beef or pork), *roskilde landevej* (cold cuts), cheese and eggs, wrapping all in waxed paper and then in newspaper to be handed to the men on their way to work. Marinus helped get breakfast for all, *havregrod* (oatmeal), cornflakes, eggs, bacon and pancakes, before slipping upstairs to make the beds before leaving for work himself at seven A.M.

Mathilde served up the breakfast and then, after the men had departed, tackled the dishes, cleaning, laundry, baking, meal planning and food preparation, plus caring for two children. Her boarders ate well. She baked all her pies and cakes from scratch. No one complained of her *rodkal, Fleskestej, firikadeller* or other goodies. She always served desserts: Jell-O, puddings and fruit, in addition to the pastries.

Endless quantities of sheets and towels, all boiled before being placed in the washing machine, billowed weekly from the clotheslines that Mathilde strung in the front, side and backyards of the house. The roomers' personal laundry, however, she gave to the Kimball Laundry man.

In the spring, the same clotheslines often held her rugs which, in the days before efficient vacuum cleaners, she beat with a special wire beater that resembled a giant fly swatter. For everyone, personal cleanliness was difficult at best. Until an additional washstand, stool and tub were placed in the basement in the late 1920s, the boardinghouse afforded only one of each such facility for all, both Thorups and guests.

On Saturdays the Thorups shopped. With children in tow, they took the streetcar downtown to Buehler Brothers Meat Market, where they could command quality meat. Then it was on to Haydens, a multiple-floor department store on Sixteenth and Dodge streets. There in the basement, amid the moist odors of grinding coffee, cheese and fish, Mathilde could buy a quantity of the latter (*sild*) to pickle for her boarders.

Until the 1930s, when they bought an electric refrigerator, the Thorups preserved their food with block ice. From an ice house two-and-one-half blocks away, Ruth and Roy often used their little wagon to carry home a large hunk for the family's basement icebox.

The new refrigerator, now on the main floor, was a godsend, for it made possible the economy of food purchases in much greater quantities.

The men who ate all this food returned daily from work around five-thirty P.M., most of them on the streetcar. Marinus came home at the same time, often to be met by his two children looking for a Planter's Peanut Bar from his lunch box.

By six P.M., the boarders were all sitting at one large table eating family style. Mathilde hovered over her "sons," serving food, enforcing table manners and seeing to it that they took no more meat than was a fair share. Any complaints, albeit infrequent, received her advice: *Hvis du klager, pa kosten, kan du rejse til den forste.* (If you complain, you can move the first of the month.)

For all this loving board and room, the men paid seven dollars per week.

Dinner table talk covered a variety of subjects such as who had the hardest job and whether working conditions were better in Chicago than in Omaha. Sometimes the talk heated up, such as when politics got involved, and the subject matter turned to who would make a better president, Al Smith or Herbert Hoover.

After dinner, everyone gathered in the living room to listen to the radio or play cards. Sometimes they played ball with the neighborhood kids in the alley; at other times, liking to drink, and this being the time of Prohibition, they helped Marinus make home brew or root beer for Ruth and Roy.

On some Sunday afternoons the Thorups went on picnics, Mathilde making the sandwiches and the men with cars furnishing the transportation. On other Sunday afternoons the four Thorups would have their own outing—a long streetcar ride to Florence for some ice cream and a long streetcar ride home.

But the most fun was on Thursday evenings and Sunday afternoons when, with living room rugs rolled up, Danish "aunts," domestics of West Omaha employers, would come to the Thorups on their days off to dance with the "uncles" to tunes rolling out of

Danes

Marinus's Victrola. The girls normally stayed for dinner, helped with the dishes and spent the evening with the Thorups. They went monthly to the Danish church for a meeting of *Vaegteren*, a Danish young peoples' group, before returning to their homes.

The men who added so much to the fellowship of the Thorups' home and provided so much joy to their children came from many places in Denmark, each for his own reason. One fled to escape the vengeance of a man who had vowed to kill him; most came for less dramatic personal or family reasons or just to seek a better life.

These uncles found employment with many different Omaha companies and in many different fields. Some, like Marinus, worked for the Union Pacific; others worked at local creameries or in the Ford Assembly Plant at Sixteenth and Cuming streets. Many were tradesmen who had learned their skills in Denmark: bricklayers, carpenters, tailors, cement finishers and dairymen. While one became a driver for a Danish-owned coal yard, another became a

The former Thorup home, 1117 Park Avenue, 1999

motorman on the streetcars, the transportation of the day.

Several of the men were uncles in every sense of the word and became members of the Thorup family. One, who came from Odense in the late 1920s, was an outstanding cabinet maker. One Christmas he made for Roy a perfectly constructed and professionally finished pool table and for Ruth an ornate doll bed. It was natural for Mathilde to serve as a mother-in-law to the eventual wives of these men and as a grandmother to their children.

Several of the roomers built a four-car garage across the back of the Thorups' property, allowing them to receive an additional monthly rent of one dollar for each stall. Like brothers, the men also helped one another. One lent his roommate money to reach an out-of-town job; another lent his tools to a fellow roomer who needed them in order to get work.

By 1932 immigration had slowed to a trickle, and the roomers had drifted away. Only two remained when Roy was killed in an accident just before Christmas. His death was followed by a heart attack suffered by Marinus, which brought on rapidly declining health. In those terrible days the uncles were there in force to rally around and help Mathilde. During an earlier bout of Marinus's sickness, they had offered to pay her in advance in order to provide needed funds, reminding her that she had carried them when they were out of work.

During all his years in America, Marinus worked on his English. He perfected it to such an extent that his Danish accent faded away. He took pride in pronouncing and spelling English words. Later in life, he worked in less strenuous jobs, a sales person with the Lefler Shoe Company and a maintenance man with C.B. Brown, one of Omaha's foremost jewelers. How proud it made him feel, he an immigrant Dane, to be sought out by his employer, himself, for the meaning or pronunciation of an English word.

Ruth, the little "niece," grew up to engage in a myriad of Danish-American activities. These culminated in her 1997 recognition as Outstanding Dane of the Year by Nebraska Lodge Number One of

Danes

the Danish Brotherhood of America. A background of extensive education allowed her a thirty-year career as a teacher and an administrator in the Omaha Public Schools. In 1978, she finished things up with a Ph.D. degree from Walden University, Florida. Over time she took on a host of duties with her Lutheran church and with all sorts of Danish societies and events, and was especially proud of her work with the Oaks Indian Center in Oaks, Oklahoma, originally sponsored by Danes. Her biography is summed up in **Who's Who: American Women**.

The tiny country in Northern Europe that points her nose into the North Sea has given celebrities to the world out of proportion to its size, among others entertainer Victor Borge and atomic physicist Niels Bohr. Yet one might claim for its finest gifts the acts of the Danish king and dedicated Danes during World War II.

First, in the face of an order by invading Nazis that all Danish Jews shall wear yellow stars of David on their clothing, the king decreed that *all* Danes shall wear the same. Second, courageous Danes risked their own lives, directly under the noses of the Nazis, to whisk hundreds of fellow countrymen, all Jews, to safety across the water in neutral Sweden.

This is the land of Hans Christian Andersen, the author of delightful fairy tales, that sent Ruth all her "uncles," many with faces similar to those dusty blue and gray ones found on Royal Copenhagen plates and figurines. As the years have gone on, the early days are but a memory to the little girl who shared their love.

Today she sees them no longer, yet many of their progeny are her close friends. All of them are constant reminders of the loving relationships formed in the Park Avenue boardinghouse. By their contribution to the coloring of the Omaha canvas, they have enriched the portrait.

REFERENCES

BOOKS

Hale, Frederick. **Danes in North America.** Seattle, WA: University of Washington Press, 1984.

Larsen, James H. and Barbara J. Cottrell. **The Gate City: A History of Omaha**. Boulder, CO: Pruett Publishing, 1982.

Nielsen, George R. **The Danish Americans**. Boston, MA: Twayne Publishers, 1981.

INTERVIEW

Nielsen, Ruth Herman. Interview by Donald H. Erickson. November 1998.

MISCELLANEOUS

Nielsen, Ruth Herman. **Lots of Danish Uncles Growing Up in a Boardinghouse**. Lecture. May 1989.

NEWSPAPER

McMorris, Robert. *The People Who Make Up Omaha: The Danes*. **The Omaha World-Herald**. November 26, 1981.

THE MEXICANS

Even though she faces toward Europe, the Statue of Liberty sends her message to every realm. Close at hand is Mexico, whose "tired and poor" America has embraced for years.

Indeed, some Mexican-Americans didn't come to the United States at all; the United States came to them. Many lived in what is now Texas, New Mexico and Arizona. Under the Treaty of Guadalupe Hidalgo, which ended America's 1846 war with Mexico, the border of the United States shifted south of them. These Mexicans merely stayed where they were. Who migrated to whose country, the Mexicans or Uncle Sam?

Modern-day Mexicans, some almost pure descendants of Aztecs and Mayans, are a handsome race. With their coal-black hair, copper-brown skin and shiny dark eyes, they confront you with a certain air of pride. Even the humblest worker inherently senses that his ancestry rivals anything the Old World has to offer. He challenges anyone who has studied his pre-Columbian civilization, Aztec pyramids, Mayan ruins and other artifacts, to conclude otherwise.

The 1990 Census reported over sixteen thousand persons of Mexican descent living in the three counties of Douglas, Sarpy and Pottawattamie, a thirty-eight percent increase over 1980. By U.S. Census estimates, in 1997 over thirty-one thousand Latinos lived in the Omaha metropolitan area. The turn of the century saw many more.

Omaha's fastest growing minority group contrasts sharply with the small group of Mexicans (solos) who first came to Omaha in the 1860s to drift in and out of the city during the next four decades working for the Union Pacific and Burlington Railroads.

The first migration of any size arrived in 1910 following political upheaval and unrest in Mexico. Many came to Omaha from labor in the sugar beet fields of Western Nebraska, the only group of immigrants willing to do this backbreaking work on a regular basis.

Mexicans

In time, some of these Mexicans brought their families to Omaha, establishing homes near the tracks of the Burlington Railroad at Gibson, a station on the banks of the Missouri River near First and Hascall. As many as fifty such families from the 1910s through the Depression took residence there in three company houses, including a rundown boardinghouse and a row of boxcars.

By the 1920s, some signs of Mexican settlement in the city appeared at three other main locations: Seventh and Pierce, South Omaha and Brown Park. Those living at Seventh and Pierce, while mainly railroad workers, also tended small shops or worked as white collar employees. Mostly Roman Catholic, along with Italians, Syrians and Hungarians, these families attended St. Philomena Cathedral, (later renamed St. Frances Cabrini) at Tenth and William.

South Omaha was the location of the largest Mexican community, over six hundred persons, the first workers settling in boardinghouses on Q and R streets and in hotels. Four Mexican restaurants appeared between Twenty-fourth and Twenty-fifth on Q Street. By the 1930s, increasing numbers of Mexican immigrants moved into the Czech community of Brown Park.

Like other ethnic immigrant groups, these new arrivals longed for their own church with services in their native language. The focal point of their yearning became Our Lady of Guadalupe Church, which Fr. Leonardo Ascona, OAR, organized in 1919 when he began holding services in St. Agnes Church School Hall. This group of faithful members later were to worship in a bakery until their priest was called away in 1923.

Even later, when the church was reorganized under Fr. Mario Alba in 1928 and its membership increased to two thousand, it had only a rented storefront at 5027 South Twenty-fourth for its place of worship, and the congregation had to hold its catechism classes in members' homes.

At last in 1951, many dimes, quarters and bake sales later, the parishioners were able to move Our Lady of Guadalupe into a lovely new building at Twenty-third and O streets. Today, together with schools and social halls, it serves an ever-growing church population with three Spanish language Masses each Sunday.

Spanish-speaking churches of denominations other than Roman Catholic also have appeared in South Omaha in recent years: Lutheran, Pentecostal, Jehovah's Witnesses and others. In part, such churches have gathered adherents by recruiting from Mexico and other Latin countries ministers who are truly Spanish-speaking and fully acquainted with the Mexican culture.

Not only did the Mexican-Americans found churches, but they formed a variety of other organizations to meet their needs. Two of these were for mutual assistance and social activities: *Comision Honorifica* organized by Gregerio Aguilera in the 1920s and *Esperanza* (Hope). In 1922, *Esperanza* merged with the Mexican

Magdalena Garcia Thomson of El Museo Latino,
4701 South Twenty-fifth Street

287

Mexicans

Mutual Society founded by Joseph Carrillo at 2917-19 Q Street. Its function was to unify the Mexican residents and acquaint them with their Mexican heritage, as well as to instruct them in the history, geography and political constitution of their new country.

Today, a vibrant Chicano Awareness Center serves the economic, political and cultural needs of a growing Omaha Latino community. The center strives to afford its members equal access to all alternatives, opportunities and resources of American society while maintaining their own cultural values. Upstairs in its building at 4821 South Twenty-fourth Street are its administrative headquarters, fully staffed, and rooms for education and counseling. Downstairs is a brightly decorated Head Start bilingual preschool for three- and four-year-olds, with a life-sized Big Bird cutout to greet them.

In 1993, a great cultural gap was filled by Magdalena Garcia Thomson who spearheaded the formation of El Museo Latino, a museum featuring art from south of the border. First lodged in the Livestock Exchange Building, it now finds a home in a brick building at Twenty-fifth and L streets that long served as the Polish Home. El Museo has become the leading organization in the Midwest to promote Latino culture and art.

Of course, many persons from Latin American lands other than Mexico have come to Omaha to live. Especially during the turmoil of recent years, they have arrived from every nation in Central America, as well as from Cuba and Puerto Rico. Although there are cultural differences between the Mexicans and these Hispanics, at least all share Spanish as a native language and all face the problems of learning English as a second language. Unlike the Mexicans, they tend to live, not in South Omaha, but throughout the city.

Early on, strong personalities emerged in the Mexican-American community. An apt representative is Jose Ramirez, who came to Omaha as a permanent resident in 1950. He previously had fled with his parents from Jalisco, Mexico to the United States as a young

Jose Ramirez

boy in order to escape religious persecution. He returned with them to Mexico during the Depression.

When he later reappeared in Omaha to find work in construction and as a packinghouse employee, Ramirez began serving his community as a minority advocate. He was able to do some real good. For example, in a 1952 meeting with Omaha's Catholic archbishop and Mayor Eugene Leahy, he complained about the administrative requirement that all police officers be at least five-feet-nine-inches tall, a regulation that precluded most Mexican-Americans from joining the force. Leahy got the regulation changed; Mexican-Americans became policemen.

In 1952, Ramirez met and married his wife and settled down as a packinghouse labor leader. Ashamed to admit to his union that he was unable to vote, he studied to be a naturalized American citizen and in 1960 gratefully received both citizenship papers and voting power. Yet he is ever mindful of his Mexican heritage. His cry of *"Viva!"* each year on Independence Day rekindles a feeling of pride in those Omahans who have not one, but two American countries.

Eight years of formal education in a Roman Catholic seminary in Mexico, as well as night courses at the University of Omaha where he perfected his English, made it possible to be ordained as deacon of Our Lady of Guadalupe Church. His services are

Mexicans

especially beneficial to his fellow Mexican-Americans who in ever-increasing numbers seek pastoral care from a limited number of bilingual religious leaders. The Omaha Archdiocese is especially grateful for his translation of church documents from English into Spanish.

Today, when more and more Mexican immigrants are attending services provided by South Omaha's St. Agnes church (traditionally a place of worship for Irish immigrants, but now dubbed Santa Inez, the Spanish equivalent of St. Agnes), Ramirez is there to aid with the Spanish Masses.

As a member of the Human Relations Board of the city, the Greater Omaha Community Action Board and the Urban League, Ramirez has been a militant voice against discrimination, not merely for Mexicans but for all minorities. He has spoken against it early and often. Sometimes his advocacy has proved too strong for certain community members who have accused him of wanting to be a *patroncito*, a sort of self-appointed boss. Yet, like most everyone, his militancy has moderated with his waning years, and today he is universally beloved.

Ramirez involved himself deeply in the English as a Second Language Program of the Omaha Public Schools. In the beginning, it involved three hundred students; now it concerns three thousand, a majority of them of Mexican origin. As to the assertion by some that Mexican-Americans don't want to learn English, Ramirez has this to say: "We are not stupid. We know that if we don't learn English, we can't get an education and thus will be barred from all professional fields and any good job."

Recently he spoke of a speech he gave at Creighton University. He was told to speak on a non-controversial subject, nothing negative "like the fact that the United States once stole one-half of Mexico." "I can do this very easily," he said.

When I came to Omaha in 1950, I met this young lady whose parents had fled Mexico during the revolution. My wife's father found himself in front of a firing squad but was able to get away and come to the States. He had four children. He came to the States and struggled. Ultimately he had twelve kids. All of them went to high school. Now their children are university educated. One is an airline pilot, another a State Department official and still another, an electrician. This is the contribution he has made to this nation.

If you don't already know it, the Mexican-Americans are very patriotic. Even here in Omaha, if you would just visit the City Hall you would find a plaque listing the Medal of Honor persons from Omaha. Including Senator Robert Kerrey, there are six. The five others are John Joseph Parle, Robert John Hibbs, Edward Gomez, James W. Fous and Miquel Keith. Two of these are Mexican-Americans. We are proud to be Americans.

Mexican Fiesta, 1980

Mexicans

Not all Mexican-American residents of Omaha are new arrivals from Mexico or other Latin countries. Having been reared elsewhere in the United States, some are second- and third-generation Americans of Mexican descent. Two such persons are Paul Gutierrez and his wife, Alice, who both grew up near San Antonio, Texas.

Although Paul's grandfather on his father's side came from Mexico as a boy, his paternal grandmother was born in a San Antonio mission. Reared bilingually, she taught her husband English. When not engaged as a local or itinerant field worker, this grandparent would sell personally-butchered meat to a Mexican-American list of customers.

Paul's maternal grandparents and his mother and father were born in the United States. Despite the fact that his mother spoke scarcely any English, there were few language barrier problems for him and his seven siblings. Like his grandfather, his father was a dirt farmer with little formal education. He sometimes was a migrant worker, moving his family with the harvest to Indiana, Alabama and Mississippi; at other times he was a construction worker or operated a bar.

Although Paul and Alice are, of course, American citizens, their heritage is strictly Mexican, including the Spanish language plus lots of food and fiesta traditions. Reared with these customs, they cling to them and rejoice that the recent influx of Mexican immigrants brings a new invigorating influence from the mother country. They deplore watching the traditions fade away in their own children and in their nieces and nephews, all of whom speak little Spanish and devote themselves to American fast food.

The second youngest child in his family, Paul was born about the time his oldest brother died during World War II. He grew up in San Antonio, graduated from high school there in 1961 and soon afterward joined the Air Force. Sent to Offutt Air Force Base for a four-year hitch, he returned to San Antonio only to bring his new wife back to Omaha.

Finding his enlisted pay inadequate for the couple's needs, Paul applied for Officer's Candidate School, but in vain. He lacked the necessary college credit hours. As a stopgap, he moonlighted as a janitor for a commercial office cleaning service. This led to a career. When he was discharged from the Air Force in 1965, Alice and he paid over everything they had to purchase the contracts and equipment which included six accounts, a few vacuum cleaners and floor buffers, of the Midwest Equipment Company, whose owner wanted to retire.

The Gutierrez family

They were in business. Or a least Paul was, for Alice had to take care of the offspring that soon appeared. Although Paul had no background in how to run the company, it slowly grew. The seller had given him a few hints: what costs to look for, how to bid a job and how to process the contracts entered into.

Formal training helped. Having always hungered for a college degree, he found Bellevue College enticing. Somehow he took the time during his non-working hours to get a degree in accounting, management and marketing. Alice followed suit. Both now have degrees.

After a while, the couple was able to build a home on an acre in Sarpy County between Bellevue and Papillion. Attending church schools in St. Bernadette parish, their three children were able to grow up in a rural setting.

But one day the flock left the nest. Having retired and transferred control of the business to one daughter and her husband, Paul and

Mexicans

Alice chose to return to worship in Our Lady of Guadalupe parish, where they could be closer to the Mexican-American people and Mexican-American influence.

Although they now spend their winters in Carmel, California, they both love Omaha, finding it a city of good values and a great place to raise kids. They are happy so many Mexican immigrants have come to the community.

More descriptive of the average Mexican immigrant is the story of the Valenzuela family. Arturo Valenzuela, born across the border from El Paso, Texas in Juarez, Mexico, had the same struggles as almost every newcomer from Mexico.

During his tender years, Arturo, together with his older brother and sister, was reared by a single mother, Leonor Valenzuela, who early on decided to leave her children in the care of an uncle and aunt and move to Los Angeles with her sister. There she could find work and send money back for the support of the children. Arturo spent his early years in Juarez with his siblings and cousins under the care of Uncle Alberto Valenzuelo. For spending money, he picked cotton.

All went well until Leonor became sick and required surgery. When the money to Mexico stopped, the children suffered accordingly. After she recovered, Leonor heeded the advice of friends who directed her to Omaha. She could find work in the packinghouses, they told her.

Arriving in Omaha, she encountered a climate and a culture vastly different from the one she had left, even the one in Los Angeles. She wasn't used to the cold weather and didn't even have a coat when she came. Furthermore, she didn't speak any English. Although she lived in South Omaha, in the 1960s it was hard for a woman to find a job in one of its packinghouses.

Blue Star Foods in Council Bluffs gave her a job. At first she walked to work over the Thirteenth Street South Omaha Bridge (now Veterans Bridge). Later she took the bus. Eventually she got her permanent visa (green card) and a husband, Pete Kobos. Then she was able to send for her children. At age fourteen, Arturo was among them when they came to Omaha in 1970 to share for a while their mother's suffering from snow and cold weather.

Living directly across the Rio Grande from El Paso, Arturo had picked up a few English words, but had had no formal training in English. When he arrived in Omaha, although he was old enough to attend high school, it was impossible for him without adequate English.

He enrolled at Marrs Junior High School where he found caring teachers patient enough to guide him in the new language. No longer a small child, picking up English was not easy for him. Like many others before and after him, his gravest burden were the taunts of thoughtless fellow students who mocked his efforts.

He even sought help though military service. At age seventeen, he enlisted in the army and was sent to Fort Jackson, South Carolina. It was warmer there, and his English did improve. But not well enough. After two-and-a-half months, he was back in Omaha with an honorable discharge. At least he had learned that there were many persons whose English was worse than his, and he had lost his fear of trying. He began carrying a dictionary with him at all times.

New immigrants get all the menial jobs. When its regular dishwasher failed to show up for work, the Omaha Club, a private club at Twentieth and Douglas, gave Arturo the job. Not much English was needed. Then about a month later when one of the cooks suddenly walked out, the chef asked Arturo to replace him.

Although he knew nothing about cooking, he started anyway— merely following the chef's orders. He figured the absent cook would get over what was bothering him and return the next day. He didn't. The chef told Arturo to continue to work in his place and to learn from the other cooks how to do things like making soups and basic sauces. For the next four to six weeks he cooked and, in his spare time, washed dishes.

The club announced that it was closing for two weeks for

Mexicans

Arturo Valenzuela at the Omaha Club, 2002 Douglas Street,
closed on January 1, 2000

employee vacations. It would serve members only soup and sandwiches. Arturo and one or two others would remain to serve. With the chef gone, the club manager asked Arturo to take charge. "Just create something out of whatever you have there, like all chefs do," he said.

Charged up, Arturo got creative. Every day he and his coworkers served more and more club members who apparently approved of their soup and sandwiches. When they ran out of food, Arturo nervously ordered more from the wholesale grocer, whose kindly service representative took his time to help him with the order.

After two weeks, when the vacationing head chef failed to return, the club hired Walter Hecht, a Swiss chef with sparkling credentials. Hecht had lived for a few years in Puerto Rico and had learned enough Spanish to communicate well with Arturo. He took a liking to him and saw to it that he received a pay raise.

Speaking English most of the time, Hecht taught him many things—new food preparations, new techniques. "Hecht could create just about anything," Arturo says, "and he taught me how to do a lot of it."

For six or seven years, Arturo worked for Hecht both at the Omaha Club and at various restaurants that Hecht later established in the community. Ultimately Arturo became a good enough chef to be hired by the Marriott Hotel chain for its hotels both in Omaha and El Paso, Texas.

Then one day his sister told him that the Omaha Club was looking for a *sous* chef. Not only did the club hire him, but three months later promoted him to executive chef. It was 1986, and he was only thirty years old.

For nearly fourteen years in this role, until the Omaha Club closed January 1, 2000, he catered meals for many club members, as well as many visiting VIPs. This included a breakfast for a twosome, Vice President Dan Quayle and Mayor Hal Daub.

In 1979 Arturo married Kathy Steinbloch. They have two children. Arturo Gabriel, eighteen, is enrolled at the University of Nebraska at Lincoln; Carlos Jesus, sixteen, still living at home, attends Westside High School.

Arturo embraces a simple philosophy: work hard and learn. His Mexican friends say, "We outwork the Americans, yet we are poor."

> *This is not enough,* he tells them, *you must outthink them, too. Their genius has created a superstructure that permits their wealth. Their education permits them to enjoy the good life without the hard work most Mexicans endure both here and in their native land. If the Mexican-American wants to enjoy the good life, he must educate himself, or at least insist that his children do.*

Mexicans

Fully acclimated, Arturo loves Omaha and would not live anywhere else. Today his English, if not impeccable, is better than that of many Americans born and reared in his adopted land. Nobody makes fun of him now.

REFERENCES

BOOKS

Grajeda, Ralph F. **Mexicans in Nebraska**. Lincoln: Nebraska State Historical Society; Nebraska Mexican-American Commission, 1998.

Larsen, Lawrence H. and Barbara J. Cottrell. **The Gate City: A History of Omaha**. Boulder, CO: Pruett Publishing, 1986.

INTERVIEWS

Ramirez, Jose. Interviews by Harry B. Otis. May and September 1998

Sill, Mary. Interview by Harry B. Otis. May 1998

NEWSPAPERS

Freed, Kenneth. *Latin Flavor Enlivens Spanish Mass at Eleven*. **The Omaha World-Herald**. October 7, 1998.

Freed, Kenneth. *Hispanics Test Catholic Mission*. **The Omaha World-Herald**. October 7, 1998.

Gauger, Jeff. *1980s Paint Different Face on Omaha's Hispanic Community*. **The Omaha World-Herald**. December 6, 1992.

Wright, Kristi. *El Museo Latino is First in Midlands*. **The Omaha World-Herald**. September 17, 1995.

THE JAPANESE

Japan is a small country geographically, yet it is the sixth most populous, with one hundred and twenty-five million inhabitants packed into an area the size of Montana. It has but few natural resources, yet it is one of the most affluent and economically productive nations in the world.

This has not always been so. Until the mid-nineteenth century, Japan chose to isolate itself. For two hundred years it shunned most trade with the West, as well as any Western influence on its culture. Only after U.S. Commodore Matthew C. Perry anchored in Edo (Toyko) Bay in 1853 was there a chink in the armor. On March 31, 1854, a Treaty of Kanagawa formalized relations between the two countries.

As time went on, however, increased emigration of Japanese to the United States caused negative reactions from West Coast workers, as well as a general anti-Japanese prejudice and discrimination. Relationships between Americans and Japanese-Americans, both *Issei* (those born abroad) and *Nisei* (those born in the United States) did not improve—particularly in the early years of World War II.

Kaz Takechi

Then the public learned of the remarkable war record of the all-*Nisei* 442nd Regimental Combat Team that fought in Italy. The regiment was the most decorated unit in the war. In 1946 Harry Truman awarded it a Presidential Unit Citation.

It was not until 1937 that the Takechi family would come to Omaha to give it their bright color of civic accomplishment. First to arrive was Kazuo (Kaz) Takechi

299

Japanese

from Pocatello, Idaho, in time to become a respected jeweler, watch repairman and importer of fine oriental gifts. Soon to join him was his wife, Kimi, with their new-born son, Richard. Over the next fifty years, Kimi would work hand-in-hand with Kaz in the couple's stores, all the while caring for an additional four children.

Takechi is an honorable Japanese name. Kaz's ancestors were Samurai, the warrior protectors of the Japanese emperor. When, in 1853, Commodore Perry entered Tokyo Bay to help open up Japan to Western trade and customs, one consequence was the gradual disappearance of feudalism in Japan and with it the Samurai. When the Samurai disappeared as a class, its members tended to become blacksmiths or locksmiths.

Kaz's grandfather became a locksmith. Japanese custom decreed that being the second son in his family, Kaz's father, Shigeyoshi, be adopted by his mother's family and assume his mother's last name in order to preserve it. As a Takechi, he became both a locksmith and a missionary.

Born in 1913 in Kochi, Japan, Kaz immigrated to America in 1930. He came with Shigeyoshi, who had been sent as a missionary to establish a church in Seattle. The following he represented was the Tenrikyo Church, a monotheistic faith that arose in Japan during the nineteenth century. As a teenager, Kaz's life was filled with odd jobs and studies in Seattle where he attended Pacific High School, which had special English classes for immigrants.

Kimi, Kaz's future wife, was born in Pocatello in 1917 of parents who also had immigrated from Kochi, Japan. Leasing plots of ground owned by Native Americans, they had established vegetable and potato farms and were as successful as anyone could be during the Depression of the 1930s. When Kimi's father died in 1930, Kaz's father moved to Pocatello to help her family out. Kaz went with his father to find such work as he could, while pursuing English studies at Pocatello High School.

It was inevitable that Kaz and Kimi would marry. The wedding took place in a Tenrikyo church in San Francisco.

Japanese

In 1937, Goro (Harry) Watanabe, who owned a wholesale importing company in Omaha, needed a bilingual person of Japanese descent to run his warehouse. Through a mutual acquaintance he discovered Kaz, who, following an interview in Omaha, accepted the job offer. For a while he was diverted to Sioux City to manage Watanabe's gift shop in that city; however, a year or so later, accompanied by Kimi and baby Richard, he came to Omaha as a permanent resident.

During the years prior to World War II, Kaz and Kimi occupied apartments in Pocatello, Sioux City and Omaha. But by 1942, they were able to buy their first house, one at Thirty-first and Decatur streets. With a German family on one corner of the block, a Swedish family on the other and an Italian family next door to them in the middle, the Takechis found nothing but loving acceptance by all their neighbors.

Harry Watanabe, an astute man of affairs, gave Kaz good lessons on running a business, and working with Harry allowed Kaz to learn many new specialized English words, such as Hummel figurine. Every day he learned something new. As his salary increased, he could send to his mother in Japan regular sums of money for food and clothing. At that time one dollar equaled two yen. Ten yen would buy one hundred pounds of rice, enough to sustain a family of four for many months.

Then came Pearl Harbor. In 1941, while Kaz was in Florida on a business trip for his company and Kimi was back in Pocatello awaiting the birth of their second son, Steve, Japan struck Hawaii. Disregarding the strong anti-Japanese reaction this triggered in the American public, Kaz was able to drive, somewhat frantically, back to Omaha.

But how could he get to Kimi in Pocatello? Following the air strike, Japanese were not allowed to travel on public transportation without a permit, and for a person of Japanese descent to drive to Pocatello was increasingly dangerous in those hysterical days.

Kaz sought out a friend, Joseph Votava. As the U.S. district attorney for Nebraska, he secured a permit allowing Kaz to take the train to Idaho. By then the nation was beginning to intern Japanese. Fortunately, Kimi's family lived a few miles east of the demarcation line west of which all persons of Japanese descent, citizens or not, faced this fate. Kaz and Kimi later were able to return with their newborn to their Omaha home.

Before World War II, few Japanese resided in Nebraska, even fewer in Omaha. The first group to come was in 1904 when Kinya Okajima, on behalf of the packinghouses, recruited about one hundred and twenty laborers from Wyoming and Colorado mines.

By 1910, there were two hundred Japanese in the area, half of them working for the Cudahy Packing Company. They lived in a house called the Home of the Good Shepherd and organized their social lives in a Japanese Association with officers and a paid bilingual secretary who helped with their language problems. At the same time, some found lodging in a boardinghouse run by a Mr. Hashimoto, who boarded twenty of them at his establishment on Eleventh Street between Harney and Farnam.

By 1920, the number of Japanese residents had increased further. A Mr. Kiyoka operated a Japanese restaurant employing ten people. Furthermore, Joe Watanabe (no kin to Harry), a colorful individual, ran the Uptown Café near Thirteenth and Douglas. Joe, who came to be known as the "King of Skid Row," customarily sported a white suit, white bowler hat, a cigar and a large diamond ring. Together with a daughter, Martha, the issue of a Caucasian wife, he did a thriving business in his restaurant, dishing out good food to poor pensioners with meal tickets and feeding free any hungry person who sought his help and couldn't pay.

Another Japanese settler appearing during the 1920s was Harry Matsuo, a photographer, who for many years would provide the graduates of Central High School and other secondary schools with photographs for their treasured yearbooks. Matsuo eventually would train Ihachi Ishii in the art.

Born in Kaita-machi, Hiroshima, Japan, Ishii came to Omaha

from labor in a Mexican diamond mine. Along with other Japanese, he found work with the Cudahy Packing Company. The men boarded in a hotel at Thirty-sixth and L streets. Eventually Ishii became a professional photographer, married a Czech girl and reared a family at 2926 Castelar Street. Their son, Edward, a World War II Army Air Corps veteran, remembers as a youngster being able to recite a prayer in Bohemian in St. Adalbert Catholic Church, whose members were largely Czech immigrants.

Other early Japanese in Omaha were Chuichi Taso and Shin Kichiro Yoden, who established a retail shop at Eighteenth and Farnam named the Nippon Importing Company. To help them, they brought to Omaha many young people from California. Among them were Taso's nephew, Goro (Harry) Watanabe, George Yamasaki, S. Oshimo and Jiro Akamatsu.

When Taso returned to Japan, his nephew, Harry, opened up the wholesale concern, Oriental Trading Company, and helped Yoden in his retail store. A few years thereafter Harry moved his wholesale company to Eleventh and Farnam. Many years later he moved it to its present location at 4206 South One hundred eighth Street.

Few Omaha companies can match the success of Oriental Trading Company. In 1994 it reported sales of more than two hundred million dollars. Harry Watanabe ran the firm until 1977, before turning its operation over to his son, Terry, who has carried it to new heights. During the thirty years that Harry ran the company from its Farnam Street location, it dealt mainly in such carnival items as Kewpie dolls, plush animals, hand buzzers and hula skirts.

The Oriental Trading Company became a child of ingenuity. When World War II cut off Harry's imports, he was required to make his stock in trade himself. With the assistance of Japanese released from internment camps under work permits, he produced the Kewpie dolls and other cheap novelties

By 1970, annual sales had reached Harry's announced goal of seventy million dollars. Ready to retire, he handed control to his

Japanese

Terry Watanabe at the Oriental Trading Company

twenty-year-old son who was ready, willing and very able to start it skyrocketing. He certainly had the experience. To quote Terry Watanabe:

> *[My dad] started me as a cashier when I was six years old. At seven, I was doing typing; at eight, bookkeeping; at ten, U.S. Customs entries; at twelve, talking to customers; and at fifteen, I was overseas buying.*

Terry's move was to broaden the business beyond carnivals and fairs. His method involved direct mail and lots of it. His targets were churches, schools, clubs and other retail customers. His new direction required a huge number of employees. In 1994, twenty-five hundred expanded to four thousand during the peak season of the months of September through December. It also required an immense storage capacity in three Omaha locations, as well as in Underwood, Iowa, and Fremont, Nebraska, for the likes of feather boas (27,000), tiaras (115,000), sets of chattering teeth (18,000) and whoopee cushions (500,000).

Although he continued to work for the Oriental Trading Company for a short while after the war started, Kaz decided to buy Joe Watanabe's Uptown Café. He had a reason. Kimi's relatives, who had owned a Seattle restaurant, had sent their children to be cared for by Kimi's mother and brother on their farm near Pocatello. To help them, Kimi, with Kaz's blessing, brought some of these children to Omaha to her own home. The Uptown provided a place for them to work.

At this time, Kaz learned that the war had led to a scarcity of watch repairmen, although there still existed in Omaha watch repairmen of Japanese descent, among them: Tak Misaki, Roy Hirabayashi and Gary Zaiman. An Elgin, Illinois school advertised for students. His friend, Misaki, talked him into attending. Despite Harry Watanabe's pleas to remain with him in Omaha, he traveled to Elgin and learned the art. Upon his return, he worked for two years with the Edward Jewelry Company before starting his own business.

Not the type to let anyone down, while in Elgin, Kaz responded to a plea by Watanabe's wife to return to Omaha to run his business. Her husband had become ill. By this time Watanabe had brought to Omaha many interned Japanese. Knowing his services were needed, Kaz answered the call, yet returned to Elgin to finish his training when Harry recovered.

Now, as an accomplished watch repairer, Kaz had another career in mind. Following his employment with Edward Brodkey, he leased space on the tenth floor of the former Woodmen of the World Building at Fourteenth and Farnam streets for the purpose of wholesale watch repair. His customers were other jewelers from Omaha and surrounding cities. Later he started a retail store next to the Western Union Company on the main floor of the Woodmen Building for the retail sale of fine gift items and jewelry.

Working for theWartime Relocation Authority, Adah Eier and

Japanese

Frances Hotz enabled many displaced Japanese to come to Omaha during this period. Boys Town's Father Flanagan also found Omaha jobs for many evacuees. And an interesting by-product of World War II was the appearance of many war brides, the wives of returning GIs.

At the onset of the war, some Japanese left Omaha; however, by 1947, with the formation of the Japanese American Citizens League, there were one hundred and fifty or so in the city. In addition to the Takechis, founders of the league were the families of Okura, Nakadoi, Matsunami and Kaya. About that time, the Kaya family established the Mt. Fuji Restaurant.

After internment at the Santa Anita Race Track in Los Angeles, Pat Okura ultimately served as a Douglas County probation officer. On one occasion, during a talk given to a service club, he wryly remarked that although many times before the war he had bet on horses at the California track, he never dreamed he would have to live there.

During the 1950s, Kaz Takechi moved his retail store into space in the Paxton Hotel across Fourteenth Street and also into quarters

Kaz Takechi (on the right) at Takechi's Jewelers, 1609 Farnam Street

306

previously occupied by the B.Q. Haines Company in the north side of the Orpheum Theater Building. By that time his sons, Richard and Steve, were old enough to run this store.

Then, sometime during the 1960s, Kaz and Kimi closed the B.Q. Haines store and moved into space in the Kilpatrick Building on Farnam Street, formerly the Thom McCann Shoe Store. Ultimately, they would move into their present location on Farnam Street between Sixteenth and Seventeenth streets.

During all this moving experience, when the law in 1954 allowed him to do so, Kaz became a naturalized citizen, and Kimi continued to deliver children: Jane, Julie and Jeri. Jeri's husband, Mark, also of Japanese descent, was trained by Kaz as a watch repairman and has found a career as a watch repairer for the Borsheim Jewelry Company.

Although born and reared in the United States, Kimi speaks Japanese fluently. Her family spoke it while she was growing up. Nevertheless, she and Kaz spoke it in the home only when they were saying something the children didn't need to hear. Both Richard and Steve have traveled to Japan to study the language and now speak it fluently.

Omaha has treated the Takechis well, and they have more than returned the favor. Following service on the Omaha City Council, Richard is now the Register of Deeds for Douglas County. Kimi, with all her duties in rearing a family and working in the various stores, has found time for service with the YWCA, her church and many other activities.

Especially after his family was able to help him operate his stores, Kaz has engaged in many civic affairs. Among these are roles as a charter member of the Japanese American Citizens League and advisor to the Omaha Sister City Association that made Shizuoka, Japan, our sister city. Together with Kimi he founded the Omaha Chapter of Ikebana International, a flower arranging society. Kaz also is a recipient of the annual Good Neighbor award and in 1987 received from the University of Nebraska at Omaha an honorary

Japanese

degree.

As a member of the Downtown Rotary Club and the International Committee on Foreign Relations, in 1971 Kaz really put Omaha on the map by helping the then-mayor, Eugene Leahy, promote the Japanese-American College World Series. Baseball is so popular in Japan that a Japanese newspaper with a huge circulation was able to spread the word about Omaha to millions of enthusiastic citizens. Unfortunately for Omaha, this college world series failed to remain here.

At a 1984 celebration dinner honoring him, Kaz received through the counsel general of Japan the Fifth Class of the Order of the Sacred Treasure, an honor conferred by the emperor of Japan and presented only twice a year. He was the first Nebraskan to receive the award which is given to a foreign or Japanese individual who has rendered extraordinary service to the promotion of closer friendship and bonds between Japan and a foreign nation.

What is the secret of Kaz's success? Why has he had no problems anywhere he has traveled in the United States, even during World War II? With gracious humility he says:

> *Because I have always smiled at people . . . and they have always smiled back at me. . . . I love America and Americans, and the beautiful qualities of both this and my native land.*

REFERENCES

BOOKS

Herman, Masako, compiler and editor. **The Japanese in America: 1843 to 1973.** Dobbs Ferry, NY: Oeana Publications,1974.

Meyer, Milton W. **Japan: A Concise History.** New York: Rowman and Littlefield, 1993.

INTERVIEWS

Takechi, Kazuo and Kimi Takechi. Interview by Donald H. Erickson. February 1999.

Takechi, Kazuo and Kimi Takechi. Tape-recorded interview by Donald H. Erickson and Harry B. Otis. March 1999.

NEWSPAPERS

Celebration for Takechi's. **The Omaha Star.** December 25, 1969.

Getschman, Suzi. *Metropolitan Profile: A Man Like Water.* **Metropolitan.** June 28, 1989.

Out of Diamond Mine to Photography. **Rocky Mountain Jiho.** June 8, 1988.

Schinker, Nick. *Emperor Honors Omahan.* **The Omaha World-Herald.** June 21, 1984.

CONCLUSION

Some wise person once said that when people start waiting in line to get out of America instead of waiting in line to get in, we can start worrying about our system. Before we complain about America, we should remember it's one of the few places where most people don't want to move to another country.

Every newcomer to the United States seeks primarily one thing: Freedom. It always has been our big attraction. The immigrant is just as able to find it in Omaha as anywhere else in the country. From its earliest hour our city has delivered it, just as it provides a refuge today for those who might otherwise face persecution and death in their own countries: Sudanese, Vietnamese, Cubans and a host of others.

These stories of Omaha's immigrants offer strong evidence that all men are brothers who can live together without rancor. They illustrate that the right mix of law, order and tolerance over the years has allowed all ethnic groups to live peaceably side by side.

Our experience in preparing this book revealed to us that each group is eager to show others how they live, worship and play. While they are proud and happy to be living in America, they remain proud of their heritage. We believe that the more we learn about all of them, the more we may help to dissipate the hatred and bigotry of the few that arise out of an unfounded fear of persons they perceive to be different from themselves.

We urge everyone to join us in our study by making the acquaintance of someone of a different background. Go into his home when possible, visit his beautiful church or synagogue and enjoy his fiesta. He will love you for your interest and make you proud to be part of a municipality where we are all, in one way or another, fellow immigrants.

PHOTO ACKNOWLEDGEMENTS

Cover & title page: *Lithograph of early Omaha, circa 1875, from a photo by Charles Savage.* Graphic work by Bob Bailie. Courtesy of Historical Society of Douglas County. B2038.

page 12: *Sod dwellings.* From Fletcher, Alice C. **Historical Sketch of the Omaha Tribe of Indians in Nebraska**. Washington, D.C.: Judd & Detweiler, 1885. Plate 1.

page 13: *Part of an Omaha village, circa 1860.* Photo by William Henry Jackson. Courtesy of Historical Society of Douglas County.

page 18: *Chief Logan Fontenelle.* Courtesy of Historical Society of Douglas County. B23.

page 20: *Reginald Buckman and the Ponca Health and Wellness Center sweat lodge.* Courtesy of **The Omaha World-Herald**.

page 23: *General George Crook.* Courtesy of Historical Society of Douglas County. B527.

page 24: *Chief Standing Bear.* From Fletcher, Alice C. and Francis La Flesche. **Twenty-seventh Annual Report of the Bureau of American Ethnology**. Washington, D.C.: Government Printing Office, 1911. Plate 5.

page 28: *Early pioneers of Omaha.* Graphic work by Bob Bailie. Courtesy of Historical Society of Douglas County.

page 28 inset: *Byron Reed's office.* Photo by William Henry Jackson. Courtesy of Historical Society of Douglas County. Jasper Hall Album.

page 31: *Cyrus Morton.* Courtesy of **The Omaha World-Herald**.

page 36: *View of Capitol Hill from downtown Omaha.* Photo by William Henry Jackson. Courtesy of Historical Society of Douglas County. Jasper Hall Album. B2033.

page 42: *Telegraph line construction.* Courtesy of Historical Society of Douglas County.

page 44: *Piper Denny Moriarty and Dualta dancers.* Courtesy of **The Omaha World-Herald**.

page 46: *Father Flanagan.* Courtesy of Historical Society of Douglas County.

page 51: *John Mulhall.* Courtesy of **The Omaha World-Herald**.

page 56: *The Goreliks.* Courtesy of the Jewish Historical Society.

page 57: *Julius Meyer.* Photo by William Henry Jackson. Courtesy of

Photo Acknowledgements

Historical Society of Douglas County. Jasper Hall Album.

page 58: *Temple Israel*. Courtesy of the Jewish Historical Society.

page 60: *Rabbi Grodzinsky*. Courtesy of the Jewish Historical Society.

page 62: *Baruch, David & Joseph Fishel*. Personal photo.

page 69: *Joseph Fishel*. Personal photo.

page 73: *Augustus Kountze*. Courtesy of Historical Society of Douglas County.

page 75: *German float*. Courtesy of Historical Society of Douglas County. K936

page 77: *Val Peter family, 1927*. Courtesy of the Peter family.

page 79: *Theodore Reese*. Courtesy of the Peter family.

page 80: *Omaha Daily Tribune office and employees*. Courtesy of the Peter family.

page 82: *Val Peter family, 1953*.Courtesy of the Peter family.

page 83: *809 Pine Street residence*. Courtesy of the Peter family.

page 84: *Saengger-Halle*. From the Bostwick-Frohardt Collection owned by KMTV and on permanent loan to the Durham Western Heritage Museum.

page 90: *Joe Wah Lee*. Photo by Louis Bostwick. **The Illustrated Bee**. August 19, 1900.

page 92: *Mandarin Cafe*. From the Bostwick-Frohardt Collection owned by KMTV and on permanent loan to the Durham Western Heritage Museum.

page 93: *Interior, King Fong Restaurant*. From the Bostwick-Frohardt Collection owned by KMTV and on permanent loan to the Durham Western Heritage Museum.

page 95: *Jeanette & Carl Chin*. Courtesy of **The Omaha World-Herald**.

page 103: *Father Jusevicius*. Courtesy of Al Praitis.

page 107: *Totilas family portrait*. Personal photo.

page 113: *Lithuanian dancers*. Photo by and courtesy of Al Praitis.

page 117: *Lithuanian float*. Photo by and courtesy of Al Praitis.

page 121: *The Jerry Shores family*. Courtesy of Nebraska State Historical Society. Solomon D. Butcher Collection. RG 2608-1231.

page 124: *W.L. & Essie Myers*. Personal photo.

page 129: *St. John AME Church*. Omaha City Planning Department.

page 131: *Urban League Meeting*. From the Bostwick-Frohardt

Photo Acknowledgements

Collection owned by KMTV and on permanent loan to the Durham Western Heritage Museum.

page 134: *Robert & Bertha Myers*. **North Sun Newspaper**. March 11, 1965.

page 138: *Mary & Alex Morar*. Personal photo.

page 139: *Congregation at St. Cross Church*. Personal photo.

page 142: *Traian Posa*. Personal photo.

page 149: *St. John the Baptist Church*. Photo by and courtesy of Lynn Meyer, Omaha City Planning Department.

page 152: *Nicholas Payne*. Personal photo.

page 156: *The Virginia Cafe*. Personal photo.

page 159: *Nicholas Payne pouring coffee*. Personal photo.

page 163: *Danita & Doreen McKenney at Czech Festival, 1989*. Courtesy of **The Omaha World-Herald**.

page 167: *American citizenship class at Brown School*. From the Bostwick-Frohardt Collection owned by KMTV and on permanent loan to the Durham Western Heritage Museum.

page 169: *Sokol dancers at Sokol Hall*. Courtesy of Historical Society of Douglas County. B363.

page 172: *Senator Roman Hruska*. Photo by John S. Savage. Courtesy of Historical Society of Douglas County. BC108-4.

page 179: *Scottish Piper*. Personal photo.

page 183: *E.L. Holland*. Personal photo.

page 184: *Ada Holland*. Personal photo.

page 189: *Dora Holland*. Personal photo.

page 195: *St. Philomena Cathedral*. Photo by Louis Bostwick.

page 199: *Sam & Rose Seminara*. Personal photo.

page 204: *Little girl eating spaghetti*. Photo by Robert Wintersteen.

page 207: *Santa Lucia*. Photo by Robert Wintersteen.

page 214: *Father Zaplotnik*. Courtesy of Sts. Peter and Paul Church.

page 216: *Rose & Blaz Cupich*. Personal photo.

page 218: *Cupich children in ethnic dress*. Courtesy of **The Omaha World-Herald**.

page 221: *Sts. Peter and Paul Church, 1918*. Courtesy of Sts. Peter and Paul Church.

page 223: *Monsignor Blase Cupich and parents*. Courtesy of **The Omaha World-Herald**.

Photo Acknowledgements

page 227: *Father Vojin Dosenovich in church*. Personal photo.

page 230: *Waterfall*. Personal photo.

page 234: *Dosenovich home in Sanski Most*. Personal photo.

page 242: *Father Vojin & Nadine Dosenovich*. Photo by Jim Kascoutas. Courtesy of Fr. Vojin Dosenovich.

page 247: *Mayor Dahlman & Sheelytown Mayor, Nick Dargaczewski*. Courtesy of Tom Buras.

page 248: *Immaculate Conception Church*.

page 249: *Nick Dargaczewski*. Courtesy of Tom Buras.

page 251: *Stanley & Anna Nykiel*. Personal photo.

page 254: *Polish dancers at St. Stanislaus Church*. Courtesy of **The Omaha World-Herald**.

page 258: *John Engdahl*. Personal photo.

page 263: *Olga Engdahl*. Personal photo.

page 264: *Engdahl Top & Body Co*. Personal photo.

page 266: *Swedish folk dancers*.

page 271: *Thorup family cutout at the Durham Western Heritage Museum*. Personal photo.

page 275: *Mayor A.V. Sorensen*. Photo by John S. Savage. Courtesy of Historical Society of Douglas County. BC84-3.

page 276: *Sophus Neble and the **Danish Pioneer***. Courtesy of **The Omaha World-Herald**.

page 280: *Former Thorup home*. Photo by Bob Bailie. Courtesy of Historical Society of Douglas County.

page 287: *Magdalena Garcia Thomson at El Museo Latino*. Courtesy of **The Omaha World-Herald**.

page 289: *Jose Ramirez*. **Sun Newspaper** photo.

page 291: *Mexican fiesta*. Courtesy of **The Omaha World-Herald**.

page 293. *Gutierrez family*. Personal photo.

page 296: *Arturo Valenzuela*. Personal photo.

page 299: *Kaz Takechi*. Personal photo.

page 304: *Terry Watanabe at the Oriental Trading Co*. Courtesy of **The Omaha World-Herald**.

page 306: *Kaz Takechi at Takechi's Jewelers*. Personal photo.

Index

Index

Index

Index

Index

Index

326

Index